Language Testing: The Social Dimension

Blackwell
Publishing

Language Learning Monograph Series

Richard Young, Editor
Nick C. Ellis, General Editor

Schumann:
The Neurobiology of Affect in Language

Bardovi-Harlig:
Tense and Aspect in Second Language Acquisition: Form, Meaning, and Use

Kasper and Rose:
Pragmatic Development in a Second Language

Seedhouse:
The International Architecture of the Language Classroom: A Conversation Analysis Perspective

McNamara and Roever:
Language Testing: The Social Dimension

Language Testing:
The Social Dimension

Tim McNamara and Carsten Roever
The University of Melbourne

Blackwell
Publishing

© 2006 Language Learning Research Club, University of Michigan

Blackwell Publishing
350 Main Street
Malden, MA 02148
USA

Blackwell Publishing, Ltd.
9600 Garsington Road
Oxford OX4 2DQ
United Kingdom

Library of Congress Cataloging-in-Publication Data

McNamara, T. F. (Timothy Francis), 1949-
    Language testing: the social dimension/Tim McNamara and Carsten Roever.
    p. cm. – (Language learning. Monograph series)
    Includes bibliographical references and index.
    ISBN 1-4051-5543-4 (pbk. : alk. paper)
    1. Language and languages–Ability testing. I. Roever, Carsten. II. Title.

P53.4.M359 2006
418.0076–dc22   2006021660

Contents

Series Editor's Foreword

Finding out how well someone knows a second language is no simple undertaking. What is meant by 'knowledge' of a second language? Does it mean what a person demonstrates of that knowledge in conversation or in writing? Or does knowledge mean something mental that is only poorly represented in actual use? And what is meant by 'a second language'? That is a big question which, thanks to developments in linguistics, we can now see as combining several separate questions: questions of form about pronunciation, vocabulary, grammar; and functional questions about effective language use in social situations that give the intended meaning and that give off desired meanings about a person's identity and beliefs. And when we decide what 'knowledge' means and what aspects of a second language we want to find out about, there remains the procedural problem of how to go about finding out what we want to know. The procedural problem is the subject of a wide ranging literature in psychometrics, and many authors of books on language testing concentrate their efforts on the twin procedural questions of how successfully a test measures what it is supposed to measure and how dependable a measurement tool it is.

It is perhaps remarkable that academic and professional languages testers should be so concerned with these two issues, but underlying both is a fundamental question of equity: Is a test unfairly discriminating against certain people? Perhaps aspects of the second language that some test takers know differ from the majority (they might, for instance, have a good command of the spoken language but not be so good at discriminating between the elements that make for good language and those that are ungrammatical). Or perhaps particular items in the test imply cultural knowledge that some test takers don't command (a reading comprehension question about automobiles may, for instance, refer to makes and types of cars that are unknown to some people, or to concerns about fuel consumption that are prevalent in some societies but not in others).

Such concerns about test fairness often motivate discussions of measurement, especially when the people who take a test come from such a wide variety of backgrounds as do takers of language tests. It is a small step from concerns with the internal equity of a test to the realization that all language testing occurs in a social context that is much broader than the test itself. The social context of language assessment includes not just the designers and takers of a particular test, but also the purposes for which the test is designed, the purposes for which people take the test, and the ends to which the results of the test are put. These broader political questions are rarely addressed in the language assessment literature and the present volume is a necessary expedition into this unfamiliar territory. Why is it necessary? Because in our intercultural societies and in our world of cross-border migration, the requirement to distinguish between *them* and *us* has increased. This political dimension of language testing was famously recorded in the Book of Judges in the Hebrew Bible. Around three thousand years ago in a war between Hebrew tribes, the Gileadites killed forty-two thousand Ephraimites who had crossed secretly into Gilead territory. The Ephraimites were given a simple language test: Pronounce the Hebrew word for 'ear of grain' תלובש. The Shibboleth test was designed to distinguish the Ephraimites whose dialect lacked a /ʃ/ sound (as in shoe) from Gileadites whose dialect did include the sound. Those who did not pronounce the /ʃ/ sound were put to death.

Many more recent versions of the Shibboleth test are recorded in the language assessment of immigrants, asylum seekers, and those who wish to become citizens, but the political context of language testing is just as pertinent in more widespread but less fatal language testing enterprises that have resulted from the No Child Left Behind Act in the United States and the Common Framework of Reference for Languages in Europe. Each of these frameworks is designed to achieve a policy goal. In the case of No Child Left Behind, the policy is designed to improve education for all by allowing communities to identify those schools whose students do well on tests from those schools where students perform poorly, and to direct financial resources to those schools with good testing results and, over the long term, to sanctions those with consistently poor results. Although the Common European Framework was initially developed with the goal of facilitating the recognition of language credentials across national boundaries, the framework's promulgation of one particular theory of language knowledge and its establishment of a progressive set of standards have produced effects felt throughout education in Europe and elsewhere. In both the American and European cases, the establishment of a particular assessment framework has had a very significant effect on teaching and learning, as a result of process that language testers know well: washback.

Because language assessments like these serve the purpose of distributing scarce resources such as jobs, higher education, and financial support to those who desire them, the question of how to distribute those resources fairly is by no means academic. The developers of language tests have indeed been aware of the necessity for internal equity in their tests, and there is a long and distinguished psychometric tradition of research in this area. Institutional testing agencies and professional associations of language testers have also responded to the need for fairness in the testing enterprise by the development of professional codes of ethics and institutional codes of practice. In many cases, however, such codes are responses to legal challenges to institutions or are intended to provide protection for members of the profession. Such measures undoubtedly reflect the concern of language testers for the fate of testing and test takers in the community, but these concerns have been inward-looking and have so far lacked a foundation in description or research into the political consequences of language testing. The present volume is important in opening a dialogue on the political consequences of language testers' professional activity.

Tim McNamara and Carsten Roever's "Language Testing: The Social Dimension" is the fifth volume in the *Language Learning Monograph Series*. The volumes in this series review recent findings and current theoretical positions, present new data and interpretations, and sketch interdisciplinary research programs. Volumes are authoritative statements by scholars who have led in the development of a particular line of interdisciplinary research and are intended to serve as a benchmark for interdisciplinary research in the years to come. The importance of broad interdisciplinary work in applied linguistics is clear in the present volume. McNamara and Roever survey the work that language testers have done to establish internal equity in assessment, and they describe the consequences of language testing in society as a whole and in the lives of individuals. Language is rooted in social life and nowhere is this more apparent than in the ways in which knowledge of language is assessed. Studying language tests and their effects involves understanding some of the central issues of the contemporary world.

Richard Young
University of Wisconsin-Madison

Acknowledgments

We would like to thank our series editor, Richard Young, for his support, constructive suggestions, and most of all for keeping us on track. It is invaluable in undertaking a project as large as this to be gently but firmly reminded of the time frame, and Richard struck a perfect balance between letting us roam free and keeping us on the path to timely completion.

We are also grateful for the extremely useful and insightful comments by our reviewers, which helped us fill important gaps in our work.

Carsten would like to thank the Department of Second Language Studies at the University of Hawai'i at Manoa for hosting him for part of his 2005 sabbatical, during which most of his contribution was written. As always, he is particularly grateful to Kevin Yang, whose love and support make it all worthwhile.

Tim wishes to thank Brian Lynch and Alastair Pennycook for initially challenging him to think more deeply about the relevance of social theory to the concerns of applied linguistics. As always, discussions with Bernard Spolsky are illuminating on language testing and language policy, as on so many other subjects. And Tim's thanks go most of all to Elana Shohamy, whose originality, courage, and passion always challenge him to push the envelope further.

Dedications

TMcN: For Elana

CR: For Christine Klein-Braley, who inspired my interest in language testing

CHAPTER ONE

Introduction

Language testing has a long history as a social practice but only a relatively short one as a theoretically founded and self-reflexive institutional practice. When language testing became institutionalized in the second half of the 20th century, it did so as an interdisciplinary endeavor between Applied Linguistics and psychometrics. In fact, psychometrics became the substrate discipline, prescribing the rules of measurement, and language was virtually poured into these preexisting psychometric forms. Psychometrics has remained the basic foundation for language testing: it has the appeal of its rigorous methods and anchorage in psychology, a field much older than applied linguistics, with a correspondingly wider research base. However, through marrying itself to psychometrics, language testing has obscured, perhaps deliberately, its social dimension. This is not to say that psychometrics has no awareness of the social context of assessment, but mainstream work in the area is firmly oriented toward assessment instruments with little systematic research on broader issues. In fact, the most socially motivated research in psychometrics on bias and differential item functioning still generally follows an ideal of improving tests so that they measure more precisely and more purely the construct under investigation.

Within the practice of testing, it is, of course, necessary to acknowledge the contribution that psychometrics, despite its limitations, has made and continues to make to socially responsible language testing. Given that modern societies will necessarily use tests, adherence to the fundamental rules of what makes a "good test" is indispensable for ensuring the quality of assessments and the defensibility of conclusions drawn from them. Following the rigorous prescriptions of psychometrics and measurement theory inherently serves to reduce bias and unwanted social impact. However, and this is a core tenet of our argument, a psychometrically good test is not necessarily a socially good test. In fact, there is no correlation between the two: Any assessment can have far-reaching and unanticipated social consequences. It is precisely these social consequences and the general lack of systematic research on them that we are concerned with in the present volume. This is not a new concern; in fact, the advent of modern testing in the 19th century was accompanied by a vigorous critique of its social and educational implications, as eloquently pointed out by Spolsky (1995) in relation to language testing, reflecting a theme recognized within the more general educational literature represented by, for example, Madaus and Kellaghan (1992). This critique became subdued, certainly within language testing, following the triumph of psychometrics in the 1950s, and this volume represents in a sense only the revoicing of an old issue.

The existence of a social dimension of assessment might well be more striking in language testing than in assessments measuring general cognitive abilities because language is a social medium and any measurement of it outside of a social context tends to be at odds with the increasing acceptance of social models of language within Applied Linguistics more generally. Of course, language tests for a long time ignored the social use dimension of language and followed traditional psychometric methods of measuring isolated pieces of grammar and vocabulary knowledge. However, with the rise of the communicative competence paradigm in second language teaching, the measurement of the ability to use language in social contexts has become increasingly important, as indicated by recent work on oral proficiency interviews (Brown, 2005; Young & He, 1998), performance tests (McNamara, 1996), and tests of pragmatics (Liu, 2006; Roever, 2005). However, here, too, the individualist, cognitive bias in psychometrics has obscured or even hindered the issues at stake in these assessments, as our discussion shows.

Testing social aspects of language use is only one facet of the social dimension of language tests. The much broader consideration is the role and effect of language testing in society. One of the most pervasive functions and consequences of language tests throughout history is their use as sorting and gatekeeping instruments. These tests, imposed by a more powerful group on a less powerful one, tend to have severe, life-changing, and not infrequently life-ending consequences for their takers, from the Biblical shibboleth test followed by the immediate slaughter of those failing it to the modern language tests that form a precondition for promotion, employment, immigration, citizenship, or asylum. Although the consequences of failure might be less immediate and deadly for the modern tests (except, perhaps, for refugees), they are, nonetheless, high-stakes situations for test takers with the power to define their identity: Passing the test means that one can become a civil servant or a Dutch citizen, incorporating a new facet in one's identity. Also, although modern language tests are frequently administered not by sword-wielding guards but in an orderly, regulated, and lawful fashion in well-lit, carpeted test centers, they are just as much the result of political processes and value decisions as the shibboleth test was. Who should be allowed to immigrate? What standard of language proficiency should be required to grant someone citizenship or allow them to practice medicine in another country? What deeper social and political values are at stake in the implementation of policy through tests in these areas? Social values and attitudes fundamentally determine the use of tests.

Another area in which the consequences of language testing are particularly and sometimes painfully obvious is educational systems. Government-imposed standards and test instruments resulting from them strongly impact what is taught and have a reverberating effect throughout the system, an issue recognized in response to the introduction of such practices within state-sponsored education in the 19th century, itself reflecting an older tradition of concern dating to the 15th century at least (Madaus & Kellaghan, 1992). From the Common European Framework, which controls language testing and teaching throughout Europe, to the No Child Left Behind Act in the United States, with its special emphasis on English as a second language populations and its grave consequences for various stakeholders, testing in educational systems continues to raise issues of the consequential and social effects of testing, most of which remain the subject of only scant contemporary reflection.

1.1 Structure of This Volume

Our argument is framed in relation to contemporary approaches to validity theory, which we sketch in chapter 2. We describe Messick's (1989) view of validity and validation, including his conceptualization of test consequences, which establishes the social effects of test use as a part of the overall argument for or against a test's construct validity. We consider Messick's influence on his successors: Mislevy's influential Evidence-Centered Design framework (Mislevy, Steinberg, & Almond, 2002, 2003), which implements Messick's approach but focuses on test construction and ignores the consequential facet of validity, in contrast with the work of Kane (Kane, 1992, 2001; Kane, Crooks, & Cohen, 1999), which places decisions based on test scores centrally in his discussion of test validity. We then discuss validity theory in language testing, especially the work of Bachman (Bachman, 1990, 2004; Bachman & Palmer, 1996), in which the influence of Messick and, more recently, Kane is very evident. We argue that despite the creative and sophisticated nature of such discussions, the social role and function of tests is inadequately conceptualized within them.

In chapter 3 we explore the testing of social aspects of language competence. Our argument here is that the individualist and cognitive bias of psychometrics and the linguistics that most neatly fitted it has meant that 40 years after the advent of the communicative movement, the field still encounters difficulties in conceptualizing and operationalizing the measurement of the social dimension of language use, a problem that was recognized more or less from the outset of the testing of practical communicative skill. We support our argument by considering tests of second language (L2) pragmatics and oral proficiency interviewing. These two measures contrast in interesting ways: Pragmatics tests are rarely used, but their theoretical basis is the subject of much discussion, whereas oral proficiency measures are frequently used with comparatively little reflection. Only four larger measures of L2 pragmatics exist, all focused on English as a target language. These instruments measure speech acts for Japanese learners of English (Hudson, Detmer, & Brown, 1995) or Chinese learners of English (Liu, 2006), as well as implicature (Bouton, 1994), and the only test battery in this area covers routines, implicatures, and speech acts (Roever, 2005). Tests of pragmatics struggle with the necessity of establishing adequate context while keeping the test practical in administration and scoring. Also, the traditional instrument of the discourse completion test (DCT) has been shown to be problematic and there are serious concerns about tearing speech acts out of the context of coherent discourse and atomizing them for testing purposes. Oral Proficiency Interviews take place in the domain of face-to-face interaction, which has been the subject of intense research and theorizing, particularly in the study of language in interaction or Conversation Analysis. One of the central findings of this research is that performance is inherently social and co-constructed, not simply a projection of individual competence; this means that there can be no reading back of individual competence from the data of performance. Schegloff (1995, p. 192) called for a recognition of "the inclusion of the hearer in what [are] purported to be the speaker's processes." The implications of this position for a project that aims at the measurement of what are understood to be individualized cognitive attributes are still being recognized and worked through. Studies are now emerging exploring this issue empirically in detail—for example the research of Brown (2003, 2005), which shows the implication of interlocutor and rater in the scores attributed to individual candidates, a point that had been raised in principle many years before, for example, in comments by Lado at a symposium in Washington in 1974 (Jones & Spolsky, 1975).

In chapter 4 we discuss ways in which traditional psychometric approaches to testing have handled certain aspects of the social context of assessment. Within this tradition, the issue is conceptualized as one of social fairness, and attention is primarily given to avoiding bias in favor of or against test takers from certain social groups, particularly minorities. Investigation of the psychometric properties of items is done in order to detect items that function differentially for different groups. A variety of statistical techniques have been employed to detect differential item functioning (DIF), ranging from nonparametric cross-tabulations to complex model comparisons based on item response theory. We will describe some of these approaches, together with generalizability theory and multifaceted Rasch measurement, both of which can detect unwanted influences of test-taker background variables at the level of the whole test. Although all of these techniques help detect bias in items or tests, they do not offer much insight into the causes of such unwanted item or test functioning. We discuss this as a shortcoming of traditional DIF and bias analyses and we critically review some of the value decisions made in setting up these analyses.

Although bias avoidance recognizes a social dimension in assessment, it is still fundamentally constructed as a psychometric enterprise. In chapter 5 we consider other aspects of conventional approaches to dealing with the social embeddedness of testing, in the form of procedures of fairness review and the promotion of codes of ethics. Fairness review is a formal process that some test makers operate with the purpose of identifying and eliminating possibly biased items during the test construction process. However, as we show, fairness review is also a response to social and societal pressures on test makers and serves a parallel function of keeping test content uncontroversial to ensure wide acceptance of scores. Similarly, codes of ethics serve as a way for the testing profession to provide transparency to stakeholders and reassure them of the profession's commitment to ethical conduct. Although there are no effective sanctions for breaches of the ethics code, such codes are useful for guiding ethical decisions and protecting testers from stakeholder pressures to take actions that contravene professional conduct.

In chapter 6 we broaden our scope and discuss ways in which language tests are involved in the construction and defense of particular social identiies. Because language indexes social group membership, language tests can be used to classify test takers and this classification is frequently motivated within potentially or actually conflicted intergroup settings and is thus highly consequential. We describe various examples of this social practice from ancient history to the present day, including the Biblical shibboleth test, the Battle of Worcester between Cromwell and Charles II in 1651, the massacre of Haitians in the Dominican Republic in 1937, and the Canadian Mounted Police's "fruit machine" to identify (and exclude) homosexual recruits in the 1950s. We discuss specifically the modern role of language tests in citizenship and immigration contexts, in which they are used to adjudicate the claims of asylum seekers, control legal immigration, and grant or refuse full membership in a society as a citizen. We use this discussion to reflect on the use of language tests as instruments of subjectivity in modern societies.

We then turn in chapter 7 to the pervasive use of tests in educational settings. Standards have long been used to enforce social values throughout educational systems, and tests are the instruments that implement and operationalize such standards. We provide examples of the impact of values and standards in educational systems through the rejection by teachers of an oral component in senior high-school entrance examinations in Japan, as well as in a very different setting, the impact of the Common European Framework of Reference for Languages on language teaching throughout Europe. Increasingly, tests are also used as accountability measures with potentially drastic consequences for various stakeholders and entire educational systems, a use that was first recognized as early as the 15th century in

Europe. This is the case for the No Child Left Behind Act (NCLB) in the United States, where test results determine the fate of entire schools. The test-driven nature of the NCLB has unforeseen collateral effects on various areas of school education in the United States, and the debate about this resurrects debates that have been going on since at least the 19th century.

Finally, in chapter 9 we discuss the implications of our discussion for research and training, most notably a need to devote more research to the social dimension of language testing and to ensure that academic training in language testing balances an appreciation of the achievements of the psychometric tradition and a greater awareness of the social dimensions of language testing.

1.2 Concluding Statement

We feel that language testing is beyond the teething stage and ripe for a broader view of assessment and its social aspects. This includes coming to grips with the theoretical and practical difficulties involved in testing the social side of language use, but testers need again to engage in debate on the increasingly consequential application of their tests and to reflect on test use both during test development and when tests are operational. Language testing has a real impact on real people's lives, and we cannot cease our theoretical analyses at the point where the test score is computed. Just like language use, language testing is and has always been a social practice; the very power of tests has a mesmerizing effect on consciousness of their social character. This volume aims to reawaken that consciousness.

CHAPTER TWO

Validity and the Social Dimension
of Language Testing

In what ways is the social dimension of language assessment reflected in current theories of the validation of language tests? In this chapter we will consider the theories of validation that have most influenced current thinking in our field, in the work of Messick (following Cronbach) and his successors Mislevy and Kane, and its interpretation within language testing by Bachman, Chapelle, Lynch, Kunnan, Shohamy, and others. Contemporary validity theory has developed procedures for supporting the rationality of decisions based on tests and has thus addressed issues of test fairness. However, although validity theory has also begun again to develop ways of thinking about the social dimensions of the use of tests, many issues are still unresolved, and in fact, it almost feels as if the ongoing effort to incorporate the social in this latter sense goes against the grain of much validity theory, which remains still heavily marked by its origins in the individualist and cognitively oriented field of psychology.

2.1 Cronbach

Contemporary discussions of validity in educational assessment are heavily influenced by the thinking of the American Lee Cronbach; it is only a slight overstatement to call Cronbach the "father" of construct validity. He was part of the American Psychological Association's Committee on Psychological Tests, which met between 1950 and 1954 to develop criteria of test quality. Their recommendations became the precursor of the present-day Standards for Educational and Psychological Testing (American Educational Research Association, 1999), and during the committee's work, a subcommittee with Meehl and Challman coined the term "construct validity." Cronbach and Meehl (1955) explicated the concept in detail in their classic article in the *Psychological Bulletin*. Whereas criterion-related validity (also known as predictive or concurrent validity) was the standard approach at the time, there was also increasing dissatisfaction with its shortcomings (Smith, 2005), and Cronbach and Meehl framed their new concept of construct validity as an alternative to criterion-related validity:

> Construct validity is ordinarily studied when the tester has no definite criterion measure of the quality with which he [sic] is concerned and must use indirect measures. Here the trait or quality underlying the test is of central importance, rather than either the test behavior or the scores on the criteria. (Cronbach & Meehl, 1955, p. 283)

Note that the language of "trait" and "underlying quality" frames the target of validation in the language of individuality and cognition. One of the major developments in validation research since Cronbach and Meehl's article is the increasingly central role taken by construct validity, which has subsumed other types of validity and validation. There is also clear recognition that validity is not a mathematical property like discrimination or reliability, but a matter of judgment. Cronbach (1989) emphasized the need for a validity argument, which focuses on collecting evidence for or against a certain interpretation of test scores: In other words, it is the validity of inferences that construct validation work is concerned with, rather than the validity of instruments. In fact, Cronbach argued that there is no such thing as a "valid test," only more or less defensible interpretations: "One does not validate a test, but only a principle for making inferences" (Cronbach & Meehl, 1955, p. 297); "One validates not a test, but an interpretation of data arising from a specified procedure" (Cronbach, 1971, p. 447).

Cronbach and Meehl (1955) distinguished between a weak and a strong program for construct validation. The weak one is a fairly haphazard collection of any sort of evidence (mostly correlational) that supports the particular interpretation to be validated. It is in fact a highly unprincipled attempt at verification by any means available. In contrast, the strong program is based on the falsification idea advanced by Popperian philosophy (Popper, 1962): Rival hypotheses for interpretations are proposed and logically or empirically examined. Cronbach (1988) admitted that the actual approach taken in most validation research is "confirmationist" rather than "falsificationist" and aimed at refuting rival hypotheses as researchers and test designers try to prove the worth of their instruments.[1]

In his most influential writings on validation within measurement, Cronbach never stressed the importance of the sociopolitical context and its influence on the whole testing enterprise; this is in marked contrast to his work on program evaluation (Cronbach et al., 1980), in which he strongly emphasized that evaluations are sites of political conflict and clashes of values. However, in his later writings, possibly through his experiences in program evaluation, Cronbach highlighted the role of beliefs and values in validity arguments, which "must link concepts, evidence, social and personal consequences, and values" (Cronbach, 1988, p. 4). He acknowledged that all interpretation involves questions of values:

> A persuasive defense of an interpretation will have to combine evidence, logic, and rhetoric. What is persuasive depends on the beliefs in the community. (Cronbach, 1989, p. 152)

And he concurred with Messick (1980) that validity work has an obligation to consider test consequences and help to prevent negative ones. Cronbach also recognized that judgments of positive or negative consequences depend on societal views of what is a desirable consequence, but that these views and values change over time (Cronbach, 1990). What we have here then is a concern for social consequences as a kind of corrective to an earlier entirely cognitive and individualistic way of thinking about tests.

Cronbach's difficulty in integrating his psychometrically inspired work on construct validity, originating within educational psychology, and his concern for social and political values, originating in his work in the policy-oriented field of program evaluation, has remained characteristic of both the fields of educational measurement and language testing, as we will see. This difficulty in integrating these concerns is also characteristic of the work of Messick, to which we now turn.

2.2 Messick

The most influential current theory of validity of relevance to language testing remains that developed by Samuel Messick in his years at Educational Testing Service, Princeton from the 1960s to the 1990s, most definitively set out in his much-cited 1989 article (Messick, 1989). Although this framework has been discussed in detail elsewhere (Bachman, 1990; McNamara, 2006) and is well known in language testing, it is important to discuss the issues that it raises in the context of the argument of the present volume.

Messick incorporated a social dimension of assessment quite explicitly within his model, but, as with Cronbach, it is grafted (somewhat uneasily, as we will see) onto the tradition of the psychological dimensions of measurement that he inherited and expanded. Messick, like Cronbach, saw assessment as a process of reasoning and evidence gathering carried out in order for inferences to be made about individuals and saw the task of establishing the meaningfulness and defensibility of those inferences as being the primary task of assessment development and research. This reflects an individualist, psychological tradition of measurement concerned with fairness. He introduced the social more explicitly into this picture by arguing two things: that our conceptions of what it is that we are measuring and the things we prioritize in measurement, will reflect values, which we can assume will be social and cultural in origin, and that tests have real effects in the educational and social contexts in which they are used and that these need to be matters of concern for those responsible for the test. Messick saw these aspects of validity as holding together within a unified theory of validity, which he set out in the form of a matrix (Figure 2.1).

We can gloss the meaning of each of the cells in such a way as to make clear the way in which Messick's theory takes theoretical account of aspects of the social dimension of assessment (Figure 2.2). It will be clear from this gloss that aspects of the social context of testing are more overtly present in the model, in the bottom two cells of the matrix. One addresses the social and cultural character of the meanings attributed to test scores; the other considers the real-world consequences of the practical use of tests. The question naturally arises of the relationship of the fairness oriented dimensions of the top line of the matrix to the more overtly social dimensions of the bottom line, a question it could be argued that Messick never resolved and remains a fundamental issue facing our field.

Messick's insistence on the need to investigate the overtly social dimension of assessment, particularly the consequences of test use, has, of course, been controversial. Although many figures

	TEST INTERPRETATION	TEST USE
EVIDENTIAL BASIS	Construct validity	Construct validity + Relevance / utility
CONSEQUENTIAL BASIS	Value implications	Social consequences

Figure 2.1. Facets of validity. From Messick (1989, p. 20).

	WHAT TEST SCORES ARE ASSUMED TO MEAN	WHEN TESTS ARE ACTUALLY USED
USING EVIDENCE IN SUPPORT OF CLAIMS: TEST FAIRNESS	What reasoning and empirical evidence support the claims we wish to make about candidates based on their test performance?	Are these interpretations meaningful useful and fair in particular contexts?
THE OVERT SOCIAL CONTEXT OF TESTING	What social and cultural values and assumptions underlie test constructs and hence the sense we make of scores?	What happens in our education systems and the larger social context when we use tests?

Figure 2.2. Understanding Messick's validity matrix.

have endorsed this position (Kane, 2001; Linn, 1997; Shepard, 1997), pointing out the long history of discussions in validity theory of validation of the *use* of test scores, others (Mehrens, 1997; Popham, 1997) object on the grounds that it is not helpful to see this as part of validation research, which they prefer to restrict to descriptive interpretations rather than decision-based interpretations, to use Kane's terms (see next section). In fact, however, both Popham and Mehrens agreed that the consequences of test use *are* a subject requiring investigation; they simply do not want to call it "validation" research. In some ways, therefore, this is a dispute more over wording than substance; Popham has in fact published a book (Popham, 2001) on what he sees as the damaging consequences of school and college testing in the United States.

In what follows, we will consider how validity theorists following Messick, and informed by his thinking, have interpreted and elaborated his approach, including its social dimensions. We will begin by setting out Messick's own thinking on construct validity in greater detail and then see how it has been subsequently interpreted by two leading theorists: Mislevy and Kane. The concept of construct validity has traditionally dominated discussion of test validation, and it is important to understand what the issues are and in what way they involve social dimensions of assessment in terms of a concern for fairness.

Construct validity an

2.2.1 Messick on Construct Validity   *Social issues*

Setting out the nature of the claims that we wish to make about test takers and providing arguments and evidence in support of them, as in Messick's cell 1, represents the process of construct definition and validation. Those claims then provide the rationale for making decisions about individuals (cells 2 and 4) on the basis of test scores. Supporting the adequacy of claims about an individual with reasoning and evidence and demonstrating the relevance of the claims to the decisions we wish to make are fundamental to the process. Because of its centrality to assessment, and its complexity, this aspect of validation continues to attract considerable theoretical and practical attention, to the point where, for some authors, it becomes synonymous with validity, as we have seen.

For example, consider tests such as the International English Language Testing System (IELTS; British Council, IDP: IELTS Australia, and University of Cambridge ESOL Examinations, 2005) or the Internet-based test version of the Test of English as a Foreign Language Test (TOEFL iBT; Educational Testing Service, 2005), which are used to help decide whether a prospective international student should be admitted to an English-medium educational and social environment, or a test such as the Occupational English Test (McNamara, 1996) used to determine whether a health professional whose first language is not English should be allowed to practice under supervision in an English-medium clinical environment. The decisions here are clearly highly consequential for the individuals involved and for the institutions that will admit them. Decisions in such cases are based on a belief about whether the person concerned will be able to cope communicatively once admitted and about the demands that they are likely to make on the institutional setting in terms of support, risk of failure, adjustment to routine procedures, and so on.

The path from the observed test performance to the predicted real-world performance (in performance assessments) or estimate of the actual state of knowledge of the target domain (in knowledge-based tests) involves a chain of inferences. This cannot be avoided: There is no way for us to know directly, without inference, how the candidate will perform in nontest settings. Usually, this is as simple as the fact that the candidates are not in such settings yet and cannot be observed there. However, you might say, what about situations in which students and health professionals are given temporary admission to the setting in question and are placed under observation? Is not the observation a form of direct inspection? However, even in these cases, we cannot observe the student in all contexts of interest and must sample from them, acknowledging also that if the student knows he or she is being observed, his or her behavior might be modified accordingly. We cannot tell the extent of this modification, as we have no benchmark of unobserved behavior against which we can measure the observed behavior. In principle, then, and in fact, how the person will fare in the target setting cannot be known directly, but must be predicted. Deciding whether the person should be admitted then depends on two prior steps: modeling what you believe the demands of the target setting are likely to be and predicting what the standing of the individual is in relation to this construct. Clearly, then, both the construct (what we believe "coping communicatively" in relevant settings to mean) and our view of the individual's standing are matters of belief and opinion, and each must be supported with reasoning and evidence before a defensible decision about the individual can be made.

The test is a procedure for gathering evidence in support of decisions that need to be made and interpreting that evidence carefully. It involves making some observations and then interpreting them in the light of certain assumptions about the requirements of the target setting and the relationship of the evidence to those assumptions. The relationships among test, construct and target are set out in Figure 2.3.

Tests and assessments thus represent systematic approaches to constraining these inferential processes in the interests of guaranteeing their fairness or *validity*. Validity therefore implies considerations of social responsibility, both to the candidate (protecting him or her against unfair exclusion) and to the receiving institution and those (in the case of health professionals) whose quality of health care will be a function in part of the adequacy of the candidate's communicative skill. Fairness in

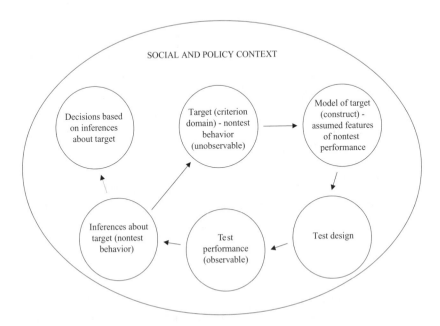

Figure 2.3. Target, construct, and test as the basis for inferences leading to decisions.

this sense can only be achieved through carefully planning the design of the observations of candidate performance and carefully articulating the relationship between the evidence we gain from test performance and the inferences about candidate standing that we wish to make from it. Test validation steers between the Scylla and Charybdis of what Messick called *construct underrepresentation*, on the one hand, and *construct-irrelevant variance*, on the other. The former warns of the danger that the assessment requires less of the test taker than is required in reality. We will give examples of this later. The latter warns that differences in scores might not be due only to differences in the ability being measured but that other factors are illegitimately affecting scores. It is under this rubric that the psychometrically driven work to be considered in chapter 4 also addresses social issues.

For example, if scores can be shown to systematically vary by gender when the variable being measured is required to be insensitive to gender, then construct-irrelevant variance has been detected and has to be eliminated by redesigning aspects of the test. Chapter 4 on test bias will investigate this issue in depth. The general point here, then, is that through its concern for the rationality and consistency of the interpretations made on the basis of test scores, validity theory is addressing issues of fairness, which have social implications: The quality of a test mediates the relationship between the test user and the test candidate. In this sense, the developers of tests are like others such as doctors and lawyers on whose professional skills the public relies, and this forms the rationale for the codes of professional ethics, based largely in validity theory, that will be discussed in chapter 5. We will go on to argue, however, that this aspect of the social dimension of tests, although crucial in its own right, is only one aspect of a much larger question that theories of validity have not adequately encompassed.

Given the complexity of the effort required for construct validation, practitioners have needed guidance as to how to set about it from both a theoretical and a practical point of view. Recent work has tried to set out the logical and practical steps involved, and we will consider that work in detail now.

2.2.2 Construct Definition and Validation: Mislevy

The work of Mislevy and his colleagues provides analytic clarity to the procedures involved in designing tests. As we have seen, central to assessment is the chain of reasoning from the observations to the claims we make about test takers, on which the decisions about them will be based. Mislevy calls this the "assessment argument" (Figure 2.4). This is needed to establish the relevance of assessment data and its value as evidence.

According to Mislevy,

> An assessment is a machine for reasoning about what students know, can do, or have accomplished, based on a handful of things they say, do, or make in particular settings. (Mislevy, Steinberg, & Almond, 2003, p. 4)

Mislevy has developed an approach called Evidence Centered Design (Figure 2.5), which focuses on the chain of reasoning in designing tests. This approach attempts to establish a clear relationship between the claims we wish to be able to make

Evidence		Assessment argument		Claims about test takers
(Observations; assessment data)		(Relevance of data; value of observations as evidence)		(Inferences from observations)

Figure 2.4. The assessment argument.

DOMAIN ANALYSIS	
valued work task features representational forms performance outcomes	valued knowledge knowledge structure and relations knowledge-task relations

⇓

DOMAIN MODELING (SUBSTANTIVE ARGUMENT)		
CLAIMS	**EVIDENCE**	**TASKS**
The characteristics of students and aspects of proficiency they reflect	The characteristics of what students say and do— what would a student need to say or do to establish a basis for the claim about them?	Kinds of situation that might make it possible to obtain this evidence, which minimize construct-irrelevant variance.

⇓

CONCEPTUAL ASSESSMENT FRAMEWORK (TECHNICAL BLUEPRINT)				
Student model	Task model	Evidence model	Assembly model	Presentation model

⇓

OPERATIONAL ASSESSMENT

Figure 2.5. Evidence Centered Design.

about test candidates and the evidence on which those claims are based.

A preliminary first stage, *Domain Analysis*, involves what in performance assessment is traditionally called job analysis (the testing equivalent of needs analysis). Here the test developer needs to develop insight into the conceptual and organizational structure of the target domain.

What follows is the most crucial stage of the process, *Domain Modeling*. It involves modeling three things: *claims*, *evidence*, and *tasks*. Together, the modeling of *claims* and *evidence* is equivalent to articulating the test *construct*. A detailed example of the use of this approach in a test development project is given in chapter 7 of this volume.

Step 1 involves the test designer in articulating the *claims* the test will make about candidates on the basis of test performance. This involves conceptualizing the aspects of knowledge or performance ability to which the evidence of the test will be directed and on which decisions about candidates will be based. Mislevy sees the purposes that tests are to serve, including the decisions that they are to support, as influencing the formulation of claims—yes/no decisions, as in decisions about admission, are different from pedagogic decisions about what features of language to focus on in remedial work. The granularity of claims will vary according to their function and the audience to which they are addressed (a point to be covered in detail in the discussion of standards-based assessment in chapter 7). As a result, claims might be stated in broader or narrower terms; the latter approach brings us closer to the specification of criterion behaviors in criterion-referenced assessment (Brown & Hudson, 2004). Some practically worded claims make simple, common-sense reference to real-world activities in the target domain—for example, "can follow a lecture on a topic in an academic context" or "can communicate with a patient about relevant aspects of their medical history" or "can deal with a routine customer complaint," and so on. Other claims might be somewhat more clearly based on a theory of the domain: "can read texts of a given level of difficulty as defined in terms of parameters such as lexical density or vocabulary level." It is important to note that performance-based claims about what a person can do communicatively in real-world settings, which appeal to a certain "naturalness," in a way defer an elaboration, necessarily theoretical, even if only implicitly, of how this aspect of real-world behavior is understood and of what it consists; this is spelled out more clearly in the next stage.

Step 2 involves determining the kind of *evidence* that would be necessary to support the claims established in step 1. For example, in relation to the claim that the candidate could "communicate with a patient about relevant aspects of their medical history," this would mean that the candidate would have to follow the steps in a narrative both when it is presented as a neat sequence and when it is not, would have to interpret correctly references to relevant lifestyle features that have implications for the history, could cope with idiomatic language used to refer to body parts and disease symptoms, and could interpret culturally embedded humor and irony when relevant to the presentation of the history. This stage of test design clearly depends on a theory of the characteristics of a successful performance—in other words, a construct that will also typically be reflected in the categories of rating scales used to judge the adequacy of the performance.

Step 3 involves defining in general terms the kinds of *task* in which the candidate will be required to engage so that the evidence set out in step 2 might be sought. Clearly, in the example we have just considered, the most directly relevant task would be a complete sample history-taking. In clinical education and assessment, this is made manageable by simulating the event using actors trained to present as patients with a typical history and range of symptoms. This might be unrealistic on logistic grounds; for example, in the case of the Occupational English Test (McNamara, 1996), an Australian test of professionally relevant language proficiency for health professionals, the test is administered outside of Australia to health professionals wishing to emigrate to Australia, under circumstances in which this sort of complex simulation would be impossible to organize. In any case, on cost grounds, the use of complex simulations, even if they are available, will normally be ruled out. As a result, less direct ways of gathering the evidence might need to be envisaged; these might involve testing separately the various aspects of history-taking listed earlier—for example, by completing tasks while listening to a recording of a consultation, being given a test to measure recognition of relevant colloquial or specialized vocabulary, and so on. The validity of inferences from these separate tasks to integrated performance then becomes a necessary subject of investigation; this is a possible example of construct underrepresentation; that is, if the performance requirement of real-world communication involves real-time integration of different components and this skill cannot be predicted from measures of control of the components separately, then the demands of the target use situation are not being adequately represented in the construct and the demands of the test.

All three steps precede the actual writing of specifications for test tasks; they constitute the "thinking stage" of test design. Only when this chain of reasoning is completed can the specifications for test tasks be written. (See Figure 7.2 in chapter 7 of this volume for an example.)

In further stages of Evidence Centered Design, Mislevy goes on to deal with turning the conceptual framework developed in the domain modeling stage into an actual assessment and ensuring that the psychometric properties of the test (involving analysis of the patterns of candidate responses to items and tasks) provide evidence in support of the ultimate claims that we wish to make about test takers. He proposes a series of statistical models in which test data are analyzed to support (or challenge) the logic of the assessment. The discussion here is highly technical and deals in particular with the requirements in terms of measurement, scoring, and logistics for an assessment to implement the relationships in the domain modeling.[2] The final outcome of this is an operational assessment.

Mislevy's conceptual analysis is impressive. Note, however, that its consideration of the social dimension of assessment remains implicit and limited to issues of fairness (McNamara, 2003). For example, Mislevy does not consider the context in which tests are commissioned and, thus, cannot problematize the determination of test constructs as a function of their role in the social and policy environment. As we will see in chapter 7, the conceptualizations on which assessments are ultimately based might be determined from outside as part of a policy that might not involve input from applied linguists or experts on language learning at all. Nor does Mislevy deal directly with the uses of test scores, the decisions for which they form the basis, except insofar as they determine the formulation of relevant claims, which, in any case, is taken as a given and is not problematized. Perhaps he is deliberately circumscribing the scope of his enterprise; this, however, is not acknowledged.[3]

2.3 Kane's Approach to Test Score Validation

Kane has also developed a systematic approach to thinking through the process of drawing valid inferences from test scores. Kane points out that we interpret scores as having meaning. The same score might have different interpretations. For example, scores on a test consisting of reading comprehension passages might be interpreted in very different ways, such as "a measure of skill at answering passage-related questions," "a measure of reading comprehension defined more broadly," "one indicator of verbal aptitude," or "an indicator of some more general construct, such as intelligence" (Kane, 1992, p. 533). Whatever the interpretation we choose, Kane argues, we need an argument to defend the relationship of the score to that interpretation. He calls this an *interpretative argument*, defined as a "chain of inferences from the observed performances to conclusions *and decisions* included in the interpretation" (italics added) (Kane, Crooks, & Cohen, 1999, p. 6). The general character of an interpretative argument is illustrated in Figure 2.6.

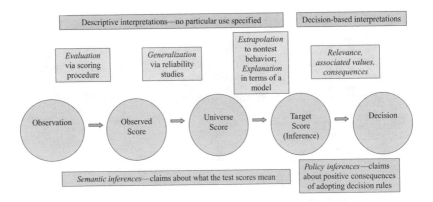

Figure 2.6. Kane: Steps in an interpretative argument.

Kane proposes four types of inference in the chain of inferences constituting the interpretative argument. He uses the metaphor of bridges for each of these inferences; all bridges need to be intact and crossed safely for the final interpretations to be reached. The ultimate decisions are vulnerable to weaknesses in any of the preceding steps; in this way, Kane is clear about the dependency of valid interpretations on the reliability of scores. Let us go through the types of inference in turn and consider the issues that they raise. (Because of the complexity of the model, the reader might prefer to refer to the simpler presentation of the chain of inferences presented in Figure 2.7.)

The first inference is from observation to observed score. In order for assessment to be possible, an instance of learner behavior needs to be observable. This could be the production of a spoken or written text resulting from participation in a communicative event, making marks on a page indicating the choice of answer in a forced choice test, and so on. This behavior is then scored. The first type of inference is that the observed score is a reflection of the observed behavior (i.e., that there is a clear scoring procedure and that it has been applied in the way intended: that criteria are clear and are understood, that the correct scoring key has been used, that scorers conform to the required scoring procedure, and so on).

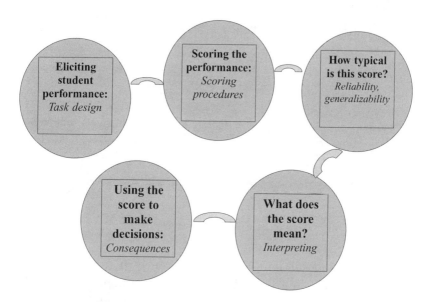

Figure 2.7. Chain of inferences.

The second inference is from the observed score to what Kane called the universe score, deliberately using terminology from generalizability theory (Brennan, 2001). This inference is that the observed score is consistent across tasks, judges, and occasions. This involves the traditional issue of reliability and can be studied effectively using generalizability theory, item response modeling (e.g., in Rasch measurement or other approaches), and other psychometric techniques. A number of kinds of variable typical of performance assessments in language can threaten the validity of this inference, including raters, task, rating scale, candidate characteristics, and interactions among these (cf. the model and discussion in McNamara, 1996).

Here, language testing is like science:

> Consistent with the broader nomothetic view of science from which it arises, the goal of psychometrics is to develop interpretations that are generalizable across individuals and contexts and to understand the limits of those generalizations. Core methods in psychometrics

involve standardized procedures for data collection.... These methods promise replicability and experimental or statistical control of factors deemed irrelevant or ancillary to the variable under study.... Meaningful interpretations are to be found in the patterning of many small, standardized observations within and across individuals. (Moss, Pullin, Gee, & Haertel, 2005, p. 68)

In Messick's words:

The major concern of validity, as of science more generally, is not to explain any single isolated event, behavior or item response, because these almost certainly reflect a confounding of multiple determinants.... Rather, the intent is to account for consistency in behaviors or item responses.... It is important to recognize that the intrusion of context raises issues more of generalizability than of interpretive validity. (Messick, 1989, pp. 14–15)

Kane pointed out that generalization across tasks is often poor in complex performance assessments: that because a person can handle a complex writing task involving one topic and supporting stimulus material it does not necessarily mean that the person will perform in a comparable way on another topic and another set of materials. If task generalizability is weak, or if the impact of raters or the rating process is large, then this "bridge" collapses and we cannot move on in the interpretative argument. For Kane, an interpretative argument is only as strong as its weakest link. In performance-based language tests, the impact of such factors as task, rater, interlocutor, and so on has been consistently shown to be considerable (McNamara, 1996), and an aspect of the social responsibility of testers is to report efforts to estimate the impact of these factors and to control them, for example, through double rating and so on.

The third type of inference, from the universe score to the target score, is that commonly dealt with under the heading of construct validity and is closest to the first cell of Messick's validity matrix. This inference involves *extrapolation* to nontest behavior—in some cases, via *explanation* in terms of a model.

We have seen how complex it is to establish the relationship between test and nontest behavior, a relationship which goes to the heart of tests and which is the basis for Mislevy's elaboration of what is involved.

The fourth type of inference, from the target score to the decision based on the score, moves the test into the world of test use and test context; it encompasses the material in the second, third, and fourth cells of Messick's matrix. Interpreting test scores to form the basis of real-world decisions about individual test takers involves questions of relevance (cell 2), values (cell 3), and consequences (cell 4) (the terms are clearly chosen to reflect Messick's language and concerns). (Bachman, 2005, suggests the term *utilization* to characterize what is involved in this stage.) Decisions involve *decision rules* (e.g., that a student will be admitted to a program of study in an English-medium university with a TOEFL iBT score of, say, 90 or an IELTS score of, say, 7; students scoring below those levels will not be admitted directly, and so on). According to Kane, the argument justifying the decision will be in terms of the positive consequences of the adoption of the decision rules.

Kane thus distinguishes two types of inference (*semantic inferences* and *policy inferences*) and two related types of interpretation. Interpretations that only involve semantic inferences are called *descriptive interpretations*; interpretations involving policy inferences are called *decision-based interpretations*. That is, we might, on the one hand, evaluate the quality of interpretations of test scores (together with the inferences on which they are based) without reference to the context of the use of the test. He calls such interpretations descriptive, and he calls the inferences that they involve semantic. However, when we cross the bridge into actual test use on the other hand, we are engaged in decision-based interpretations and policy inferences.

The question of decision-based interpretations and policy inferences has grown in prominence in Kane's discussion of validity in more recent articles (e.g., Kane, 2002) in response to the continuing prominence of tests as instruments of policy—a topic to be dealt with in chapter 7. Kane argues that just as policy initiatives involving the introduction of programs need to be evaluated, so the use of tests as a policy initiative needs to be evaluated in the same way. Using the example of high-school graduation tests, he writes:

> The use of high-school graduation tests to promote achievement in certain content areas is clearly an educational policy, much like the adoption of a new curriculum. The focus is not on measurement per se, but on achieving certain goals. The test is being used to implement a policy, which will have consequences, some positive and some negative. The test-as-policy should be evaluated in terms of its perceived effectiveness. (Kane, 2002, p. 38)

He is critical of the restriction of validation in such policy contexts to descriptive interpretations:

> I think that much of the current practice in the validation of high-stakes testing programs including high-school graduation tests is seriously flawed, because only part of the interpretive arguments is evaluated. The validity arguments developed to support [the] ... claims [for the success of the policy] seldom go beyond the initial stages in the interpretive argument. ... I do think it would be prudent to investigate the assumptions built into the interpretations assigned to the high-school graduation tests before we subject a generation of high-school students to a potentially powerful treatment. (Kane, 2002, p. 40)

It can be seen then that Kane fully endorses Messick's argument about the need to consider values and consequences as part of defending the interpretation of test scores when those scores are used as the basis for actual decisions in the world. Although, like Messick, he distinguishes between two aspects of validation (policy-related and non-policy-related), both writers are committed to including the social and political dimensions of assessment within the scope of validation of test score inferences. It is also interesting that it is within the discourse of program evaluation that Kane, like Cronbach, found the rationale for conceptualizing the social and policy dimensions of assessment.[4]

The question remains, however, as to who has the authority to insist on the evaluation of policy inferences in an interpretative argument, and it is here that we encounter some of the limitations of the tradition represented by Messick and Kane in addressing the social context of assessment. Kane seems to assume that this kind of evaluation will be authorized routinely:

> If the primary purpose of a testing program is to promote certain outcomes, rather than simply to estimate certain variables, the testing program is functioning as an educational intervention, and therefore merits evaluation of the kind routinely mandated for any new educational program. (Kane, 2002, p. 40)

Wheres this assumption might hold true in some political systems in some settings, it is in fact because of the political *values* of that setting that such evaluations (and the commitment to accountability that they imply) are "routinely mandated"; they actually do not simply happen by default. For other tests that are not simply interventions into publicly accountable educational systems, no such assumption can be made, and evaluation might be resisted. In any case, program evaluations never occur outside a policy setting; the competing interests of stakeholders determine their shape and whether they happen at all. The broader social context in which tests are located is not theorized, but is taken for granted, in this approach; but as we will see in chapters 6 and 7, we need a theory of the social context to understand test use. We will return to this point in the concluding part of this chapter.

2.4 The Social Dimension of Validity in Language Testing

How have discussions of validity in the general educational measurement literature been taken up in language testing? Some of the implications for assessment of the more socially oriented views of communication represented, for example, in the work of Hymes (1967, 1972) were more or less immediately noted in publications at the time (Cooper, 1968; Spolsky, 1967). However, the most elaborated and influential discussion of the validity of communicative language tests, Bachman's landmark *Fundamental*

Considerations in Language Testing (1990), builds its discussion in significant part around Messick's approach to validity. Previous standard language testing references, especially Lado (1961) and Davies (1977), had reflected the existing modeling of validity in terms of different types: criterion validity (concurrent/predictive), content validity, and construct validity. Following Messick, Bachman presented validity as a unitary concept, requiring evidence to support the inferences that we make on the basis of test scores. An example of the immediate relevance of Bachman's presentation of Messick was his reminder (following Messick) of the limits of content-related validity evidence, important given that the European version of the communicative movement in language testing had stressed authenticity of test content—for example, in the British tradition of EAP testing, including the work of Weir on the Test of English for Academic Purposes (TEAP; Weir, 1983) and Alderson and others on the English Language Testing System (ELTS, the precursor to IELTS: Alderson, 1981). A focus on content in the interests of authenticity could not guarantee inferences about individuals based on the test.

Most memorably, Bachman (1990) introduced the Bachman model of communicative language ability, reworking and clarifying the earlier interpretations by Canale and Swain (1980) and Canale (1983) of the relevance of the work of Hymes (1972) on first languages to competence in a second language. The model involves a double level of abstraction. As we have seen, conceptualizing the demands of the target domain or criterion is a critical stage in the development of a test validation framework. In communicative language testing, the target of test inferences is performance of a set of communicative tasks in various contexts of use. How will this target domain be characterized? Bachman does this in two stages. First, he assumes that all contexts have in common that they make specific demands on aspects of test-taker competence; the complete repertoire of aspects of competence is then set out in the famous model of communicative language ability, the Bachman model. This then acts as a kind of menu to be drawn upon to model the context of use. Bachman handled characterization of specific target language use situations and, hence, of test content in terms of what he called test method facets. The section of the volume on characterizing the target language use situation recapitulates the chapter on communicative language ability, because context is characterized in terms of that ability. This is deliberate, as Bachman argues that the target language use context and, hence, test content have to be characterized in terms of the general model of ability in order for inferences about that ability to be retrieved from engagement with test content. The duplication feels somewhat unwieldy, a feeling that is also a function of the complexity of the model itself, which, being general, also needs to be exhaustive.

This a priori approach to characterizing the social context of use in terms of a model of individual ability obviously severely constrains the conceptualization of the social dimension of the assessment context. Although the terms in which communicative language ability is discussed include social dimensions such as sociolinguistic appropriateness, drawing on the ethnographic work of Hymes, the model is clearly primarily cognitive and psychological, a reflection of the broader traditions both of linguistics and educational measurement in which Bachman's work is firmly located. (In fact, an incommensurability between psychological and social orientations to competence was a problem inherent in Hymes's own work, a fact pointed out by Halliday, 1978). The social context of the target language use situation is conceived from the perspective of the language user (i.e., defined in terms of its demands on the learner's abilities). There is thus a feedback loop between context and ability: The target language use situation is conceptualized in terms of components of communicative language ability, which, in turn, is understood as the ability to handle the target language use situation. The situation or context is projected onto the learner as a demand for a relevant set of cognitive abilities; in turn, these cognitive abilities are read onto the context. What we do not have here is a theory of the social context in its own right, as it were (i.e., a theory that is not primarily concerned with the cognitive demands of the setting on the candidate).

A decade and more of grappling with the operationalization of a validity framework as complex as that proposed by Messick and as interpreted by Bachman has led to debate about the feasibility of the project of validating inferences from scores on language tests. Chapelle (1998) considers how to frame a validation argument in terms of Bachman's model and gives fully worked examples in relation to the testing of vocabulary (see also Chapelle, 1994). However, those who have used the test method facets approach in actual research and development projects have found it difficult to use (Clapham, 1996) or have acknowledged it in a very general sense (Commonwealth of Australia, 1994), and it has in fact been implemented in relatively few test development projects (Davies, 1995). Bachman's approach appears to be more successful as a powerful intellectual framework for considering validity in language tests—for example, acting as a conceptual mold within which a number of very helpful books have been written (Alderson, 2000; Bachman, 2004; Buck, 2001; Douglas, 2000; Luoma, 2003; Purpura, 2004; Read, 2000; Weigle, 2002) on various aspects of language testing, in a series edited by Bachman and Alderson.

One influential attempt to make language test development and validation work more manageable has been proposed by Bachman (Bachman & Palmer, 1996) via an overarching notion of *test usefulness*, which requires a trade-off among six aspects: *reliability, construct validity, authenticity, interactiveness, impact,* and *practicality*. Note here that a metanarrative of "usefulness" has replaced Messick's construct validity, a fact that the authors acknowledge: "Authenticity, interactiveness and impact are three qualities that many measurement specialists consider to be part of validity" (p. 41); among such "specialists," we must include the earlier Bachman. The price of manageability is a certain loss of theoretical coherence, although that might not be of primary relevance to practitioners.

The desire to make test validation a manageable process is reflected again in a series of recent publications from Bachman in which he turns to the work of Mislevy and Kane. For example,

> In this chapter I will describe the process of investigating the validity of test use, which we call validation, in terms of building an interpretive argument and collecting evidence in support of that argument. This perspective draws on the work of Michael Kane (Kane, 1992; Kane, 2002; Kane, Crooks, & Cohen, 1999), who describes validation in terms of an interpretative argument, and Robert Mislevy (Mislevy, 1996; Mislevy, Steinberg, & Almond, 2002, 2003) who describes assessment as reasoning from evidence. In this perspective, the process of validation includes two interrelated activities:
>
> 1. articulating an interpretive argument (also referred to as a validation argument), which provides the logical framework linking test performance to an intended interpretation and use, and
>
> 2. collecting relevant evidence in support of the intended interpretations and uses.
>
> The advantage of this perspective, I believe, is that it provides a transparent means for linking the dominant theoretical view of validity as a unitary concept, as described by Messick (1989) and Bachman (1990), with a plan and set of practical procedures for investigating the validity of the uses we make of scores from a particular language test. That is, this perspective enables us to link an abstract, theoretical and general conceptualization of validity with the concrete, specific and localized procedures that are required in the validation of a particular test use. (Bachman, 2004, p. 258)

Note that this position reflects a return to the metanarrative of validity and follows Kane in accepting that test use is part of the validation argument. The concern for manageability no longer involves a loss of theoretical coherence. Bachman goes on to describe in detail procedures for validation of test use decisions, following Mislevy et al. (2003) in suggesting that they follow the structure of a Toulmin argument (i.e., a procedure for practical reasoning involving articulating claims and providing arguments and evidence both in their favor [warrants or backing] and against [rebuttals]).

Following Bachman, Chapelle, Enright, and Jamieson (2004) used Kane's framework as the basis for a validity argument for the new TOEFL iBT, arguably the largest language test development and validation effort yet undertaken. They explain how research commissioned as part of the development project can be seen as providing evidence in support of assumptions and inferences at each stage of the development of the test. The studies they cite were restricted at the time they were writing, prior to the implementation of the test, to descriptive interpretations and semantic inferences, to use Kane's terms; they argue that decision-based interpretations and policy inferences about utility and washback "await the operational phase" (p. 16).

To date, no studies of such interpretations and inferences for language tests have been reported within a Kanean framework, although Bachman (2005), elaborating the position set out in Bachman (2004), argues for the potential of Kane's model in validating decision-based interpretations and policy inferences in language tests and proposes the concept of an *assessment use argument*. In his earlier work, Bachman (1990), following Messick, had acknowledged the need to make explicit both the role of values implicit in test constructs and the consequences of testing practice as necessary aspects of validity research, but this was in minor key in that volume. Now, Bachman engages explicitly and in detail with these issues:

> An assessment use argument is an overall logical framework for linking assessment performance to use (decisions). This assessment use argument includes two parts: an assessment utilization argument, linking an interpretation to a decision, and an assessment validity argument, which links assessment performance to an interpretation.[5] (Bachman, 2005 p. 1)

Although Bachman clearly adopts the Kanean framework for considering decisions and use as part of the responsibility of test developers, he appears to maintain a distinction between "validity" and "test use" as applying to different domains, both when discussing his own approach and in discussions of other writers (Kunnan, 2003; Lynch, 2001; Shohamy, 1998, 2001) whom he rightly sees as sharing his interest in the relationship between validity and use. In this he differs from Kane, who importantly conceives of the interpretative argument (including decisions) as a single multistage process, each stage of which needs to be validated; decisions are simply another sort of interpretation, requiring validation like all of the others.

Kane's integration has certain advantages, in that it sees test use and test consequences as aspects of validity, although the distinction between semantic inferences and policy inferences upholds a separation that survives even into Messick's matrix, where it reflects, as we have seen, the development of validity theory from its relatively asocial psychometric origins. In the language testing literature, there has been considerable research on test consequences under the headings of *test washback* (Alderson & Wall, 1996; Cheng, Watanabe, & Curtis, 2004; Messick, 1996), usually referring to the effect on teaching in subject areas that will be examined, and *test impact* (Clapham & Corson, 1997; Wall, 1997), referring to broader sorts of impacts in the school and beyond. Summaries of discussions of the consequential aspects of language test validation can be found in McNamara (1998, 2006). It should be noted in passing that the popularization of the concept of washback following the influential early article by Alderson and Wall (1993) represents the reemergence of a much earlier tradition of critique of the influence of tests within educational systems (Latham, 1877; Sutherland, 1973; White, 1888; useful general discussions are available in Madaus and Kellaghan, 1992, and Spolsky, 1995). Kane integrated such concerns into the structure of the interpretative argument, under the heading of policy inferences. One such policy-related inference raised by Kane is the effect on instruction of assessments used to achieve policy goals. Using again the example of high school graduation tests, he considers unintended consequences:

Does the high-school dropout rate increase after the introduction of a test? Does the number of students taking art, music, physical education, and other courses not directly related to the [test] decrease? Does participation in extracurricular activities (sports, clubs) go down? Are students spending a lot of time and effort on test-preparation activities? (Kane, 2002, pp. 38–39)

Integrating studies of washback and impact into a larger interpretative argument has the advantage of framing the significance of such studies more clearly in terms of investigating the policy assumptions involved in testing programs.

2.5 The Broader Social Context: The Limits of Validity

In both the work of Kane and in work in language testing, with one or two notable exceptions, the wider social context in which language tests are commissioned and have their place is still not adequately theorized. For example, Bachman (2004) writes:

Language tests have become a pervasive part of our education system and society. Scores from language tests are used to make inferences about individuals' language ability and to inform decisions we make about those individuals. For example, we use language tests to help us identify second or foreign language learners in schools, to select students for admission to universities, to place students into language programs, to screen potential immigrants and to select employees. Language tests thus have the potential for helping us collect useful information that will benefit a wide variety of individuals. However, to realize this potential, we need to be able to demonstrate that scores we obtain from language tests are reliable, and that the ways in which we interpret and use language test scores are valid. (Bachman, 2004, p. 3)

What is noticeable here is that the context in which language tests are used is presented quite unproblematically; the responsibility of the tester is to make the "beneficial" information in the test as "useful" as possible.

Such optimism about the social role of tests is even reflected by Kunnan (2003), who in his writings on testing and elsewhere is concerned with broader social and policy issues. He proposes as one of the principles of his test fairness framework the following:

> Principle 2: *The Principle of Beneficence*: A test ought to bring about good in society . . .

> Sub-principle 1: A test ought to promote good in society by providing test-score information and social impacts that are beneficial to society. (Kunnan, 2003, pp. 33–34)

In sharp contrast to this liberal ameliorist position is the critical analysis of the political function of tests, a movement known as critical language testing (Shohamy, 1998, 2001). Shohamy, the originality and significance of whose work lies in the fundamental theoretical challenge it presents to existing philosophies of testing, considers the role and function of tests in the broadest political light, citing the work of Bourdieu, Foucault, and other social theorists to conceptualize that function. For example, she asks:

> The ease with which tests have become so accepted and admired by all those who are affected by them is remarkable. How can tests persist in being so powerful, so influential, so domineering and play such enormous roles in our society? One answer to this question is that tests have become symbols of power for both individuals and society. Based on Bourdieu's . . . notion of symbolic power, [we] will examine the symbolic power and ideology of tests and the specific mechanisms that society invented to enhance such symbolic power. (Shohamy, 2001, p. 117)

Lynch (2001), like Shohamy, also suggests a variety of principles to be considered in understanding the potential of tests to be sites of unfairness or injustice at the societal level. Clearly, there is nothing in Kane's model of an interpretative argument, or in its adoption within language testing, even when it focuses on test use, that would invite such reflection.

For example, in considering the application of Toulmin's argument structure (see above) for the validation of test use decisions, Bachman includes among the warrants:

> [E]vidence collected from a variety of sources, such as prior research, specific validation research to support the warrant that is conducted as part of the test development process, prevailing institutional and societal norms, government regulations, and laws. (Bachman, 2005, p. 24)

The reference to social values and policies as having a role in warrants, but apparently not in rebuttal (although this is not stated explicitly), sets this position in opposition to critical language testing, which sees an analysis of the use of tests in the light of "prevailing institutional and societal norms, government regulations, and laws" as precisely the target of critique.

Elsewhere, Bachman appears to want to quarantine such concerns from the validation process for specific tests:

> Other principles [cited by Shohamy]—such as the claim that "language testing is not neutral", the need for language testers to develop a critical view of tests and to critique the value of these, and the view of test takers as "political subjects in a political context" (Shohamy, 2001, p. 131)—are, it seems to me, premises that could well be incorporated into a code of ethics or a code of fair testing practice, rather than being articulated in an assessment use argument for a particular test. (Bachman, 2005, p. 28)

Bachman is right to suggest that it is not practical to attempt to incorporate the perspective of test takers as "political subjects in a political context" in an interpretative argument (although, we might add, so much the worse for an approach to understanding tests that restricts our thinking to the terms of an interpretative argument, fundamental to test design and construction as this might be). Nevertheless, it is surely wrong to think that such issues can be dealt with in a code of ethics or a code of practice;

although such codes are important, and have their place, as we will see in chapter 5, they simply cannot do justice to the depth and complexity of the social and political functions of language tests. Those functions are at the present time hardly discussed and not well understood, except in the work of Shohamy. In chapters 6 and 7 we will outline the kinds of intellectual perspective, far removed from validity theory as it is currently understood, or as it could, indeed, conceivably be, that make possible an understanding of the role of language tests in enforcing particular policies and in maintaining the identities and power relations that are characteristic of modern societies. If language testing research is to be more than a technical field, it must at the very least as a counterpoint to its practical activity develop an ongoing critique of itself as a site for the articulation and perpetuation of social relations. In this way, language testing research has a chance to move beyond the limits of validity theory and make a proper contribution to the wider discussion of the general and specific functions of tests in contemporary society.

2.6 Conclusion

In this chapter we have tried to set out the necessary theoretical foundation for the larger argument of the volume. We have considered the nature and main concerns of current validity theory—in particular, the influential model of Messick and its interpretation within both educational measurement and language testing. We have seen a gradual return to considering the uses of test scores and the need to bring validity evidence to bear on the decisions about individuals based on test scores. We have also seen the struggle with which the field has faced the necessity to incorporate questions involving policy and values into what was initially the secure domain of traditional psychometric considerations and constraints, from which such questions, which had been a concern from the inception of the use of tests in Europe from the 15th century, appeared to have been banished.

Understanding the social function of tests can be seen by many authors as introducing an unmanageable aspect into language testing research, opening a Pandora's box of issues with no chance of practical resolution. Implicit in Mislevy's, Kane's, and Bachman's otherwise brilliant and challenging work, for example, is a commitment to working from within, at most questioning the usefulness of tests, and refraining from going further in examining the social implications of test use. The fact that the most influential current model for thinking about language tests, outlined in Bachman and Palmer (1996), makes test usefulness (and not even validity) as the overarching criterion is significant in this regard. This is arguably a prudent ground to hold for those engaged in actual test development; but it precludes an understanding of some of the most fundamental aspects of the social meaning of tests, which simply cannot be relegated to some residual "too hard basket." Lacking in such a position is a theory of the social context of testing in its own right, or engagement with the issues of ideology and power raised by Shohamy and Lynch. These issues are also raised in the work of writers in general education such as Moss (1998), who similarly locates her concern for test consequences in a discussion of the work of Foucault, Bourdieu, and other critics of the positivism of the social sciences. In discussing the social impact of assessment practice, she states:

> This perspective on the dialectical relationship between social reality and our representation of it has implications for understanding the crucial role of evidence about consequences in validity research.... The practices in which we engage help to construct the social reality we study. While this may not be apparent from the administration of any single test, over time the effects accumulate.... While this argument has some implications for validity theory as it relates to specific interpretations and uses of test scores, the import spills over...to encompass the general practice of testing.... The scope of the [validity] argument goes well beyond...test specific evaluation practices; it entails ongoing evaluation of the dialectical relationship between the products and practices of testing, writ large, and the social reality that is recursively represented and transformed. (Moss, 1998, p. 11)

Some of the deeper social meaning of language testing as a social practice, and the conceptual tools available from outside validity theory with which to understand it, will be presented in the discussions of the social and political roles of language tests in chapters 6 and 7.

Notes

[1] In a recent review, Smith (2005) claims that construct validation has evolved beyond the "justificationist" tradition of trying to show, once and for all, that a certain test "works." He sees greater acceptance of the ongoing nature of construct validation with continual critical examination and revision of theories.

[2] Curiously, and confusingly, Mislevy calls the technical implementation blueprint a "conceptual assessment framework," although this term is more suited to the nature of the domain modeling phase.

[3] In a recent personal communication (April 2, 2006) Mislevy clarifies his position as follows:

> The main reason I focus on technical and epistemological issues is that by coincidences of training, experiences, and interest, I find myself in a position to make what I think are useful contributions along these lines—needed, I believe, to take assessment to the next level in response to advances in technology and psychology. So many problems I see in assessment, socially as well as technically, arise from inadequate conceptualizations of the assessment enterprise.

[4] Alan Davies has throughout his long career stressed the association between language testing and language program evaluation (cf. Davies, 1977, and the formulation of the goals of the Language Testing Research Centre at The University of Melbourne, of which he was the first director; these included both language testing research and work in language program evaluation). Although this association has often taken the form in practice of the use of tests to determine outcomes within program evaluations, the association goes beyond this explicit level. It reflects Davies's enduring interest in the social dimension of applied linguistics research.

[5] Bachman introduces a potentially confusing distinction between a validity argument and a validation argument ("I will use the term validation to refer to the process of collecting evidence, or backing, to support the entire assessment use argument"; p. 16). The former is restricted to what Kane calls descriptive interpretations and the semantic inferences on which they depend. The latter corresponds to what Kane calls the entire interpretative argument, which includes decision-based interpretations.

CHAPTER THREE

The Social Dimension of Proficiency: How Testable Is It?

In this chapter we will consider the way in which more socially oriented views of the construct of language proficiency pose unresolved challenges for language assessment. In this, we are addressing (in the terms set out in our discussion of validity in chapter 2) test constructs (the first cell in Messick's matrix), which involve the claims that we want to make about test takers on the basis of their test performance (Mislevy), and the following steps in the interpretative argument: generalization, extrapolation, and explanation (Kane). (In chapters 6 and 7 we will consider issues in relation to the remaining cells in the matrix.) Developments in our understanding of proficiency in language and what is required in second language (L2) communication trigger revisions to the claims that we wish to make about individuals in the light of this. The most dramatic example of such a shift are the changes in assessment associated with the advent of the communicative movement in language teaching in the mid-1970s. Perhaps the most significant contribution of the development of communicative testing was a renewed focus on performance tests. There was a shift from seeing language proficiency in terms of knowledge of structure (phonological, grammatical, lexical), which could be best tested using discrete-point, multiple-choice items, to an emphasis on the integration of many aspects of language knowledge and skill in performance, requiring evidence of the ability to comprehend and produce whole texts and to participate in face-to-face communication under real-time processing conditions. The project of communicative language testing, despite its significant achievements, remains incomplete. Current understanding of the social dimension of communication, it turns out, poses extremely difficult challenges for the conceptualization and implementation of assessment, challenges that to date have not been met. In this chapter we will set out the nature of the problem and current attempts to address it. We will consider in detail the challenges for assessment posed by two areas in which the assessment construct involves a social dimension of communication: the assessment of face-to-face interaction and the assessment of pragmatics.

3.1 Assessing Face-to-face Interaction

The advent of communicative language testing saw a growing preference for face-to-face interaction as the context in which the assessment of spoken language skills would occur. In fact, the practice was not necessarily new: Spoken performance tests already existed in the form of the U.S. Government Foreign Service Institute (FSI) test and the British tradition of examinations, but these practices were seriously undertheorized.

Communicative testing soon encountered a major theoretical hurdle. Language assessment in face-to-face interaction takes place within what Goffman (1983) called the interaction order:

> Social interaction... [is] that which uniquely transpires in social situations, that is, environments in which two or more individuals are physically in one another's response presence..... This face-to-face domain... [is] an analytically viable one... which might be titled the interaction order... [and] whose preferred method of study is microanalysis. (Goffman, 1983, p. 2)

Goffman (1964) had realized that what he called "the neglected situation" in social theory provided fundamental challenges for theories of social behavior. This social situation, "an environment of mutual monitoring possibilities," is rule-governed:

> Cultural rules . . . socially organize the behavior of those in the situation . . . . Face to face interaction has its own regulations; it has its own processes and its own structure, and these don't seem to be intrinsically linguistic in character, however often expressed through a linguistic medium. (pp. 135–136)

Following the identification of the face-to-face domain as a social domain with its own cultural rules, the nature of behavior in this domain, and the rules that constrain it, began to be systematically explored in the work of students of Goffman, Harvey Sacks and Emanuel Schegloff, who developed the study of talk-in-interaction in a field that came to be known as Conversation Analysis. For a long time, this work developed quite independently of work in language testing, until a fortuitous administrative coincidence: The establishment of strong structural links in the early 1990s between Schegloff's group in Sociology at UCLA and the distinguished Applied Linguistics program there saw a new synergy and cross-fertilization. A growing realization began to emerge of the significance of the fact that tests of oral proficiency that involved face-to-face interaction were occurring within the interaction order and, thus, were subject to its rules. What implications did this have for understanding the nature of proficiency in speaking in an L2? Students in Applied Linguistics who were supervised by Schegloff, including Anne Lazaraton and Agnes Weiyun He, wrote dissertations using Conversation Analytic techniques on data from oral proficiency interviews; this was followed by an influential edited volume on the subject (Young & He, 1998). What emerged from this confluence of research traditions was a renewed realization that for speaking tests, the presence of an interlocutor in the test setting introduces an immediate and overt social context, which presented fundamental challenges for the existing individualistic theories of language proficiency (Chalhoub-Deville & Deville, 2004; McNamara, 1997). The issue was articulated by Jacoby and Ochs (1995, p. 177):

> One of the important implications for taking the position that everything is co-constructed through interaction is

that it follows that there is a distributed responsibility
among interlocutors for the creation of sequential coherence, identities, meaning, and events. This means that
language, discourse and their effects cannot be considered
deterministically preordained . . . by assumed constructs of
individual competence.

In a sequence of three articles all bearing the title (in part)
"Discourse as an Interactional Achievement," Schegloff (1982,
1988, 1995) set out this position clearly. For example, he stated:

> It is some 15 years now since Charles Goodwin . . . gave
> a convincing demonstration of how the final form
> of a sentence in ordinary conversation had to be
> understood as an interactional product . . . Goodwin's ac-
> count . . . serves . . . as a compelling call for the inclusion of
> the hearer in what were purported to be the speaker's pro-
> cesses. (Schegloff, 1995, p. 192)

This work poses a fundamental theoretical challenge. To
adopt a social view of performance in this sense is at some level
incompatible with taking the traditional view of performance as
a simple projection or display of individual competence. Psychology, linguistics, and psychometrics assume that it is possible to
read off underlying individual cognitive abilities from the data of
performance. However, the position of Conversation Analysis is
that the interlocutor is implicated in each move by the candidate;
that is, the performance is a dance in which it makes no sense to
isolate the contributions of the individual dance partners. How
are we to generalize from these instances of use? How are we to
speak of communicative competence as residing in the individual if we are to "include the hearer in the speaker's processes"?
Halliday (1978) had pointed out this difficulty in commentary on
the work of Hymes (1972) on communicative competence when he
saw that the term "competence," a reference to Chomsky's (exclusively cognitive) notion of (linguistic) competence, had "sold the
pass," as it were, by psychologizing what was essentially a social
and cultural notion, although conceptualized very differently in
the anthropological and sociolinguistic traditions represented by

Hymes and Halliday, respectively, from the understanding of the social implicit in Conversation Analysis.

Research on this issue has taken a number of directions. Discourse analysts have focused on defining and clarifying the interactional nature of the oral proficiency interview. The Conversational Analytic tradition of research is best represented by the collection edited by Young and He (1998), which contains a number of chapters offering a Conversation Analysis account of interaction in the context of the oral proficiency interview; a book by Johnson (2001) considers the event from another interactional perspective: sociocultural theory. The result has been to emphasize the contribution of both parties to the performance, thus making it difficult to isolate of the contribution of the candidate, which is the target of measurement and reporting. Another result has been to disclose the peculiar character of the oral proficiency interview as a communicative event and to underline its institutional character. The specific interactional character of the interview was defined in an inspired early article by Van Lier (1989). In contrast to claims by the proponents of the oral proficiency interview that the interaction is fundamentally conversational in character, this research shows clearly that the interview departs from conversation in significant ways, with unequal distribution of opportunities to initiate topic changes, ask questions, and so on. In Stevenson's memorable phrase, "This is a test, not a tea party" (Stevenson, 1985). This means that any inference from the test performance to performance on conversational tasks must necessarily be indirect. Lado, in comments offered in a discussion of a paper on oral proficiency interviewing presented at a conference in Washington in 1974, was one of the earliest to recognized the issue:

> I do not agree that the interview is more natural than the other forms of tests, because if I'm being interviewed and I know that my salary and my promotion depend on it, no matter how charming the interviewer and his assistants are, this couldn't be any more unnatural. (Jones & Spolsky, 1975, p. 7)

The charge of unnaturalness and the clear differences between the interview and casual conversation are not in themselves a fatal blow to the oral proficiency interview, as the gap between the evidence obtained under test conditions and inferences about performance in nontest conditions is a given in assessment, as we saw in chapter 2. The validity of those inferences must be established, by proposing that interaction in both settings shares fundamental features that allow for the possibility of inference from performance on one to performance on the other, and empirical evidence of the ability to predict performance in nontest settings on the basis of test scores.

Language testers have tried to understand the construct, measurement, and test design implications of the joint construction of performance in oral proficiency interviews. The response from within the psychometric tradition is to maintain the goal of disentangling the role of the interlocutor by treating it as a variable like any other, to be controlled for, thus allowing us to focus again exclusively on the candidate. The research program has taken the form of trying to identify the contribution of the interlocutor, either in general, or as belonging to particular social or professional categories, including those based on gender, degree of training, professional background, native-speaker status, and so on, as a way of understanding and hence controlling for the influence of such category membership. The impact of the interlocutor on scores has also been studied. Again, this program can be seen as taking up a research agenda articulated years earlier. Lado had again identified the issues in remarks made at the 1974 conference referred to earlier:

> I think that there are questions concerning the interview from the point of view of sample, and I think that the interview is a poor sample. For example, most interviews don't give the subject a chance to ask questions. He gets asked questions, but he doesn't ask them. And it seems to me that asking questions is a very important element of communication... There's the personality of the interviewer and interviewee. There's also the fact

of accents. Sociolinguistics has shown that we react differently to different accents. For example, the Spanish accent in an English-speaking test will tend to rate lower than a French or a German accent. (Jones & Spolsky, 1975, p. 24).

The most comprehensive study of the role of the interlocutor in performances in oral proficiency interviews is that of Brown (2003, 2005), on which the following discussion draws. Brown's study design involved the same candidates completing two oral proficiency interviews with different interlocutors (one male and one female), with the performances being audio-recorded and then multiply rated independently from tape by a series of raters, none of whom was aware that the same candidate was presenting twice (the performances of interest were seeded into a larger rating task involving many candidates; the absence of a visual medium meant that visual identification was not possible). Brown first found that it was possible to identify score patterns (higher or lower scores) for candidates paired with particular interlocutors. Different interlocutors seemed to pose consistently different levels of challenge: It was harder for candidates to get good scores when they were paired with some interlocutors than when they were paired with others. What was the source of this effect? Brown went on to investigate two possible sources: the behavior of interlocutors as revealed through discourse analysis, and the comments of raters as they listened to the performances, using think-aloud techniques. Brown took a particular pair of interviewers associated with contrasting candidate score patterns and identified interactional behaviors that seemed to differentiate them. These included the topical focus and functional pitch of the questions, their questioning techniques (the use of open and closed questions and indirect elicitation strategies), the type of feedback that they provided, and their speech styles. The strategies of the interlocutor whose interviewing was associated with higher scores seemed generally supportive, as they involved selecting familiar and personal topics, eliciting mainly description, in doing so lowering the challenge to the candidate, and structuring topical sequences so that they were introduced with one or two closed questions in which the topic was introduced and background information elicited, followed by explicit requests for elaborated responses ("Tell me about..."). Regular feedback was provided in the form of news markers, echoes, assessments, and formulations, all of which are said to indicate interest and understanding.

The interactional style of the interviewer with whom candidates gained lower scores provided a clear contrast. Topical choices were less personal, thereby increasing the functional challenges greatly; in addition to description, the functions of speculation, argument, and opinion were elicited. The questioning technique used was also less explicit, involving closed questions, statements, echoes, and tokens such as "Yeah?" to try to elicit talk, despite the fact that this strategy often failed to elicit more than a minimal response. The candidate's turns elicited fewer acknowledgment or other response tokens from this interlocutor.

Given these differences, one could argue that it is not surprising that candidates achieved better scores with the interviewer whose style seemed designed to facilitate candidate performance. However, the next part of the study, using data from a retrospective recall study of raters listening to the above performances, showed that although the interactional features noted were, indeed, of significance to raters, they were in fact interpreted in a surprising way. It turned out that raters in fact tended to react negatively to aspects of the style of the seemingly more "facilitative" interviewer and other features of this interviewer such as slower speech rate, clear enunciation, and the use of exaggerated pitch and intonation movement, which were seen as lowering the challenge for the candidate and patronizing. Raters tended to compensate the candidates with higher scores on the grounds that the candidates' chances of displaying the full extent of their ability had been hampered by this interactional style. Thus, although interaction emerges as a crucial issue in this study, its impact on scores is harder to predict, thus making it harder to "manage" from a measurement point of view. A further complicating factor is that institutional needs are in line with the psychometric orientation to individual cognitive ability: What is required is not a faithful account of the interaction but a score about individual candidates that can be then fed into institutional decision-making procedures.

The study of interaction in face-to-face communication in test settings has the potential to help us rethink our understanding of the listening construct. It has long been recognized as anomalous that tests of listening usually involve noninteractive listening (the candidate is not listening while interacting), although this is, by far, the most common setting in which listening occurs. Instead, listening involves passive reception of either monologic or (at best) dialogic texts, broadcast to the listening candidates, who are then required to answer preset questions on the material to which they are listening. Here the listening construct is understood purely cognitively, an orientation which is reinforced by the administrative convenience of testing listening in this way. Sometimes comprehension is included as a score category within the rating of oral interaction (e.g., in the Occupational English Test [OET]), but research shows that raters have difficulty making judgments of comprehension under such circumstances, tending to be generous in their scoring and giving candidates the benefit of the doubt. Recently, however, a new opportunity to reconsider listening has arisen in the context of the considerable research going into an increasingly popular face-to-face format: the paired or group oral. For example, Ducasse (2006) has studied a paired oral format for beginning-level university students of Spanish as a foreign language. She has analyzed comments from raters engaged in distinguishing a series of paired performances in order to establish an empirical basis for the wording of the category "interaction" used in scoring scales for performance on this test and she has found that raters are consistently oriented to features of the interaction on the part of the listener in the pair. This important research has the potential to begin to provide a definition of the listening construct in interaction and to use this as the basis for attempts to measure it.

Although the joint construction of performance remains the prime theoretical issue facing the validity of inferences from oral interviews, an issue extensively and helpfully discussed in a series of papers by Chalhoub-Deville and Deville (Chalhoub-Deville, 2003; Chalhoub-Deville & Deville, 2004; Deville & Chalhoub-Deville, 2006), the social character of the interaction has also been conceptualized from more macrosociological points of view, as potentially being influenced by the identities of the candidate and interlocutor/rater. What is at issue here is the extent to which such features as the gender of participants, the professional identity and experience of the interviewer/rater, the native-speaker status (or otherwise) of the interviewer/rater, the language background of the candidate, and so on influence the interaction and its outcome. Qualitative research methods feature extensively in such research. A survey of the range of topics involved and the methodologies used is available in McNamara, Hill, and May (2002), which also provides detailed references for the studies.

Such studies, particularly where they involve participants in the interaction directly (interviewer and candidate, paired candidates) rather than a nonparticipant (e.g., where the rater is working from an audio-recording or video-recording of the interaction), engage with the complex issue of the presence and relevance of macrosociological categories at the micro-level of interaction. This is the subject of intensive ongoing debate in discourse studies of macrosocial phenomena (e.g., feminist discourse studies, studies of racism, the movement known as Critical Discourse Analysis in general, and discursive psychology). Those committed to understanding the ordering of the microsocial level of interaction, particularly those working within Conversation Analysis, complain that some discourse analysts read too quickly and without proper empirical foundation the relevance of macrosocial categories in the unfolding of interaction, and they insist that such influence must necessarily be mediated through the fabric of the constraints on interaction at the microsocial level. Critics of this position feel frustrated at the way in which, for them, self-evident power structures are "placed on hold" in such fine-grained analysis. The debate is illustrated by recent exchanges between Schegloff, on the one hand, and Billig and Wetherell, who work in discursive psychology, on the other (Billig, 1999a, 1999b; Schegloff, 1997, 1998, 1999; Wetherell, 1998).

Take, for example, the issue of the possible impact on scores of the gender of the interlocutors in oral proficiency interviews. This issue has been studied extensively, with inconclusive results. Brown and McNamara (2004) examine data from the study by Brown (2005) to investigate whether the interactional differences identified by Brown are associated with the gender variable. (Seeing gender as a variable potentially generating construct-irrelevant variance is how the issue would be seen from within the psychometric tradition.) They show that there was no consistent association, with female interlocutors also showing characteristics conventionally associated with male interactional behavior, and suggest that the framing of the interaction as a test, where the interviewers, who are also teachers, display "teacherly" qualities in interaction with candidates, foreground other aspects of identity than gendered ones. This corresponds to the Conversation Analysis position that the relevance of social identities in interaction needs to be demonstrated, not simply assumed, and illustrates the general problem of essentializing and dichotomizing gender. In this, language testing emerges as an appropriate site for the study of institutional and other social identities in the context of face-to-face interaction, and the value of detailed study of interaction for illuminating long-standing issues in language testing research is also demonstrated. Moreover, this applies to language testing contexts other than oral proficiency interviewing for educational purposes. In a recent study of Danish naturalization interviews, Fogtmann (2006) uses Conversation Analysis as a methodology for investigating outcomes in interviews between applicants applying for Danish citizenship and Danish police officers, in the course of which the police officer has to decide whether the applicant fulfills the naturalization language requirement: that the applicant be able to "understand and make him/herself understood."[1] She argues that the outcomes for applicants crucially depended on the behavior of the police officer conducting the interview. The use of language assessments as part of citizenship procedures is taken up in detail in chapter 6.

3.2 Assessing Second Language Pragmatics

Assessment of L2 pragmatics tests language use in social settings, but unlike oral proficiency tests, it does not necessarily focus on conversation or extracting speech samples. Because of its highly contextualized nature, assessment of pragmatics leads to significant tension between the construction of authentic assessment tasks and practicality: Social context must be established and learner responses are often productive, so simulations of real-world situations and scoring by human raters would be ideal, but they are also very costly. It is indicative of these difficulties that only few tests are available in this area.

We will begin with a brief description of L2 pragmatics, followed by a review of some of the larger assessment instruments for L2 pragmatics. We will then discuss some of the perennial issues of testing pragmatics, especially the use and misuse of discourse completion tests (DCTs), and highlight issues in testing sociopragmatics. We will also briefly explore the possibility of an L2-specific norm, and the assessment of pragmatic aptitude. We will conclude with some suggestions for future research and practice in the area.

3.2.1 Second Language Pragmatics

Pragmatics is the study of language use in a social context, and language users' pragmatic competence is their "ability to act and interact by means of language" (Kasper & Roever, 2005, p. 317). Pragmatics is a broad field, covering such diverse areas as implicature, deixis, speech acts, conversational management, situational routines, and others (Leech, 1983; Levinson, 1983; Mey, 2001). Pragmatic ability in an L2 requires offline knowledge and online control of the linguistic and the sociocultural aspects of pragmatics; following Leech, "sociopragmatic" knowledge describes knowledge of the target language community's social rules, appropriateness norms, discourse practices, and accepted behaviors, whereas "pragmalinguistic" knowledge encompasses the linguistic tools necessary to "do things with words" (Austin, 1962)—for example, produce comprehensible discourse, make requests, surrender a turn in a conversation, and so forth. Both components of pragmatic competence are equally necessary: language users who know target language sociopragmatic norms but have no pragmalinguistic tools at their disposal are prevented from even participating in interaction. Conversely, users who command a range of pragmalinguistic tools but use them unconstrained by sociopragmatic rules may unwittingly give offense, index roles and stances they do not intend to convey, or be entirely incomprehensible. Because of the connection between sociopragmatics and pragmalinguistics, it is often difficult in practice to determine whether a given error was due to pragmalinguistic or sociopragmatic deficits. For example, if an utterance is missing requisite politeness markers, this might be because the learner does not know these markers (pragmalinguistic deficit) or they might know the markers but not be aware that those markers need to be used in the given situation (sociopragmatic deficit). The situation is complicated further by learners' subjective choice: They might choose not to follow L2 discourse norms in order to assert their identity. For example, Siegal (1994) presents the case of her learner Mary, who asserts topic control in communicating with her professor in Japanese, which is normally the prerogative of the higher status interlocutor. Mary seems to want to establish a more equal relationship and be recognized as a fellow researcher, being an established high school teacher and a postgraduate student in her native New Zealand, rather than be viewed as simply another international student.

Because of the close connection between pragmalinguistics and sociopragmatics, it is difficult to design a test that tests pragmalinguistics to the exclusion of sociopragmatics or vice versa.

Still, most tests of pragmatics have focused on one or the other aspect of pragmatic competence and can be classified as oriented more toward the sociopragmatic end (testing appropriateness in the context of social relationships) or the pragmalinguistic end (testing linguistic forms necessary to achieve communicative ends). The area that has been tested the most is speech acts, and there has been some assessment of implicatures, routines, and judgment of appropriateness. Although we will emphasize formal, large-scale tests of pragmalinguistics and sociopragmatics, we will also briefly discuss some more local, smaller scale projects.

3.2.2 Tests of Second Language Pragmatics

Testing of L2 pragmatics is still a young field in need of much development: at this time, only a limited number of major projects have been undertaken in the assessment of L2 pragmatics. The largest one in terms of development and spin-offs was Hudson, Detmer, & Brown's (1995) test of English as a second language (ESL) sociopragmatics, which was also used by Yoshitake (1997) for English as a foreign language (EFL) and adapted for Japanese as an L2 by Yamashita (1996). The largest project by number of participants but the most limited in scope was Bouton's test of ESL implicature (Bouton, 1988, 1994, 1999), and the most recent ones are Roever's Web-based test of ESL pragmalinguistics (Roever, 2005, 2006b) and Liu's (2006) test of EFL sociopragmatics.

3.2.3 Testing Sociopragmatics

Hudson et al. (1995) designed a test battery for assessing Japanese ESL learners' ability to produce and recognize appropriate realizations of the speech acts request, apology, and refusal. Their battery consisted of six sections, including a written DCT,[2] an oral (language lab) DCT, a multiple-choice DCT, a role-play, as well as self-assessment measures for the DCTs and the role-play. Hudson et al. undertook a detailed and rigorous design and validation process, collecting native speakers' (NSs') and non-native speakers' (NNSs') responses and coding them according to the Cross-Cultural Speech Act Realization Project's scheme (Blum-Kulka, House, & Kasper, 1989), followed by several revisions of their items. For their multiple-choice DCT, they used high-frequency NS responses as correct answers and dissimilar NNS responses as distractors. Their oral DCT resembled their written DCT, except that responses were spoken, and their role-plays were designed to contain each one of their target speech acts in every role-play. To assess test-taker performance on the oral DCTs and the role-plays, Hudson et al. trained NSs of English on an analytical rating scale with five steps, ranging from "completely unsatisfactory" to "completely appropriate" for each target speech act (apology, request, or refusal) performed.

Although Hudson et al. do not report the statistical results of their validation, Hudson (2001) reports their findings for the role-plays, written DCT, and oral DCT, and Brown (2001) describes the findings from Yamashita and Yoshitake's studies. One clear result with strong practical consequences was the unreliability of the multiple-choice DCT: In both Yamashita's and Yoshitake's studies, the reliability of the multiple-choice DCT was far below the reliability for the other sections. Hudson et al. as well as Yamashita admit that it was extremely difficult to create response options for DCT items that were clearly wrong, and they found it nearly impossible to create distractors that were not acceptable to at least some members of the target language community. Even though they used actual responses provided by NNS that were judged to be inappropriate, this was apparently not sufficient to ensure unambiguous multiple-choice items. This shows a central problem of sociopragmatically oriented tests that focus on appropriateness: Judgments of what is and what is not appropriate differ widely among NSs and are probably more a function of personality and social background variables than of language knowledge. Whereas most NSs of a language can agree on a core of linguistic rules (grammatical, phonological, and usage) and can relatively easily determine if a given exemplar violates these rules, people's views of what is "polite" or "appropriate" are less the result of rule-based intuitions. In addition, epistemic stance is crucial in interpersonal communication and different variants of an utterance can convey different kinds of epistemic stance without being "wrong" in a clearly definable way. Indeed, what makes a request, refusal, or apology clearly inappropriate? Possibly when it is so insulting that the interlocutor would simply cease communication (although this might, of course, be the intended outcome) or when it is not recognizable as a request, refusal, or apology. However, between those extremes there is a large gray area, which complicates the development of test instruments.

3.2.4 Testing Implicature

Bouton (1988, 1994, 1999) designed a 33-item test of implicature, incorporating two major types of implicature, which he termed "idiosyncratic implicature" and "formulaic implicature." Idiosyncratic implicature is conversational implicature in Grice's terms (1975); that is, it violates a Gricean maxim and forces the hearer to infer meaning beyond the literal meaning of the utterance by using background knowledge. Bouton viewed formulaic implicature as a specific kind of implicature, which follows a routinized schema. He placed the Pope Q ("Is the Pope Catholic?"), indirect criticism ("How did you like the food?"—"Let's just say it was colorful."), and sequences of events in this category. In longitudinal studies, Bouton found that learners acquired idiosyncratic implicature over time without instruction but did not develop significantly on some types of formulaic implicature. At the same time, he found that formulaic implicature was easy to teach, whereas idiosyncratic implicature was nearly impervious to instruction. Bouton attributed learners' improved performance on idiosyncratic implicature to exposure, but as he did not compare exposed with unexposed learners (ESL and EFL groups), he confounded exposure and proficiency. Roever (2005) showed that it is actually the increase in L2 proficiency over time that leads to better performance on measures of implicature comprehension. Work on implicature is probably the least social of all pragmatics-related research. It is fundamentally based on Grice's maxims, which are philosophically rather than empirically derived, and because the interpretation of the implicature is happening in the test taker's mind, the establishment of social and relationship context is less important than it would be in the case of the speech acts.

However, the role of the test takers' background knowledge is a concern. In real-world conversation, background knowledge can be any knowledge shared by the participants, which includes general world knowledge that other members of the speech community would share as well, but also private knowledge (e.g., references to past events or conversations). The latter is obviously not replicable in a test, as it would require extensive prompts, and the former might advantage certain test-taker groups over others. In fact, Roever (2006a) found that the original Pope Q ("Is the Pope Catholic?") gave a strong advantage to test takers of German and Polish L1 background as compared to test takers of Asian language background. The bias was so strong that this item would normally be excluded from tests following established fairness guidelines (e.g., the ones used by ETS; see chapter 4). However, a modified Pope Q ("Do fish swim?") showed only mild bias, and that bias was in favor of the Asian language group. The fact that the Pope Q is easier for European test takers does not necessarily mean that it is unfair: It can be argued that the knowledge that the Pope is Catholic is a legitimate component of world knowledge in an (American) English speech community. When confronted with this implicature in real-world conversation, European test takers would doubtlessly find it easier than Asian test takers as well. Still, it is important to consider whether the inclusion of this particular exemplar is necessary or whether comprehension of the Pope Q could be tested through less culturally bound items.

3.2.5 Testing Pragmalinguistics

Roever (2005, 2006b) developed a test battery that focused squarely on the pragmalinguistic side of pragmatic knowledge. Unlike Hudson et al., who limited themselves to speech acts, and Bouton, who assessed only implicature, Roever tested three aspects of ESL pragmalinguistic competence: recognition of situational routine formulas, comprehension of implicature, and knowledge of speech act strategies. Roever tried to strike a balance between practicality and broad content coverage to avoid construct underrepresentation: His test could be delivered through a standard Web browser, took about one hr, and both the routines and implicature sections were self-scoring. Prompts were kept short to limit the effect of reading proficiency, and unlike Hudson et al. (1995), Roever used rejoinders in the speech act section. However, rejoinders served a very specific purpose in his study: They were carefully crafted to force the occurrence of certain strategies in test-taker responses, which facilitated rating because if the required strategy did not occur, the response was almost invariably unacceptable. As Roever was not primarily investigating appropriateness, he only varied the degree of imposition in his speech act items.

Roever took an overall more psychometric perspective than earlier studies and was interested in reasons for item difficulty. Like Hudson (2001), he found that the degree of imposition was a major reason for difficulty in the speech act section, and like Bouton (1999), he found that formulaic implicature was more difficult than idiosyncratic implicature. He showed that Bouton had confounded exposure and proficiency in accounting for higher levels of implicature knowledge and that it was proficiency rather than exposure that led to greater knowledge of ESL implicature. Similarly, speech act scores depended to a large extent on proficiency. For routines, the opposite was true, as Roever (1996) and House (1996) had also shown: Exposure accounted almost completely for knowledge of routines. This probably does not come as a great surprise, as routines are short, highly frequent, and linguistically noncomplex so that even low-proficiency learners might know them if they have encountered them often enough.

3.2.6 *Apologies and Requests for Chinese EFL Learners*

Liu (2006) developed a test of requests and apologies for Chinese EFL learners, which consisted of a multiple-choice DCT, a written DCT, and a self-assessment instrument. All three test papers contained 24 situations, evenly split between apologies and requests. Liu developed his instruments "bottom-up"; that is, the situations for the written DCT were generated by Chinese EFL learners from memory, the likelihood of each situation occurring was then judged by another group, and the degree of imposition for each situation was assessed by a sample of Chinese learners and English NSs, followed by a formal pilot of the draft instrument. The multiple-choice DCT was generated based on responses from NNSs on the written DCT as distracters and from NSs as correct options. Liu then collected judgments from 13 NSs of English on the appropriateness of the various response options, and he developed a draft multiple-choice DCT with three options per situation. When taken by a group of five NSs, there was no unanimous agreement on the correct answer for 12 of the 24 situations, which Liu revised and gave to another three NSs, who then agreed on the correct answer for all situations.

The final version of the test was completed by 200 EFL learners in China, together with a TOEFL to ascertain learners' English proficiency. Liu (2006) found satisfactory reliabilities for all sections, with the multiple-choice DCT in the .8 range and the self-assessment paper and the written DCT in the .9 range. He also conducted a Rasch analysis on the multiple-choice DCT and did not find any misfitting items. His many-facet Rasch analysis for the written DCT showed consistent differences in rater severity and less than optimal functioning of rating scales. Factor analysis showed a "request" factor, an "apology" factor, and a TOEFL factor, but an analysis of variance (ANOVA) did not

find significant score differences on the subtests based on learners' proficiency. This is not an unexpected finding, as soci4prag-
matic knowledge of appropriateness is less dependent on proficiency than pragmalinguistic knowledge would be. As would be
expected, high-imposition items were consistently more difficult
than low-imposition items, although, interestingly, the difference
was not significant for requests in the multiple-choice DCT. Liu
also conducted verbal protocols with 12 learners and found that
test tasks generally engaged pragmatic knowledge.

Liu's (2006) findings are interesting, particularly with regard to the multiple-choice DCT, which has much better reliability in his study than in Yamashita's (1996) or Yoshitake's
(1997) study, both of which relied on the instruments developed
by Hudson et al. (1995). One obvious difference between the test
construction processes that Hudson et al. and Liu used is Liu's re-
liance on situations generated by members of the same EFL population for which the test was designed. In other words, whereas
in Hudson et al.'s case, the situations were tester-generated, they
were provided by members of the target population themselves
in Liu's case and were then double-checked for plausibility by
another group of members of the target population and NSs of
the target language. So one reason could be that Liu has established context in a way that his test takers were more able to
relate to than Hudson et al.'s. At the same time, Liu's approach
is potentially problematic, as his incorrect distracters were taken
from NNS responses, but his correct response options were taken
from NS responses. So it is possible that test takers are really
reacting to the idiomaticity of the utterance, rather than its appropriateness. Another effect in Liu's instrument that is difficult
to explain is the disjunct between request and apology knowledge:
The factor analysis shows that the sections testing apology on the
multiple-choice DCT, written DCT, and self-assessment instrument have very little in common with the section testing requests
on these instruments. Why should that be? Would knowledge of
L2 speech act performance not be expected to be approximately
similar for different speech acts? In other words, if a learner

has sociopragmatic competence, should that competence not feed judgment of appropriateness and production of appropriate speech act realizations across speech act types? It is difficult to think of a case in which a learners' knowledge of requests is in no way predictive of their knowledge of apologies; this makes for a very complicated construct, and it is nearly impossible to explain in acquisitional terms, which is a point that Liu does not address.

As Liu (1996) stated quite clearly, his test exclusively targets Chinese EFL learners so its usability for other first language (L1) groups is unclear. It also only considers one aspect of L2 pragmatic competence—speech acts—so that conclusions drawn from it and decisions based on scores would have to be fairly limited and re-stricted. Although the high reliabilities that Liu reached for his multiple-choice DCT are heartening and renew hope that such an instrument is, indeed, possible, a more thorough investigation of his instrument would be useful for confirming that it was his thorough test development that made the difference, rather than other factors.

3.3 The Tension in Testing Pragmatics: Keeping It Social but Practical

If pragmatics is understood as language use in social set-tings, tests would necessarily have to construct such social set-tings. It is not just contextual variables that would have to be established: Speech acts are carried out over various turns and their exact shape takes into account interlocutor reactions. In other words, conversation is co-constructed by both interlocutors, which is something that can never be simulated with DCTs. So the usual method of DCTs of cramming all possible speech act strategies into one gap is highly inauthentic in terms of actual conversation.

The obvious alternative would be to test pragmatics through face-to-face interaction, most likely role-plays. In this way, speech acts could unfold naturally as they would in real-world interac-tion. However, such a testing approach carries its own problems,

most notably practicality. Role-plays take substantial time to conduct and they require multiple ratings. Additionally, there is a
standardization issue as well because every role-play would be
somewhat unique if the conversation is truly co-constructed, and
this would make it very difficult to compare one role-play performance with another.

How can this dilemma be solved? One way to approach it
is to acknowledge that pragmatics does not exclusively equal
speech acts. Speech acts are certainly the most researched area of
pragmatics, and they are arguably the most social, as their real-
world realization depends very much on co-construction. However, speech acts are not the only area of pragmatics, and it is
possible to test other aspects of pragmatic competence without
simulating conversations. For example, routine formulas are by
their very nature one-shot utterances, not requiring extensive, co-
constructed negotiation. This is not to say that they cannot be part
of such an extended conversation, but they can certainly stand
on their own. Similarly, implicature is certainly omnipresent in
extended discourse, but instances of it can be isolated for interpretation by test takers. Thus, certain aspects of pragmatics can
be tested more easily in isolation than others.

However, such a limitation begs the question of construct
underrepresentation; in other words, if a test conveniently tests
Vietnamese routines by multiple-choice questions, can the results
be generalized to the entire domain of Vietnamese pragmatics?
So, if learners can order coffee in Vietnamese, does that mean
they can communicate appropriately in any situation with any
interlocutor? The answer is, we do not know. Maybe they can;
maybe they cannot. Such a test would only tell us about learners'
knowledge of routines but nothing about their ability to produce
apologies, comprehend implicature, or use address forms correctly
(beyond the ones covered in the test items). However, this situation is analogous to language testing in general: A grammar test
that focuses on tenses and articles cannot be used to draw conclusions about test takers' ability to produce coherent discourse in
speaking or writing, use comprehensible pronunciation, or have

a good command of collocations. Valid conclusions from a test are only possible with regard to knowledge and skills that have actually been tested.

Given that pragmatics is a fairly broad area, it is difficult to design a single test that assesses the entirety of a learner's pragmatic competence. Again, in analogy to testing in general, it is possible to attain broader content coverage and test an appreciable chunk of pragmatic competence by using a test battery, but testing "pragmatic competence" as a whole is just as complex, time-consuming, and impractical as it would be to test "language competence" as a whole. Depending on the purpose of the test, different aspects of pragmatic competence can be tested, and for some purposes, it might be unavoidable to use role-plays or other simulations of social situations because conclusions are to be drawn as to the learner's ability to produce speech acts in discourse. For other purposes, it might be enough to focus on a specific subarea of pragmatics, such as routines, implicature, or address terms, and test comprehension or ability to recognize appropriate speech. Similarly, it might be sufficient sometimes to focus on learners' knowledge of building blocks for speech acts (strategies and their linguistic realizations) rather than their ability for use in real-world-like settings.

In the following section we will show how such a more limited view of pragmatics assessment can breathe new life into an old favorite of researchers (and testers) that has recently been broadly discredited: the DCT.

3.4 DCT Items in Pragmatics Tests: A Case Study in Limiting the Construct

Discourse completion test items are attractive to pragmatics researchers and testers alike, mostly because they look like they elicit something akin to real-world speech act performance and because they are still somewhat practical despite the need for rating—at least they can be administered to large numbers of test takers at the same time. The problem is that they are in fact very limited in what they can do and are beset with numerous problems.

First and foremost, DCTs do not neatly replicate actual speech. As Golato (2003) has convincingly shown, people do not use language in DCT responses in the same way that they use language in real-world communication. They might subjectively feel that their DCT responses are written versions of their real-world language use, but in fact some language items used in DCTs do not occur in real-world conversation or at least not at the same frequency, whereas language present in real-world conversation does not occur in DCTs or only rarely. In addition, as we discussed earlier, speech acts do not happen in the one-shot format that DCTs require. Rather, speakers distribute strategies over various turns, monitoring their interlocutor's reactions and adjusting their talk accordingly. Additionally, of course, there are many differences between written and spoken language with regard to hesitation phenomena, tone of voice, facial expression, gesture, and a number of other nonverbal cues that interlocutors use to contextualize their utterance and convey meaning. None of these are available in DCTs, or any written instrument for that matter.

So does this mean DCTs are useless for assessing L2 pragmatics? The answer is: Not entirely. Like any instrument, there are certain constructs that can be assessed with this instrument and others that cannot. A DCT can elicit semantic formulas, but it will not necessarily elicit all semantic formula that learners know and it does not allow conclusions as to what formulas they would actually use in reality. DCTs also do not show whether a learner can implement a speech act appropriately and effectively over various turns, and they do not provide any information about learners' ability to participate in conversations in real time, take turns, or generally be skilled communicators. However, they do provide information about whether learners have semantic formulas at their disposal to realize certain speech acts, and to a limited extent, they might also provide some information about learners' sociopragmatic awareness (e.g., with regard to address terms), but other instruments are more suitable for measuring sociopragmatic awareness. Although DCTs (and most multiple-choice measures) measure knowledge and do not allow direct predictions of real-world performance, they can be thought of as measuring potential for performance, as knowledge is arguably a necessary precondition for performance. In other words, learners who have knowledge of speech acts might not necessarily be able to use that knowledge under the pressures of a communicative situation, but they are far closer to using it than learners without any knowledge.

So whereas the purpose of the test is to assess learners' off-line knowledge or repertoire of semantic formulas, DCTs are an appropriate instrument, but this limited use of DCTs for the elicitation of pragmalinguistic knowledge is an application specific to the *assessment* of pragmatics. Because they do not necessarily reflect real-world language use, DCTs might not be useful as instruments for pragmatics survey research, which tries to uncover how people actually use language. Survey research tends to be interested in the frequency of occurrence of certain semantic formulas, but this may matter much less in assessment, where the question may simply be whether a formula provided by a learner is targetlike.

3.5 Methodological Issues in DCTs

The fact that conversation, real or imaginary, is not necessary if the use of DCTs is limited to the elicitation of semantic formulas does not imply that conversational contextualization is useless. Roever (2005) used rejoinders to limit the range of allowable responses a DCT item can elicit and thereby facilitate rating. Consider the following item from his test (Roever, 2005, p. 130).

> Ella borrowed a recent copy of *TIME Magazine* from her friend Sean but she accidentally spilled a cup of coffee all over it. She is returning the magazine to Sean.
>
> Ella: ....
>
> Sean: "No, don't worry about replacing it, I read it already."

Without the rejoinder, a wide variety of utterances are possible for Ella, and there would be very little grounds for penalizing one but rewarding another. For example, test takers could let Ella use a strategy of hoping Sean will not notice or will not care and have her say: "Here you go" without any further ado; or they could enter a verbose and overly apologetic "Sean, I'm so very sorry. I was clumsy and spilled coffee over your magazine. You must be mad at me but please, find it in your heart to forgive me. . ." However, the rejoinder constrains the range of possible responses: Although the situation requires an apology, the rejoinder forces an offer of repair because otherwise it would no longer fit Ella's utterance. A simple "I'm sorry" is not enough here; test takers need to enter something along the lines of "I'm sorry, I'll buy you a new copy." It is debatable and probably up to rater judgment whether an explanation plus offer of repair would be adequate ("Sean, I ruined your magazine. I'll buy you another one.").[3]

In both his original study and a follow-up (Roever, 2005), Roever had very high interrater reliabilities in the .9 range after fairly little training, which confirms the practical usefulness of the rejoinders, but it does not mean that the raters always agreed. Most of their disputes were centered on the acceptability of atypical semantic formulas or cases in which some raters felt that the response did not convey the intended illocutionary force.

At the risk of sounding repetitive, it is important to stress that learners' performance on this type of DCT item does not mean that they can successfully participate in conversations. It simply means that they know which semantic formula they need to use. By the same token, Hudson et al.'s (1995) comment (also echoed by Johnston, Kasper, & Ross, 1998) that rejoinders made test-taker responses inauthentic misses a key difference between assessment and a survey instrument: If we were striving for authenticity, DCTs could not be used at all. All that DCTs can offer is knowledge elicitation.

However, another authenticity issue identified as a problem for survey DCTs deserves serious consideration. As Rose (1994) and Rose and Ono (1995) have found, participants might feel forced to respond in a DCT, whereas, in reality, they would prefer to remain silent (e.g., not make a request that they would evaluate as too face-threatening). In real-world situations, they also have other means at their disposal; for example, instead of refusing directly, they might superficially comply with a request, but in fact perform whatever is requested less than enthusiastically. In a test, it is not really possible to allow test takers to opt out because such opting out would be indistinguishable from simply not knowing the correct response. So does this mean tests are inauthentic because they require performance that would not occur in real-world communication? An argument can be made that this is not the case. For one thing, opting out is most likely to occur on items at the extreme end of the politeness continuum (i.e., where the imaginary interlocutor is much higher in power and the imposition is great, making the performance of the speech act extremely face-threatening). Not many items of this type, however, should appear in any test of pragmatics, so the effect of any construct-irrelevant variance introduced this way should be small. In tests of pragmalinguistics, such items should not appear at all because there is no reason to vary sociopragmatic variables to a great extent if the focus is on eliciting strategies.

In any case, as already mentioned earlier, there is a distinct difference between eliciting language for survey purposes or for certain assessment purposes. On a survey instrument, researchers try to elicit what the respondent would actually say in real-world communication, and forcing them to respond in a way in which they would not normally respond lowers the validity of findings. However, on a test, testers may simply try to assess whether test takers have a certain knowledge, skill, or ability or are, in principle, capable of performing in certain ways, but test takers are, of course, free to choose not to make use of their knowledge in the real world. As an analogy, learners might choose not to make use of the present perfect progressive when they speak

English, but it is still legitimate to assess their knowledge of it on an ESL test. In the same way, it is legitimate to ask learners to show that they know certain strategies and can produce a range of politeness levels.

The above argument in favor of DCTs should not be mistaken to mean that they are easy to make and use. We still know far too little about how much background information about the situation and the social relationship between the imaginary interlocutors is necessary for respondents to respond confidently to a prompt, although this problem is likely to be smaller in a pragmalinguistically oriented DCT. Providing more context in the prompt might look like an attractive option, but it is unclear on which aspects of the prompt test takers focus. In addition, lengthening prompts threatens to contaminate scores with construct-irrelevant variance from different levels of reading proficiency even more than is already the case.

What is fairly clear is that the use of multiple-choice DCTs for the assessment of sociopragmatic knowledge remains a challenge, and they are likely just as unsuitable for pragmalinguistics, but probably for different reasons. Whereas it is difficult to design response options that are clearly inappropriate without being off-the-wall ridiculous in sociopragmatics tests, it is likely just as difficult to design ones that are clearly wrong but not too obvious in pragmalinguistics tests. In other words, would it not be fairly noticeable if a semantic formula is missing and the conversation does not make sense? This is really an empirical question, and to our knowledge, no research exists on it.

3.6 Testing Sociopragmatics: Role-Plays and Appropriateness Judgments

The extensive discussion of DCTs above was motivated by their strong prevalence in pragmatics research but their often misguided use as instruments that elicit sociopragmatic knowledge (i.e., learner utterances that are then judged to be more or less appropriate). However, how can sociopragmatic knowledge and even the ability to speak appropriately in extended discourse be tested?

As mentioned earlier, role-play is a valid option. Hudson et al. (1995) designed eight role-play scenarios, each containing a request, apology, and refusal. Participants played all eight scenarios with an interlocutor, and Yamashita (1996) reported that this took about 30 min per participant. Although both the participants and the interlocutor used role-play cards with the scenario written out, Hudson et al.'s role-plays did not rely on scripts for the interlocutors; rather, the role-play instructions for the interlocutor specified which speech act to perform but not how it was supposed to be performed verbatim—for example, "accept request to move the furniture next Sat[urday]" (Hudson et al., 1995, p. 157). This leaves the role-play open to criticism with regard to comparability, but it also probably makes it much more similar to an actual conversation, although this is really an empirical question. There is little research on the similarities and differences between role-plays and real-world conversation (the topic is covered to a small extent in Young and He, 1998). Obviously, a role-play cannot establish context in the same way as the real world; there are no real-world stakes involved and the presentation of self (Goffman, 1959) is not actually of the test taker being themselves but rather the test taker pretending to be another person. Still, more detailed investigations of the extent to which role-played conversations resemble actual conversations or differ from them would make for very interesting discourse analytic work.

Hudson et al. (1995) videotaped test-taker performances and later had them rated by three raters. The raters judged each targeted speech act in each situation and rated its appropriateness on a Likert scale of 1 to 5. It must be noted that the rating was only focused on the speech acts, not the candidate's ability (or lack thereof) to carry on a conversation. However, general proficiency factors like fluency might have influenced ratings, and as there were no interviews with raters or verbal protocol reports of their work, it is unclear to what raters attended. Yamashita (1996) obtained an interrater reliability of .88, which indicates quite strong agreement among raters.

One concern with Hudson et al.'s (1995) instrument and most other tests (and research instruments) in interlanguage pragmatics is that they atomize sociopragmatic ability at the level of a speech act, but, clearly, there is more to the ability to speak appropriately in social situations than performance of specific speech act; address terms, honorifics, backchannels, and conversational management come to mind. An interesting aspect of sociopragmatic competence that is rarely assessed was highlighted in a study by Cook (2001). She investigated whether Japanese as L2 learners were able to distinguish between polite and impolite speech styles in Japanese. In Japanese, the social relationship between speaker and listener is morphologically encoded in spoken production; for example, lower status speakers are expected to use humble forms when speaking to higher status interlocutors. The absence of required morphology makes an utterance immediately highly inappropriate, regardless of the referential content of the utterance.[4] Cook played tape-recordings of three Japanese self-introductions by job applicants for a position of bilingual (English-Japanese) sales clerk to her participants, who were supposed to indicate which job candidate would be most suitable for a position that involves extensive contact with Japanese customers. One candidate's self-introduction contained several incongruities between her claim that her Japanese is strong and her lack of humble speech style and morphology appropriate to a higher status hearer. Although this candidate's formal qualifications appeared slightly stronger than the other candidates', her lack of appropriate speech made her entirely unsuitable for work in a customer service position. To her surprise, Cook found that 80.8% of her group of 120 university-level Japanese as a foreign language learners did not recognize the rather glaring inappropriateness of this candidate's spoken production and chose her as the most suitable person for the job.

Cook's (2001) study shows an interesting example of assessing learners' ability to make judgments about sociopragmatic appropriateness at the discourse level. The concept of speech style is particularly interesting because it is highly relevant in communication with native speakers and the appropriateness or inappropriateness of a speech style depends on a range of definable factors.

3.7 Foreigner-Specific Norms?

Research on pragmatics assessment tends to be referenced to target language norms (based on NS intuitions), and greater convergence of learners toward these norms is taken as an indication of greater competence. This view is not unproblematic, however. Pragmatic performance serves an indexical function as well, and nativelike performance might be interpreted by NSs as a claim to group membership. Where such a claim is evaluated as inappropriate or preposterous, group members might exclude learners rather than applaud their nativelike competence. In the terminology of accommodation theory (Giles, Coupland, & Coupland, 1991), linguistic convergence can lead to psychological divergence.[5] In some cases, it might actually be preferable for learners to "do being foreigner" (i.e., follow a norm specifically for foreigners and conform to NS expectations of how foreigners behave). This not only avoids sanctions from group members, but it might also give the learners more freedom and absolve them somewhat from strict adherence to L2 pragmatic norms. A foreigner who is clearly recognizable as such enjoys a certain degree of what is so aptly called "Narrenfreiheit" in German. Literally translated as "fool's freedom," it describes the tendency of interlocutors to be more forgiving of nonnormative behavior if it is shown by out-group members (who just do not know any better), whereas the same behavior by in-group members would not be tolerated, because they should know better. The introduction of foreigner-specific norms accompanied by an added degree of tolerance for non-target-like pragmatic performance as well as less tolerance for behavior that would be perceived as *too* targetlike by NSs would, of course, greatly complicate assessments of L2 pragmatics. It is also somewhat unclear at this point what foreigner-specific norms might exist in various languages and how far the tolerance for non-target-like behavior would stretch.

In addition, any kind of tolerance for non-target-like behavior would be constrained by comprehensibility concerns. Where a learner is so off course in terms of L2 norms that the message or stance that they are trying to convey is no longer "readable" to NSs, communication is likely to fail. This applies particularly to verbal, paralinguistic, and nonverbal contextualization cues, as illustrated in Gumperz's cross-talk work (Gumperz, 1982a, 1982b), Young's (1994) work on discourse structure, and Cameron's (2001) example of British teachers scolding pupils of Caribbean background, who convey respect and remorse by looking at the floor whereas the teacher interprets their behavior as disrespectful and dismissive.

Conversely, where a learner is so NS-like in their general proficiency that NSs do not realize or forget over time that the learner is not one of their own, this learner will be fully expected to comply with group norms and be subject to the same sanctions as any group member who disobeys these norms. Such "passing" as an NS might be less likely if the learner looks different from other group members (e.g., a high-proficiency user of L2 Mandarin of Caucasian ethnic background among ethnically Chinese NSs of Mandarin). However, with increasing international mobility, interethnic marriage, and people growing up or living long term in other countries, it will become more common worldwide to have NNSs who are NS-like for all practical purposes, possibly except under conditions of extreme fatigue or stress. They might even view themselves as members of the target speech community or have a bicultural identity, at which point they could no longer be said to be "passing" as members of the target speech community: Assuming acceptance by that speech community, they simply are members.

We are, of course, acutely aware of the homogeneity fiction with regard to NS behavior. Obviously, not all NSs are the same, react the same, and interpret behavior the same way. In particular, those who have a great deal of contact with foreigners might be more attuned to nonnormative behaviors and might be more willing and able to do extra work in comprehending non-target-like language production. They might give NNSs the benefit of the doubt when learners do not conform to norms or seem to claim too much group membership. Certainly, there are also personality factors at work: Some people are more open to new experiences, give others more leeway, and search for the best possible interpretation of a behavior or utterance, whereas others are simply less tolerant and less able or willing to compensate for interlocutors' communicative shortcomings.

3.8 Assessing Pragmatic Aptitude

Obviously, the more pragmalinguistic and sociopragmatic knowledge a learner has and the more accurately the two are mapped onto each other, the more likely it is that the learner will be successful in cross-cultural communication. However, is it easier for some people to acquire this knowledge than for others? In other words, is there a predisposition, even an aptitude, for successful cross-cultural performance? If so, how can it be measured?

Because much of pragmalinguistic competence is fed by general L2 knowledge, learners with a high general L2 aptitude should have an easier time building their pragmalinguistic competence (for recent discussions of aptitude, see Robinson, 2002a, 2002b, 2005; Skehan, 2002). Sociopragmatic competence, however, has much to do with interpersonal relations, understanding why people react the way they do, and fundamentally caring about what other people think. Some learners are extremely good at establishing rapport despite limited general L2 competence, mostly because they interact in a way that is felt to be positive and engaging. Schmidt's (1983) case study of Wes comes to mind, in which the L1 Japanese-speaking Wes was quite successful in his English-language interactions, despite gaps in his general command of English. What leads to high sociopragmatic competence in learners like Wes?

Work in this area has often focused on cross-cultural adaptability and identified personality factors that can facilitate or
hinder acquisition of sociopragmatic knowledge. For example,
the Cross-cultural Adaptability Inventory by Kelley and Meyers
(1993) scores prospective expatriate executives on four factors
that predict "cross-cultural effectiveness":

Flexibility / Openness: This factor is related to empathy and
cultural relativism. It incorporates the ability to withhold
judgment and willingness to try new role behaviors.

Perceptual Acuity: The degree to which learners attend to
interpersonal relations and language use for social purposes.

Emotional Resilience: This factor is mostly related to with-
standing culture shock and the unavoidable problems of re-
locating to a new cultural context.

Personal Autonomy: A personal system of values and beliefs
but the ability to respect others' values and beliefs.

Other questionnaire-type inventories include Tucker's
(1999) Overseas Assignment Inventory and Spreitzer, McCall,
and Mahoney's (1997) Prospector. All of these instruments are
generally similar, are based on theories of personality, and measure various personality traits. One problem with these inventories is that they are somewhat static; that is, they diagnose
an existing state, but they are not founded on a theory of cross-
cultural learning. The only comprehensive theory to date is Earley
and Ang's (2003) work on cultural intelligence. Earley and Ang's
theory has both process and content features and consists of three
facets: cognitive, motivational, and behavioral. In the cognitive
domain, people with high cultural intelligence have a high degree
of self-awareness and are perceptive and flexible enough to generate and integrate new aspects of identity (i.e., to modify their
concept of self). In the motivational domain, learners set realistic
goals, experience themselves as effective in achieving them, and
evaluate their success accurately while still persevering despite
obstacles. Finally, in the behavioral domain, learners are able to

acquire (often through imitation) culturally appropriate behaviors and enact them in the right setting.

Testing of such personality characteristics as Earley and Ang (2003) describe them seems to fall somewhat outside the realm of language testing, but the assessment of sociopragmatic/cross-cultural potential together with the assessment of language proficiency (or language learning aptitude) can be highly relevant to decisions with regard to international postings or assignments (e.g., for expatriate managers, foreign service officers, but also for others having a great deal of contact with interlocutors from other linguistic and cultural backgrounds). There is clearly much interdisciplinary work to be done here.

3.9 The Way(s) Forward

Clearly, much work still needs to be done in assessment of L2 pragmatics. Foundational work includes discourse analyses of the similarities and differences of language used in role-plays and natural conversations. Also, we could use more knowledge on how DCTs actually function—that is, what aspects are relevant to test-taker responses.

On a broader conceptual level, we need to move away from testing speech acts in isolation, at least for sociopragmatics, and move toward testing appropriateness of discourse production and nativelikeness of perception of appropriateness, as Cook (2001) did. At the same time, the challenge must be to construct tests that are practical, can be administered in a reasonable amount of time, and can be scored with little expense. Testing of pragmatics will not become a part of mainstream language testing if there are no practical ways to do it.

Further, conceptually, we need to be very clear about what it is that we are testing. Following test design processes along the lines suggested by Mislevy et al. (2002) would be a good way to ensure that our claims do not overreach and that our findings allow defensible conclusions to be drawn from them. A test that really only assesses learners' offline knowledge of implicature should not claim to assess their conversational ability in English. There simply are no grounds for such a claim. The question of norms is also a point that we will be grappling with for some time to come, and some groundwork would be necessary to find the foreigner-specific norms for some commonly tested languages.

One thing we really need to overcome is the design of L1-L2 specific pragmatics tests. Cases in point are Hudson et al.'s (1995) test that was specifically designed for Japanese learners of English, Yamashita's (1996) test for English-speaking learners of Japanese, and Liu's (2006) test for Chinese-speaking learners of English. Of course, it is sometimes necessary to develop tests for a specific learner population, but there really is no reason to develop pragmatics tests that are L1-specific. Again, if testing of pragmatics is to become a part of mainstream language testing, pragmatics tests must be universally usable. Their L1 neutrality can then be checked through DIF indices or G-theory studies (see chapter 4).

3.10 Conclusion

This chapter has focused on the testing of the social dimension of language use at the micro level, in face-to-face interaction. Testing of face-to-face interaction has a long history but is still relatively undertheorized. However, an understanding is developing that oral proficiency interviews are not simply unilateral displays of competence on the part of the candidate but that there is a complex interplay among candidate ability, the interlocutor's conversational style, and raters' perceptions. Assessment of L2 pragmatics illustrates the difficulty of developing assessment instruments that measure language in use. The social nature of interaction is difficult to capture in a testing setting, and what can most reliably and practically be captured are isolated pieces of a much larger mosaic. Clearly, a great deal of work is needed in both areas. This aspect of the social dimension of language testing represents an important challenge.

Notes

[1]This procedure was in place until 2002, when it was replaced by a formal language test.

[2]The DCT is a common instrument in pragmatics research. It consists of a prompt describing a situation and a gap for test takers to fill in what they would say in that situation. Optionally, the gap might be followed by a rejoinder, but Hudson et al. (1995) decided not to use rejoinders.

[3]Admittedly, Sean's response could also be read as sarcasm if Ella does not offer to replace the magazine.

[4]This is conceptually similar in many Western cultures to uttering an apology with a huge smile on one's face—the apologetic force of the utterance would be incongruous with the lack of contrition expressed by the smile.

[5]We are grateful to Gabriele Kasper for pointing out this view.

CHAPTER FOUR

Psychometric Approaches to Fairness:
Bias and DIF

In this and the following chapter, we explore the way in which the social dimension of language testing has been explored within the psychometric tradition. In this chapter, we consider the fairness of tests for particular social groups, an area known as bias. Investigations of bias are part of general work on test fairness. Test fairness is a broad area, encompassing quality management in test design, administration and scoring, adequate coverage of relevant content, sufficient construct validation work, equal learning opportunities and access to testing, and items measuring only the skill or ability under investigation without being unduly influenced by construct-irrelevant variance introduced through test-taker background factors (Kunnan, 2000; Saville, 2003, 2005; Shohamy, 2000). In this chapter we focus on the last point, the functioning of test items in ways that advantage or disadvantage groups of test takers. The potential social consequences of a systematic preference for one group of test takers over another are easy to imagine: The dispreferred group's representation in coveted college programs and jobs might be disproportionately small, whereas their representation in stigmatized "remedial" programs might be disproportionately large. Test-inherent bias distorts measurement of the construct of interest by allowing other test-taker characteristics to influence scores systematically, thereby introducing multidimensionality into the measurement. Characteristics that are commonly investigated include race, gender, socioeconomic status, and first language

(L1) background, but, theoretically, any background characteristic that some test takers possess and others do not (or not to
the same degree) can introduce systematic construct-irrelevant
variance and lead to bias.

In this chapter we first summarize the history of bias research in assessment and follow with a discussion of various ways
to detect bias, problems with bias research, and approaches to
preempt bias.

4.1 Bias and Differential Item Functioning: Definition and History

4.1.1 Bias

The use of the term "bias" in assessment research fundamentally follows its popular usage, which conveys a skewed and unfair
inclination toward one side (group, population) to the detriment
of another. The notion of bias is directly tied to fairness, in popular usage as well as assessment: A biased judgment unduly takes
into account factors other than those that should be informing it.

For assessment, bias can be seen in traditional validity terms
as construct-irrelevant variance that distorts the test results and
therefore makes conclusions based on scores less valid. Specifically, a test or an item is biased if test takers of equal ability
but from different groups score differently on the item depending on their group membership (Angoff, 1993). In this case, group
membership introduces systematic construct-irrelevant variance,
which has a consistent effect on scores. Another way to look at this
is to consider bias a factor that makes a unidimensional test mul-
tidimensional: The test measures something in addition to what
it is intended to measure, and the result is a confound of two
measurements.

Whereas any construct-irrelevant variance is harmful to
valid interpretations, bias systematically harms one group
(Shepard, Camilli, & Averill, 1981) by inflating one group's scores
and depressing the other group's scores. In a broader sense, biased
tests harm all stakeholders because students might get exempted

from language programs although they would benefit from them, others do not get admitted to a program in which they would excel, universities or employers reject perfectly qualified applicants and accept less qualified ones, and society is deprived of potentially excellent doctors, lawyers, language teachers, or electricians and must make do with mediocre ones.

4.1.2 Differential Item Functioning

Bias is a general description of a situation in which construct-irrelevant group characteristics influence scores, but because of its semantic association with societal issues like discrimination, another term was coined for more technical analyses of test items: differential item functioning (DIF). DIF identifies test items that function differently for two groups of test takers, without the discriminatory overtones of the term *bias*. Angoff (1993) admitted that there is the temptation to use the term *bias* because it is shorter and less cumbersome than the somewhat unwieldy term *differential item functioning*, but he argued for keeping the two separate and using DIF for nonjudgmental analyses of score differences between groups and using bias to discuss the larger social issues caused by DIF.

Differential item functioning is a necessary but not sufficient condition for bias because a test item that functions differently for two groups might do so because it advantages one group in a construct-irrelevant way, but there might also be legitimate reasons for differential functioning. For example, cognates of target language vocabulary in the L1 of some test takers might make an item easier for that group, but the content tested might still be completely legitimate and construct-relevant, and their L1 knowledge would confer an advantage on these test takers in the exact same way in real-world language use situations. Thus, test makers could well decide to retain such an item, arguing that it measures a necessary part of the construct and that group differences are real ability differences in terms of the construct.

Another case in which DIF does not constitute bias is where items function differently for two groups of test takers simply because the two groups differ in their ability (e.g., low-proficiency and high-proficiency English as a second language [ESL] students). These groups would be expected to score differently on most items of an ESL test. In fact, if they do not, something is wrong with the test! Thus, although items will function differently depending on whether a test taker is in the low-proficiency or high-proficiency group, it would not make sense to say that the test is biased toward the high-proficiency group.

However, the situation is usually more complicated because test-taker ability is not known in advance. What if the low-proficiency test takers are mostly international students from Europe and the high-proficiency test takers are mostly international students from Asia? A DIF analysis would then seem to show that the test is biased toward test takers of Asian background. Indeed, a native-country effect is a nondesirable source of variance in an ESL proficiency test, but in this case native country is simply confounded with proficiency. This example already highlights one of the greater challenges of DIF and bias analysis: In practice, it can be very difficult to determine the source of DIF, and only if that determination is made, can we consider an item or a whole test biased.

The above examples show how DIF analysis is usually a first step in a larger bias analysis. An item that does not show DIF is not biased, whereas an item that shows DIF needs to be investigated further to uncover the reasons for its differential functioning. Most DIF analyses compute DIF for a potentially disadvantaged group (also known as the *focal* group) compared to the potentially advantaged group (also known as the *reference* group). DIF analyses outside language testing often investigate DIF for minority groups (Blacks vs. Whites) or gender (women vs. men), whereas in language testing, group membership tends to be determined by native language and there is less a priori hypothesizing about likely disadvantages.

Although it is desirable that illegitimate DIF be minimized to ensure precise measurement, a single differentially functioning item on a multi-item test is not likely to make the entire test unfair. Only when the effect of a number of DIF items accumulates can this lead to a biased test. However, if an individual test taker's score is right at the cut score level, illegitimate DIF on a small number of items can unfairly advantage or disadvantage that test taker. It is important to note that DIF can work in both directions, so, in practice, DIF favoring the reference group is often balanced out by DIF favoring the focal group, but, of course, there is no guarantee that this will happen and an individual test form might be strongly biased toward one or the other group.

4.1.3 History

Researchers have been investigating the impact of construct-external test-taker characteristics on scores for a century. From 1905 to 1911, Binet and his associates published five studies on the effect of socioeconomic status on students' performance on intelligence tests. Originally, Binet considered "intellectual capacity" a singular innate, invariant trait (Binet & Simon, 1916), but he became increasingly aware of the complexity of this construct and the effects of schooling and environment. He tried to counter the effect of extraneous factors by eliminating items that were based too much on schooling, but, even so, he found that children from a higher socioeconomic background outperformed children from lower socioeconomic levels. The original claim that the intelligence test measured raw intellectual capacity was obviously not tenable. Stern (1914) conducted the first analysis of differences in item functioning, when he considered which items were easier and more difficult for test takers of lower and higher socioeconomic status. Weintrob and Weintrob (1912) were the first to use race as an explanatory variable in their findings, which would later become a central issue in bias analyses in the United States. Eells, Davis, Havighurst, Herrick, and Tyler (1951) provide a summary of the research from the first part of the century and report their own study with 650 high-school students, whose answers on an IQ test were used to identify and eliminate items that measured opportunity to learn rather than intellectual ability. This early work on bias and group-related differences followed a general notion of fairness, had the goal of avoiding construct-irrelevant variance, and was quite optimistic in its out-look; that is, sources of item bias could be identified, systematically eliminated, and the result would be a fair, precise, unbiased test.

In the second half of the 20th century, work on bias was informed by larger concerns of social equity and began to shift away from IQ tests to tests that provided access to educational or job opportunity. It went hand in hand with the development of more formal concepts of validity and the use of powerful statistical tools to identify biased items. Interestingly, concern also shifted from socioeconomic influences on test scores to test-taker background variables such as race and gender and, to some extent, native-speaker (NS) status. Studies that included effects of NS status often framed findings in terms of the effects of cultural differences on test scores.

The relevance of producing fair tests with little DIF was highlighted by the Golden Rule Settlement. In 1976, the Golden Rule Insurance Company sued the Illinois Department of Insurance and Educational Testing Service (ETS) for alleged racial bias in the licensing test for insurance agents. The licensing exam had caused furor in the Illinois insurance industry because the general passing rate was only 31% and it appeared that the test was "for all practical purposes excluding Blacks entirely from the occupation of insurance agent" (Rooney, 1987, p. 5). ETS modified the test and the passing rate rose to 70–75%, but when no specific steps were taken to address the allegedly disastrous impact of the test on minority test takers, Golden Rule filed suit in July 1976. The court issued an injunction stopping the test temporarily, but only based on fee issues, not on the substantive grounds that it violated the equal protection clause of the U.S. constitution. After the Illinois legislature dealt with the fee problem and ETS revised the test, the case was dismissed, but Golden Rule refiled, alleging discrimination in both the old test and the new test. The case was dismissed again, but Golden Rule appealed and the circuit court unanimously reinstated it. Whereas the subordinate court had considered ETS not liable because the company was only under contract of the insurance licensing board, the circuit court found that ETS by virtue of making the test was responsible for its effect—a finding that raised the stakes for the testing industry considerably and a practical endorsement of Messick's position on test consequences as part of validity (see chapter 2). The circuit court also argued that the defendants could be held liable for intentional racial discrimination if they had knowledge that the test was disadvantaging Black test takers but failed to remedy the situation. In other words, the court demanded that test makers monitor the effect of their test on minority test takers, and if they found deleterious effects, they needed to alleviate these effects.

The case was settled out of court in 1984, with the defendants agreeing to consider any item biased for which correct answer rates for White and African American test takers differed by more than 15%. Also, items that fewer than 40% of African American test takers answered correctly were flagged as too difficult. The test makers agreed that items would be pretested and that future test forms would be constructed to the largest extent possible from unbiased and nondifficult items. This possibility was constrained by the test's content specifications, which required that certain areas needed to be tested. For this reason, biased or difficult items sometimes needed to be included because otherwise an aspect of the construct would be underrepresented in the operational test. Allowing a difficulty difference of up to 15% indicated that the parties recognized that there could be some random measurement error as well as some true underlying difference between the groups, which was most likely related to their previous training. The agreed procedure only applied to two insurance specializations: life insurance and accident and health insurance.

The Golden Rule settlement had consequences beyond Illinois. A similar suit was settled in Alabama, imposing an even stricter standard of only 5% difference between scores of Black and White test takers. Legislatures in California, New York, and Texas discussed imposing test construction and bias-monitoring requirements (Faggen, 1987). ETS had not anticipated this wide impact, and in January 1987, then-president of ETS, Gregory

Anrig, called the settlement an "error of judgment" on his part (Anrig, 1987). Richard Jaeger, the president of the National Council on Measurement in Education, sent letters to legislators, urging them not to pass any similar provision into law (Jaeger, 1987).

A whole issue of the *Journal of Educational Measurement: Issues and Practice* was devoted to the Golden Rule settlement in 1987, and the discussion showed an interesting contrast in opinions and concerns. Whereas psychometricians were scornful of the settlement and claimed that it would harm test quality, other contributors hailed the focus on minority performance in tests that the settlement forced test makers to adopt.

From the psychometric perspective, Linn and Drasgow (1987) showed that a test following the Golden Rule settlement would be reduced in quality because it would be more likely for items with weak discriminating power to be included, lowering the test's overall reliability. For example, if all test takers were answering a certain item randomly, this item would seem perfectly unbiased, as all groups would have very similar scores. Depending on the number of distracters, it might be too difficult (four answer choices would mean that about 25% of test takers would answer correctly, three answer choices would lead to 33.3% correctness, etc.), but from a bias point of view, it would be just fine. Of course, such an item would do nothing to help discriminate between high- and low-ability test takers, as both groups would have an equal likelihood of answering it correctly.

Linn and Drasgow (1987) also pointed out that some group differences are actually real and simply reflections of different educational experiences, so tests should not be faulted for detecting such differences. In fact, they see a need for remedial action at a larger, societal scale, because an "artificial reduction of differences in average test scores might conceal this situation, but it would not rectify it" (p. 15). It is probably this position more than anything else that sets them apart from the proponents of the settlement, as psychometricians tend to take the stance that DIF (or even differential test functioning) is not in itself evidence of bias.

Only if test takers of the same ability level perform differently is there bias involved. Although this is true, the Achilles' heel of this argument is that the ability level is determined by the overall test score or the score of a criterion measure; so if the whole test or the criterion measure is biased, it will never appear that there is item-level bias because the reference and the focal group will simply seem to have a radically different ability levels.

The second weakness of this argument is that it must be possible to pinpoint reasons for the differential functioning of these items. In other words, test makers must be able to "explain away" the appearance of bias by constructing a theory about construct-relevant causes for group differences such as different educational opportunities, a higher propensity of one group to take relevant college courses, or more interest in the subject matter by one group than the other. This has never been done rigorously and has never been tested as theory. Explanations for DIF tend to be based on speculative ad hoc hypotheses, and as long as that is the case, simple bias can also function as a valid explanation.

These different arguments reflect two different stances toward test makers' responsibility: Proponents of the Golden Rule Settlement saw the score difference on the test between Blacks and Whites as evidence of the test's bias, following the underlying assumption that there is no good reason that the test scores should differ by race. In a sense, they accepted the (unproven) premise that true ability would not differ by race, and if test scores did not reflect this invariance, the test was wrong (i.e., biased).

Opponents of the settlement, on the other hand, could suggest several good reasons why test scores might differ by race: first and foremost, different educational background and opportunity. They saw the test as a faithful operationalization of a construct, and if the test found differences between the races, then that was not the test's fault but a true finding. In a sense, they accepted the (unproven) premise that the test was inherently neutral with regard to racial background, and, therefore, if test scores showed differences between racial groups, this meant that these groups actually differed in their abilities.

In fact, both can be the case. It is certainly possible for a test to be biased against a group of test takers but at the same time be a faithful operationalization of the construct. However, in fact, it is only one possible operationalization; others that might be less biased would be conceivable. At the same time, groups can differ in their ability for real-world reasons, extraneous to the test, and the test might simply detect this. Obviously, there is nothing that test makers can do about real-world differences, other than measure them. However, there is something that they can do about a test that is biased: They can search for sources of bias in the test items.

Of course, the substantive issues raised by the Golden Rule case were far-reaching and went much beyond simply finding better techniques for detecting DIF. It established that test makers are not only responsible but also legally liable for their products and that they need to take all reasonable precautions to avoid disadvantaging groups of test takers. However, the settlement did not address issues for test users: Should they take test scores as the only criterion for decision-making? What prevents them from taking other factors into account, as is commonly done in university admission in the United States? For example, a test user might decide that having a diverse population of students or insurance agents or police officers is as valuable as having this population made up of high-ability individuals. Test users can ensure this diversity in a variety of ways: by using quotas or giving extra weight to nontest factors, for example. Of course, if they were to do so, they would be making a value judgment, but by not doing so, they are also making a value judgment, namely that ability (as defined by the test) is the only issue that matters. Adducing additional criteria to make decisions is probably more defensible in situations in which the predictive validity of the test is low or in which only a minimum threshold of performance is required and other skills are learned on the job. Nevertheless, biased test items distort results and a great deal of work has been undertaken to identify such items.

4.2 The Where and Wherefore of DIF

Most DIF-related research has been done on large-scale tests like the Scholastic Aptitude Test (SAT), the Graduate Management Admission Test (GMAT), and the Graduate Record Examinations (GRE). Comparatively few studies involve testing L2 (second language) proficiency, but the ones that exist will be reviewed in more detail below. In tests with a general, non-L2 focus, we will concentrate on verbal test sections, as those are most relevant to language testing concerns. O'Neill and McPeek (1993) provided a useful overview of findings, and the following summary is based on their work.

In most general DIF studies, gender and ethnicity were the factors under investigation. For reading comprehension, men perform better than a matched group of women on texts that involve science and technical content, whereas women perform better than men on texts relating to social sciences and the humanities. Similarly, on verbal analogy and antonym multiple-choice items, women perform better on items that fit the categories of aesthetics, philosophy, and human relationships, whereas men perform better on items from science or everyday practical affairs (money, tools, mechanical objects, sports, etc.). Women also perform better than men on items that include both men and women, but there is no difference on items that only talk about men or only about women.

The obvious explanations for these findings are so gender stereotypical as to be almost insulting: Women are socialized into paying attention to human affairs and aesthetics and men are socialized into attending to scientific and practical matters. Accordingly, men know more about scientific and everyday practical content or are at least more comfortable with it, and the same is true for women and aesthetics and human relationships. It is important to remember that DIF findings are based on large groups and can only be generalized to large groups, not specific individuals: Although most women might perform worse than men on science items, there are doubtlessly some women who perform extremely well on them and some men who perform extremely poorly.

With regard to minorities, Blacks and Latinos perform better than Whites on reading passages that deal with minority concerns or contain references to minorities. Blacks perform worse than Whites on analogy items dealing with science but better on items dealing with human relationships. This tendency, however, seems to be confounded with whether the item refers to concrete objects (easier for Whites) or abstract concepts (easier for Blacks). It has also been found that Blacks and Latinos perform worse than Whites on analogy items that contain homographs.

It is easy to explain the facilitative effect of the inclusion of minority concerns: Where test takers feel that items relate to them, item content becomes less theoretical, they can integrate it more with their experiences, and they can bring more knowledge to bear on it than on other items. They also might simply be more interested, and this increase in attention stimulates working memory and leads to better performance. It is much more difficult to explain the differential performance on the analogy items.

A fundamental problem with all but the most obvious explanations of DIF is that they are highly speculative and almost never tested; just because they seem reasonable does not mean they are correct. In his response to O'Neill and McPeek's article (1993), Bond (1993) recounts an incident where he and a student devised explanations for DIF in some items from an achievement test, only to find that because of an analytical error, they had identified the wrong items. When they reran their analysis and identified items that actually displayed DIF, their new explanations were the exact opposite of the previous ones. Yet, both lines of reasoning seemed eminently plausible. It would be interesting to put explanations for DIF to an empirical test by intentionally trying to induce DIF and then having reference- and focal-group members answer the items and provide verbal protocols on their thought processes. Such empirical work would further our understanding of DIF, but it is almost never done.

We will now take a closer look at ways of detecting DIF, and we will illustrate these methods with the little DIF work that has been done in language testing.

4.3 Methods for Detecting DIF

Methods used for detecting DIF fall into four broad categories:

Analyses based on item difficulty. These approaches compare item difficulty estimates.

Nonparametric approaches. These procedures use contingency tables, chi-square, and odds ratios.

Item-response-theory-based approaches. These analyses frequently (but not always) compare the fit of statistical models that ignore possible DIF in the first step and are then recalculated to allow for it in the second step. If both models fit the data equally well, no DIF is present, but if the model that allows for DIF fits better, DIF is likely. These approaches include 1, 2, and 3-parameter IRT analyses.

Other approaches. These include logistic regression, which also employs a model comparison method, as well as generalizability theory and multifaceted measurement, which are less commonly used in classic DIF studies.

It is also possible to classify approaches as those that match test takers of the same ability level versus those that do not. Matching approaches see DIF as a systematically different performance by test takers who ought to perform similarly (because they have the same ability). Matching approaches are conceptually stronger, as DIF is irrefutably present if test takers with the same ability but from different groups have a different likelihood of answering an item correctly: In that case, the item is differentiating between the test takers in terms of group membership, not only underlying ability. However, approaches that condition on ability are more complex to carry out, and early DIF computations relied only on comparing item difficulty between groups.

4.4 Early DIF Techniques: Different Item Difficulties for Different Groups

It might seem intuitively sensible to think of DIF as a marked difference in item difficulty for two groups. In other words, if a test item is far more difficult for one group than for another, it would appear that the item functions differently for those two groups. Some early studies, as well as the Golden Rule procedure, took differences in item difficulty or total test score as automatic indications of bias.

One approach in this tradition is the transformed item difficulty (TID) index, also known as the delta plot (Angoff, 1982, 1993). This index first computes item difficulty values (p-values) for each item separately for both groups and then transforms them to a standardized metric (e.g., z-scores or ETS's delta scale). The standardized values can then be correlated and displayed in a scatter plot. An item that is very easy for one group but very difficult for the other would be located far away from the regression line and would be suspected of showing DIF.

Viewed another way, the delta plot checks whether the item difficulty estimates of one group can be predicted through the item difficulty estimates of the other group. For items where that is the case, both samples can be assumed to have been drawn from the same underlying population and no DIF is present. However, where no prediction is possible, the samples must be assumed to come from different populations. This means that the item differentiates between them on the basis of a construct-irrelevant factor (such as gender, L1, or race) and DIF is present.

A persistent issue with this type of analysis is that it assumes equal discrimination across all items (in a measurement sense, not a bias sense), and where that is not the case, items can appear to have much more or less DIF than is actually present (see Camilli & Shepard, 1994, for a detailed discussion of this point). However, equality of discrimination is an empirical assumption that can be checked, and it is probably too far-reaching to simply dismiss all difficulty-based procedures off-hand as Camilli and Shepard appeared to do. The absence of matching by ability level is a more serious problem with the TID approach.

Because of these shortcomings in DIF work based on item difficulty, such analyses have become rather rare recently, but the delta plot was used in some earlier DIF studies in language testing.

In an early study, Chen and Henning (1985) used the delta-plot method to compare the performance of 77 NSs of Chinese (all dialects) with 34 NSs of Spanish (all dialects) on the multiple-choice sections of UCLA's ESL placement test (ESLPE), consisting of 150 items. They first computed item- and section-difficulty estimates using the Rasch model, then correlated the scores of the two groups for each section and the total test, and computed regression equations to model the scores. They also produced a scatter plot of item difficulty with a regression line and a 95% confidence interval drawn around it. Chen and Henning found that only four items (3% of the test) were outside a 95% confidence interval around the regression line and that all of these items were vocabulary items. All four items favored the Spanish L1 group; that is, they were comparatively far easier for Spanish-speaking test takers than Chinese-speaking test takers. When Chen and Henning examined these items, they found that in all four cases, the word tested had a true cognate in Spanish: approximate (aproximado), animated (animado), maintain (mantener), and obstruct (obstruir). This directly explained why these items were easier for L1 Spanish test takers: They could use their L1 knowledge to answer the item, whereas L1 Chinese test takers had no such extra knowledge at their disposal. Three out of the four items were extremely easy for the L1 Spanish speakers with a difficulty of nearly −6 logits, which indicates that nearly all Spanish speakers got these items correct. Their difficulty for

Chinese speakers ranged from moderately easy to equally easy and difficult.

In this study, the L1 effect clearly led to DIF. However, does DIF equal bias in this case? Chen and Henning (1985) showed that a good case can be made that there is no bias because English does contain words that have true Spanish cognates (and words that have false Spanish cognates), so it is legitimate to test knowledge of these words. In fact, the test would be a good predictor of students' real-world success, as they would also be advantaged by their knowledge of Spanish when using English in real-world interactions. Chen and Henning cautioned that bias would be present if there is a "disproportionate number of lexical items employed for which Spanish cognates exist" (p. 162), but if the number of cognates included in the test mirrors their proportion of occurrence in the language, there is no bias problem. Of course, this view itself is highly problematic and not a little bit naïve: Not only is it difficult to determine the frequency of occurrence of a certain item in the language as a whole, but it would require intense corpus work to determine what its frequency of occurrence is in a specific domain. It is a safe bet that no language test is preceded by a corpus analysis on such a gigantic scale for every single vocabulary item.

Kunnan (1990) also used the ESLPE for a delta-plot analysis of DIF based on gender and four native languages: Japanese, Chinese, Spanish, and Korean. Similarly to Chen and Henning (1985), he calculated difficulty indexes and then created regression plots for gender and each combination of native languages. He found DIF in 9% of items in the native language analysis and 15% in the gender analysis. Some of the DIF in the native language condition could be accounted for by Spanish speakers' positive transfer from L1, and some advantages for the Japanese and Chinese groups might have occurred because of previous instructional experience with discrete-point grammar items, but other findings were inexplicable. For some of the gender-induced DIF, the major field of study was a likely explanation, with male students being more likely to study sciences and doing better on items with science content. However, again, reasons for DIF in other cases were inexplicable. Kunnan found a larger number of DIF items than Chen and Henning, which is probably due to the larger number of comparisons he made by including four native languages, as opposed to Chen and Henning's two. In general, however, his findings corroborate Chen and Henning's.

Sasaki (1991) also replicated Chen and Henning's (1985) analyses, but in addition to correlating difficulty indexes, she used Scheuneman's chi-square, a nonparametric statistic, which compares whether test takers at the same ability level were equally likely to answer an item correctly or incorrectly (Scheuneman, 1979). Sasaki's sample consisted of 262 native Chinese speakers and 81 native Spanish speakers taking the ESLPE. She found that Chen and Henning's method detected fewer items than Scheuneman's chi- square and that Chen and Henning's method identified some items as showing DIF that were extremely easy or difficult for both groups but with very slight difficulty differences. There was little overlap between methods: Out of 27 items identified, only 4 were identified by both methods. This is obviously a cause for concern, because both methods produce a great deal of type I error (finding DIF where there is none) or a great deal of type II error (not finding DIF where there is DIF). Three reasons are possible for these differences in detection rates: small sample size, arbitrary definitions of DIF, and imprecise use of the methods.

Sample size is always a concern: As Muniz, Hambleton, and Xing (2001) showed, small samples lead to underestimation of DIF, and general instability in DIF detection. The samples in all three studies (Chen & Henning, 1985; Kunnan, 1990; Sasaki, 1991) were comparatively small, which probably introduced some imprecision.

The definition of what items show DIF (viz. those outside a 95% confidence interval around the regression line) is arbitrary and, as Chen and Henning (1985) freely admitted, might be overly conservative: A lower confidence interval would have led to a much larger number of suspect items. Finally, the delta-plot (TID) method does not match test takers by ability and does not take item discrimination into account, whereas matching is at least part of the Scheuneman method. However, Scheuneman's chi-square was attacked by Baker (1981) as being too affected by sample size and not actually based on a chi-square distribution. So it appears that all three studies are questionable.

4.5 Contingency Table Methods and Other Nonparametric Approaches

Although nonparametric approaches are a powerful and practical way to investigate DIF, they do make some implicit assumptions. Because they involve frequencies of correct and incorrect answers, they essentially work with item difficulty and implicitly assume that discrimination and guessing are the same for all items. If that is not the case, results can be distorted.

Contingency table methods have the advantage that they do not require in-depth understanding of the complex mathematics of item response theory (discussed below) or complicated software. Instead, they use the odds of a correct response. For every score level, a 2 × 2 table is created that is used to compute the relative odds of a correct response for the reference group and the focal group. The odds ratios are then summed across score levels and averaged. Take the following (imaginary) example from a test. The contingency table (Table 4.1) only includes test takers

Table 4.1

2 × 2 table with correct and incorrect responses for the reference and focal groups

	Response		
	Correct	Incorrect	Total
Reference group	15	5	20
Focal group	4	6	10
Total	19	11	30

with a total score of 20. A separate table has to be computed at every score level. Table 4.1 shows that 15 members of the reference group got the item correct, whereas 5 reference-group members got it wrong. Four members of the focal group got it correct, whereas six got it wrong. We can now easily compute the odds of a correct and an incorrect response by dividing observed frequencies by total number of group members as shown in Table 4.2.

The next question is: How much more likely is a member of either group to get the item correct? This is obtained by dividing the odds of a correct response for each group by the odds of an incorrect response. So for the reference group, this would be

$$\Omega_{\text{ref}} = 0.75/0.25 = 3$$

For the focal group, it would be

$$\Omega_{\text{foc}} = 0.4/0.6 = 0.667$$

In the final step, the odds ratio (α) is computed, which answers the question: How much more likely is a reference-group member to get the item correct than a focal-group member? This is computed as $\Omega_{\text{ref}}/\Omega_{\text{foc}}$, so in this case,

$$\alpha = 3/0.667 = 4.5$$

Table 4.2

Odds of a correct or incorrect response for reference and focal groups

	Response		Total
	Correct	Incorrect	
Reference group	0.75	0.25	20
Focal group	0.4	0.6	10
Total	19	11	30

In other words, a reference-group member at this score level is 4.5 times as likely to get the item correct as a focal-group member. Put differently, for every nine times that the reference group gets this item correct, the focal group gets it correct twice. Quite a difference!

Remember, however, that this computation was only done for one score level. So to get an overall DIF value for this particular item, odds ratios at all score levels have to be computed, summed, and divided by the number of score levels. The outcome is one of the most commonly used DIF indexes: the Mantel-Haenszel odds ratio, usually written as α_{MH} (for details, see Camilli & Shepard, 1994; Dorans & Holland, 1993; Holland & Thayer, 1988). This index is sometimes transformed to fit a scale commonly used by ETS, known as the delta metric, which is centered at 0 (indicating no DIF), stretches from −13 to +13, and has a standard deviation of 4. The index is then reported as the Mantel-Haenszel delta (MH Δ), for example, by Elder (1996). Note that a positive MH Δ indicates DIF in favor of the focal group, whereas a negative MH Δ indicates DIF in favor of the reference group. Traditionally, it is the latter kind of DIF that is of most interest. Although the Mantel-Haenszel statistic gives an indication of the difference between the groups, it does not show whether this difference is significant, so there is also a significance test based on chi-square.

Probably because of its conceptual elegance, the Mantel-Haenszel statistic is very commonly used, and it is the main DIF analysis technique employed at ETS (Dorans & Holland, 1993). ETS classifies items according to their DIF scores obtained using the Mantel-Haenszel statistic. Items earn a classification of negligible DIF (Type A) if the item's MH Δ DIF is either nonsignificant at the 5% level or its absolute value is less than 1. They are classified as showing large DIF (Type C) if MH Δ exceeds 1.5 and is larger than 1 at a 5% significance level. All other items are classified as having intermediate DIF (Type B). As various combinations of reference and focal groups can exist (e.g., men–women, White–non-White, NS–NNS), items can have several DIF indexes associated with them.

4.5.1 Item Difficulty and Matched Groups: The Standardization Procedure

Another nonparametric approach that is attractive because of its conceptual elegance and simplicity is the standardization procedure (Dorans, 1989; Dorans & Holland, 1993), also known as the conditional p-value. The standardization procedure compares the proportion of test takers who answered an item correctly for the reference and focal groups at each score level. It also contains a weighting factor, giving more weight to score levels with more test takers. The result is a value between −1 and +1 (or −100% and +100%), with a result of 0 indicating no difference in difficulty between the groups. A difference of 0.1 (or 10%) means that one group has, on average, a 10% higher correct response rate on this item at all ability levels. Such a difference should be considered serious enough to warrant further investigation (Dorans & Holland, 1993). The standardization procedure is mathematically and conceptually uncomplicated, but it requires fairly large samples to be implemented profitably, as Dorans and Holland cautioned against collapsing score levels to obtain larger groups in each comparison. However, Sireci, Patsula, and Hambleton (2005) acknowledged that collapsing of score levels is sometimes unavoidable. Another strength of this procedure is that empirical response curves can be constructed, showing the different correctness rates by score level. Allowing such visual examination of the data can complement mathematical estimations of the significance and size of DIF.

4.5.2 Contingency Table Methods in Language Testing

Elder (1996) investigated DIF in the reading and listening tests of the Australian Language Certificate, an examination given to high-school students enrolled in language classes in years 8 and 9. She compared item functioning for learners who were native or heritage speakers of the target language with learners who were true L2 learners. Her sample included 1,176 learners of Chinese (22.6% NSs), 4,463 learners of Italian (8.9% NSs), and 1,224 learners of Greek (72.5% NSs). She divided learners into matched sets for each language test based on their total score, with each set covering a range of total scores and containing at least 30 learners; for example, she obtained six sets for the Chinese reading test and four sets for the Chinese listening test. She then used these matched sets to compute Mantel-Haenszel statistics for each test and language, and only considered items showing large DIF (Type C in the ETS classification). She found very strong differences in differcntially functioning items between languages: For Chinese, 65% of reading items and 70% of listening items exhibited DIF; for Italian, 30% of reading items and 27% of listening items showed DIF; and for Greek, 13% of reading items and 12% of listening items functioned differentially. After closer analysis of items showing DIF and consultation with language experts on possible reasons for their differential functioning, Elder concluded (similarly to Chen and Henning, 1985) that DIF is not bias in this case: NSs process these items differently than nonnative speakers (NNSs) and they do so in a way that is congruent with their NS competence.

Although her conclusion is reasonable, some aspects of Elder's (1996) study are problematic. For one thing, if more than two-thirds of test items show large DIF (as was the case for both Chinese tests), the use of total score as an ability measure is questionable. Elder acknowledged this but argued that a "purification" procedure (as Dorans and Holland, 1993, recommend) is not feasible: Removing all DIF items and then recalculating DIF indexes for the other items based on this nonattenuated sample would simply not leave enough items to work with, at least in the Chinese case. It is still wondrous how more than two-thirds of the items on a test could function differentially: Surely, if there is this much DIF in a test, and (at least in the case of the Chinese listening test) nearly all of it favors the NSs, should not the other items show up as functioning differentially?

One reasons for these results could be Elder's (1996) creation of matched sets, which, in effect, collapse score levels and lead to fewer contingency tables. This is precisely what Camilli and Shepard (1994) warned should be avoided: Citing Breslow (1981), they argued that the Mantel-Haenszel statistic becomes more efficient the more score levels are incorporated, which leads to more contingency tables. They suggest that frequencies in the tables are not a concern as long as the marginal totals are larger than zero, but that collapsing score levels and using fewer tables "can create a false impression of DIF" (p. 116). Elder's results might be influenced by her use of sets with collapsed score levels, but it is important to note that such collapsing is often unavoidable.

Another study with large subject numbers that used Mantel-Haenszel was Ryan and Bachman's (1992) investigation of DIF based on native language and gender in the paper-and-pencil TOEFL, consisting of a listening section, a structure and written expression section, and a vocabulary and reading section, as well as two sections of the First Certificate in English (FCE): vocabulary and reading. Ryan and Bachman's population consisted of 1,426 test takers, 575 of whom were male and 851 female. Seven hundred ninety-two were NSs of Indo-European languages and 632 were NSs of non-Indo-European languages. They used a matching variable section score rather than total test score and did not collapse any score groups. They sorted items for which DIF was detected according to the ETS system (see section 4.5) into Type A (small or no DIF), Type B (medium DIF), or Type C (large DIF). When using gender as the grouping variable, they did not find any Type C items in either test, only 4–5% of items were Type B, and the rest were Type A. However, when they used native language as the grouping variable, the picture changed significantly: On both TOEFL and FCE, 27% of items were classified as Type C, and in both cases, the section with the largest number of Type C items was the vocabulary section. Twelve percent of FCE items and 17% of TOEFL items were classified as Type B, and the rest were Type A items. Interestingly, the number of DIF items favoring the reference or the focal group was nearly completely balanced on both tests if Type B and Type C items were considered together. Ryan and Bachman found that items favoring test takers of non-Indo-European L1 background tended to have more America-specific content in the areas of culture, academia, and technology. They did not explain why this should give that particular group of test takers an advantage, showing, once again, how difficult it can be to understand reasons for DIF. However, their finding indicates that the test as a whole is not biased against a specific L1 group because advantages on both sides even each other out. Still, knowledge about possible DIF is relevant when building tests from item banks where the test paper is assembled "on the fly" and no two papers look the same. In this case, test versions could be accidentally constructed that contain only favorable or only nonfavorable items. Knowledge about DIF, however, could be integrated in the test assembly algorithm and prevent biased papers.

4.6 DIF and Item-Response Theory

Item-response theory (IRT) is an approach to DIF analysis radically different from the simple comparison of difficulty levels. By its very nature, it facilitates the matching of test takers on ability, but, at the same time, it suffers from a problem of circular reasoning by defining ability based on the total test score.

Unlike simple computations of difficulty, IRT uses three characteristics of an item to describe it: its difficulty, its discrimination, and guessing ("guessability"). These three characteristics of the item are known as parameters in IRT, and depending on whether an analysis takes into account only difficulty, or difficulty plus discrimination, or all three, it is known as 1-, 2-, or 3-dimensional IRT.

Although it is far beyond the scope of this volume to review IRT as a whole (but see Hambleton, Swaminathan, & Rogers, 1991; McNamara, 1996), simply put, it plots test-taker ability against the likelihood of answering the item correctly. This can be visualized as a curve (known as the item-characteristic curve or ICC), where test-taker ability is on the horizontal axis and likelihood of a correct response is on the vertical axis. By convention, ability is measured in logit units, usually from –4 to +4, with 0 indicating a level of ability that makes it equally likely to succeed or fail on an item of average difficulty. Likelihood of a correct response is measured from 0 to 1. Figure 4.1 shows the ICC for a medium-difficulty item from Roever's test of interlanguage pragmatics (Roever, 2005).

The ICC in Figure 4.1 shows that high-ability test takers have a very high likelihood of answering this item correctly, whereas low-ability test takers have a very low likelihood of answering it correctly. For example, a test taker at –2 logits ability has only a 10% chance of getting this item correct, whereas a test taker at +2 logits has nearly a 95% chance of getting it correct. Test takers of midlevel ability are about equally likely to answer the item correctly or incorrectly: A test taker at level 0 has a 60% chance of getting the item correct, which indicates that the item is somewhat easy.

If the sample is large and varied enough, an equation can be derived for each item, predicting the likelihood that a test taker of a certain ability level will answer this item correctly. When items differ on the difficulty parameter, it means that the

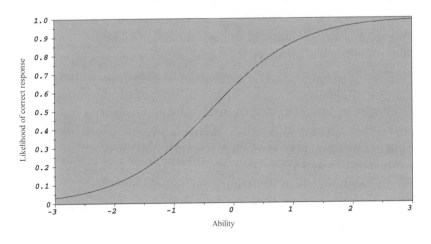

Figure 4.1. Item-characteristic curve for a mid-difficulty item.

likelihood of a correct answer is lower for a high-difficulty item than a low-difficulty item. So if a test taker has midlevel ability, that test taker would have a 50% chance of answering a mid-difficulty item correctly, but only a 20% likelihood of answering a high-difficulty item correctly. As mentioned previously, ability level is determined by total score.

The discrimination parameter describes how sharply the item distinguishes between test takers of similar ability levels. A highly discriminating item distinguishes very precisely between very similar test takers; for example, it is clearly easier for upper-intermediate test takers than for intermediate ones. However, it is nearly useless at all other levels; that is, beginners and advanced beginners will almost never get it right, and low-advanced and high-advanced test takers will almost always get it right. A less discriminating item does not distinguish as precisely between similar test takers, but it functions over a broader range of ability levels. The third parameter, guessing, can be used to adjust for guessing in multiple-choice items, but it is not usually very important in practice.

Item-response theory is radically different from classical test theory because it describes the behavior of an *item*, rather than the behavior of a population of test takers. Unlike classical test theory, IRT makes strong assumptions about item behavior, which can be used in test analysis to identify *misfitting items* that do not measure the same construct as the other items, or *misfitting persons*—those test takers whose answers to items seem inexplicable. For example, an item would be misfitting if high-ability test takers frequently get it wrong and low-ability test takers frequently get it right. A person might be misfitting if they get very easy items wrong but very difficult items correct.

Finally, because IRT focuses on items and relates likelihood of a correct response to test-taker ability, an item's characteristics are not dependent on a specific population of test takers as they are in classical test theory: Item parameters are population-invariant. Take item difficulty (p) in classical test theory: If the item is used on a low-ability population, it will appear more difficult than with a high-ability population. In IRT, it is not really the difficulty of the item that matters but the likelihood of a correct response given a test taker's ability level. It is obvious that a low-ability group of test takers would have less likelihood of giving a correct response than a high-ability group. This is where IRT becomes interesting for DIF analyses.

One problem of DIF analyses based on traditional item-difficulty estimates is that test takers are not matched for ability, so that the focal group might simply have lower ability than the reference group, which would explain the different item-difficulty indexes. From an IRT perspective, an item functions differentially if test takers at the same ability level but belonging to different groups have a different likelihood of getting the response correct. For example, take two groups of test takers at the same level of intermediate ESL proficiency: one group with Korean L1 and one with Dutch L1. Their likelihood of getting mid-difficulty items correct should be about 50%, regardless of what their native language is and regardless of whether one L1 group as a whole has a higher score on the test as a whole. It does not matter which group has overall higher ability: All that matters is that test takers at the same ability level are equally likely to get an item correct. If we find that the intermediate-level L1 Korean test takers only have a 30% likelihood of getting a specific mid-difficulty item correct, whereas the intermediate-level L1 Dutch test takers have a 60% likelihood, we have to suspect that the item functions differently for these groups.

This also shows that DIF is a matter of degree: It is easy to imagine that an item might show differential functioning for intermediate-level test takers but not for advanced ones (all of whom simply get it correct) or beginners (all of whom simply get it wrong). Also, the gap between test takers can be small or large. An item where one group has a much higher likelihood of a correct response at all ability levels than the other group would be considered to show strong DIF and would need to be examined in detail.

4.6.1 Calculating DIF in IRT Models

Although IRT models of DIF are conceptually appealing, the steepest challenge is the calculation of the actual amount of DIF and its significance. Camilli and Shepard (1994) discuss a range of formulas and approaches for calculating the amount of DIF. They consider the most promising approach to be the SPD-θ index. To calculate this index, the likelihood of a correct response for focal-group members at each ability level is subtracted from the reference-group members' likelihood. These differences are then summed and divided by the number of focal-group members. Of course, a possible concern with this index is that instances that advantage the focal group cancel out other instances that advantage the reference group, so there is also a version (UPD-θ) that simply computes all DIF, regardless of whether the focal group or the reference group are advantaged.

The most widely accepted IRT approach for detecting whether DIF is significant is model comparison (Thissen, Steinberg, & Wainer, 1993). In model comparison, the first IRT model to be created is named the "compact model" and it calculates item parameters (difficulty and possibly discrimination and guessing) for each item using the entire sample; that is, there is no distinction between reference and focal groups. Because IRT parameters try to model the data as precisely as possible, there is a goodness-of-fit statistic, which assesses how well the parameters represent the actual dataset.

The next step is done separately for each item. In this step, one item is chosen as the item of interest and, for this item alone, item parameters are calculated separately for the reference group and the focal group. For all other items, item parameters are calculated together for both groups, just as for the compact model. In other words, the parameters for one item are allowed to vary between reference group and focal group, but for all of the other items, they are kept constant. This model is named the "augmented model" because it should give a better fit to the data if there is DIF. The reason for the better fit of the augmented model is that the reference and focus groups would behave quite differently if, indeed, there was DIF. So in the compact model, where parameters are computed for both together, these parameters would be fairly imprecise: They would not model this item very well because people are not quite behaving as IRT would expect. For example, members of the advantaged group might do better than their ability suggests, whereas members of the disadvantaged group might do worse. Once the parameters of this item are computed separately for the two groups, the estimates become much more precise, which leads to the augmented model showing better fit than the compact model. The goodness-of-fit statistics for the two models are compared and if the augmented model fits much better than the compact model, DIF is present.

In contrast, in a case where there is no DIF, it does not make a difference whether the parameters of an item are computed together or separately for the reference and focal groups because the groups are not behaving differently. In that case, the compact model fits just as well as the augmented model.

These model comparisons have to be done separately for every item in the test: One compact model is computed, but there are as many augmented models as there are items. A concern is, of course, that items containing DIF might be used in the calculation of the parameters, so there might be DIF contamination in all of those models. To avoid this, a "purification procedure" is often used where items containing sizable DIF are removed after a first detection run and then the whole process is repeated without those contaminated items. Dorans and Holland (1993) point out that this principle is useful for any matching approach to obtain precise scores on the criterion measure (either the total score or an external criterion).

Altough the model comparison approach has strong theoretical foundations, it has some theoretical and practical problems. A major concern is its circularity because ability is determined by the total score on the test. Not only is there possible DIF contamination, but there is also the problem that the test is assumed to be a valid measure of the construct. A completely biased test, one where the majority of items is biased against the focal group, would not be detected by this procedure because it would appear that the focal and the reference groups differ in their overall ability. In fact, this procedure would probably identify those items that actually do *not* have DIF as being biased in favor of the focal group.

It would also not help very much to use an external criterion, such as another test, because there would be two implicit assumptions: namely that the other test measures without bias and that it measures the same construct as the test under investigation. An additional statistical assumption is that the two instruments should correlate perfectly, and this never happens, if only because of measurement error.

A further theoretical issue with practical bearing is the choice of which IRT model to use. There is some debate on the relative merits of the 1-parameter Rasch model compared to the 2- and 3-parameter IRT models, with Camilli and Shepard (1994) advising against use of the Rasch model because it makes the strong assumptions that all items have the same discrimination and the same amount of guessing, a position that is disputed by advocates of the Rasch model (McNamara, 1996). Which model to use is for some a theoretical, for others an empirical question of which model best fits the data. The fewer parameters a model has, the fewer subjects it requires, which makes the Rasch model attractive for smaller samples, but opponents of Rasch would argue there is a risk of misestimation if item discrimination varies.

The major practical problem of non-Rasch approaches lies in the large sample sizes necessary and in the mathematical and technical challenges of complex IRT models. IRT can be mathematically complex, and understanding more complex IRT models in detail takes lengthy training in psychometrics. They are also computationally intensive, and many of the programs that exist are complicated and unwieldy. Most problematic of all, they require numbers of subjects far larger than most language test users are likely to have available. When Camilli and Shepard (1994) stated that "with sample sizes as low as 400 to 600, DIF indices are likely to be highly inconsistent" (p. 131), most language testers might well feel a shiver because in the majority of language testing settings, such samples sizes would be considered large! It is enough to make the heart of any language tester sink to think that we would probably need over 1,000 test takers to have any confidence in the results of this type of DIF analysis recommended by Camilli and Shepard (1994). This has not stopped Kim (2001) from trying, but it is not likely that 2- and 3-paramter IRT models will be used to calculate DIF as a matter of routine outside large testing operations like ETS or specific research projects. The use of the 1-parameter Rasch model might be more feasible.

4.6.2 IRT and Language Testing DIF Research

Takala and Kaftandjieva (2000) analyzed gender-based DIF in a 40-item vocabulary section from the Finnish Foreign Language Certificate Examination, taken by 475 participants (182 male and 293 female) using the Rasch model. After confirming that the model indeed fits the data, they computed item-difficulty parameters by gender and then compared the parameters for each item by means of a *t*-test, based on Wright and Stone (1979). They found that 27.5% of items functioned differentially depending on gender: Six items favored men and five items favored women. In explaining their findings, they followed the common approach of hypothesizing that different life experiences conditioned by gender roles are accountable for male test takers performing better on English vocabulary items like *grease, rust,* and *rookie,* whereas female test takers performed better on *ache, turn grey,* and *jelly.* It remains mysterious, however, why women performed better on *ward* and *plot* and men performed better on *association* and *estate.* Although items favoring women and items favoring men balanced each other out on this version of the test, Takala and Kaftandjieva stressed that knowledge about differential functioning is important when creating tests from item banks, so as not to accidentally include clusters of items that favor one group without any items balancing out this effect.

Continuing in the tradition of the Rasch model, Elder, McNamara, and Congdon (2003) investigated DIF based on NS status in a test battery consisting of six components, including a cloze test, reading, vocabulary, and listening sections, as well as two writing tasks, the shorter one holistically scored and the longer one scored for accuracy, content, and fluency. Elder et al. were particularly interested in evaluating this technique's usefulness for detecting DIF in nondichotomous items like essays. Elder et al.'s participants were 139 undergraduates at the University of Auckland (New Zealand), 44% of whom were NSs of English and 56% NNSs. They generated item-difficulty estimates for both groups separately and compared them by means of a chi-square statistic. Any item more than two logits away from the mean was considered to show DIF. For the dichotomously scored sections, they found between 11% and 27% of items exhibiting DIF, most of which advantaged the NNS. When they deleted those items and recalculated the test statistics, the overall amount of DIF was reduced without affecting reliability.

The only language testing study using a model comparison approach is Kim's (2001) study with data from Bachman, Davidson, Ryan, and Choi's (1993) Cambridge-TOEFL comparability study. Her dataset consisted of 1,038 test takers who had taken the SPEAK (Speaking Proficiency English Assessment Kit) test: 571 from an Indo-European L1 background (Spanish, French, German) and 467 from an Asian language background (Thai, Japanese, Chinese). SPEAK scores were scaled 0–3 and assigned for grammar, pronunciation, and fluency.[1] This polytomous scoring complicates the use of IRT but allowed Kim to look at differences by score level using Samejima's (1969, 1996) graded response model. Kim considered each rubric as one item with three score ranges (0–1, 1–2, 2–3). She used a two-dimensional IRT model, and as suggested by Thissen et al. (1993), she first computed a compact model showing discrimination (the a parameter) for each rubric and difficulty/ability (the b parameter) for each of the three score ranges within the rubric. As a second step, she calculated three augmented models, computing separate discrimination and difficulty indexes for the Asian and the European group for one rubric but common ones for the other rubrics. She then computed likelihood ratios and found that the augmented model showed better fit for grammar and pronunciation but not for fluency. In other words, there was significant DIF in the grammar and pronunciation scores but not the fluency scores. For pronunciation, the European group was consistently favored (indicating uniform DIF) but less so at the highest ability level, so a test taker from the European group needed less ability to get the same pronunciation score than a test taker from the Asian group. For grammar, the European group was favored at low-ability levels, but the Asian group was favored at higher ability levels (indicating nonuniform DIF). Kim identified the phrasing of the rating rubrics as a possible source of DIF: The pronunciation rubric consistently talked about "phonemic errors" and "foreign stress and intonation pattern," thereby favoring European test takers just as consistently. She found that where the grammar rubric talked about grammatical errors interfering with intelligibility, the European test takers were favored, but where it did not, the Asian test takers were favored. It seemed, therefore, that raters had actually rated intelligibility rather than grammar itself.

4.7 Comparison of DIF Techniques

Muniz et al. (2001) conducted an interesting simulation study to investigate the effectiveness of DIF techniques for small sample sizes. They compared the standardization (conditional *p*-value) procedure, delta plots, and the Mantel-Haenszel procedure. To see how these procedures would operate under different conditions, Muniz et al. varied four characteristics of their datasets: sample size, ability distribution, amount of DIF, and statistical characteristics of the test items. They focused on relatively small sample sizes of 50 and 50 (reference group and focal group), 100 and 50, 200 and 50, 100 and 100, and for comparison, 500 and 500. They chose two ability distributions: one where both groups have equal overall ability and one where the focal group is one standard deviation below the reference group in overall ability. They induced three levels of DIF by building in difficulty differences (differences in the *b* parameter) of 0.5,

1.0, and 1.5 logits. For each level of DIF, they included 2 items in their 40-item dataset: 1 with low discrimination (a value of 0.5) and 1 with high discrimination (a value of 1.0). They set the guessing value (c value) for all items at 0.17, based on empirical findings.

Muniz et al. generated 100 datasets for each combination of variables: As there are 30 different combinations (5 group matches $\times$ 2 ability levels $\times$ 3 levels of DIF), they generated 3,000 datasets for this study and then used the three DIF detection techniques on these datasets to investigate how many of the six DIF items were found on average.

There were a number of useful findings:

1. The Mantel-Haenszel procedure does not show its strength unless group sizes are large. Only with reference and focal groups of 500 did Mantel-Haenszel outperform the other procedures. With small groups, it often performed worse than the other procedures.

2. Group size does not influence the conditional p-value difference and the delta-plot procedures significantly. Rather, the size of DIF is the important factor.

3. Unsurprisingly, it is more difficult to detect small DIF than large DIF, regardless of group size and equal or unequal distribution of abilities. For small DIF, all techniques only found about one-fourth of DIF cases, with the exception of Mantel-Haenszel used on large groups (500/500). Medium DIF was detected in about 50% of cases, and large DIF was detected in two-thirds of cases.

4. The standardization procedure and the delta plot performed similarly under equal ability conditions, but the standardization procedure performed much better under unequal ability distributions.

5. Both the standardization procedure and the delta plot generated more Type I errors (items identified as having DIF

that did not) than Mantel-Haenszel, except with the largest participant groups, where Mantel-Haenszel generated more Type I errors. However, Type I errors were quite low overall, never exceeding 16%.

6. Differential item functioning is easier to detect in high-discrimination items than low-discrimination items.

It appears that the standardization procedure can be reasonably used where sample sizes are small, but it is important to remember that no technique will be very good at detecting small amounts of DIF. In cases where such analyses are done with small sample sizes in a local setting, this limitation might not be of practical importance because we would be most concerned with findings items that show large DIF—those that could seriously distort test scores. The standardization procedure can detect about two-thirds of such items even with samples as small as 50 participants, and it is conceptually easy and not particularly cumbersome to compute. The Mantel-Haenszel procedure's relatively poor performance could be due to the quite strict significance level of $p < .05$, which leads to a very low Type I error, but might have caused Muniz et al. to underestimate Mantel-Haenszel potential for small samples: A level of $p < .10$ might be more appropriate.

For practical purposes, Muniz et al. recommend studying delta plots and p-value difference plots visually to identify items potentially showing DIF, which could then be confirmed statistically. Eventually, researcher judgment as to whether DIF might constitute bias and whether items suspected of it should be retained will be the deciding factor in any item analysis.

4.8 Other Approaches

4.8.1 Logistic Regression

A DIF detection technique that has recently enjoyed increased attention is logistic regression (for a detailed discussion, see Zumbo, 1999). Logistic regression is useful because it allows modeling of uniform and nonuniform DIF, is nonparametric, can be applied to dichotomous and rated items, and requires less complicated computing than IRT-based analyses. In fact, Zumbo gives several examples that only require SPSS.

Logistic regression assesses to what extent item scores can be predicted from total scores alone, from total scores and group membership, or from total scores, group membership, and the interaction between total scores and group membership.

If proficiency differences by themselves are sufficient for predicting scores with very little residual variance, there is probably little or no DIF in the data. However, if proficiency differences alone do not predict scores well and leave a large residual, and, when group membership is added into the equation, predictions become much more precise, then there is DIF present based on group membership. This is uniform DIF because test takers at any score level would be equally affected. In cases where total score and group membership still do not clear up the residual variance, the interaction term is added, which should make the model more suitable and indicates nonuniform DIF. As Camilli and Shepard (1994) point out, logistic regression is essentially a model comparison procedure because it creates and then compares three regression models.

4.8.2 Logistic Regression in Language Testing DIF Research

Lee, Breland, and Muraki (2004) used logistic regression for a study of DIF in writing prompts for the computer-based TOEFL. They faced the methodological problem that only a single prompt is answered by a test taker so that there is no total score to use for matching the reference and focal groups. Lee et al. circumvented this problem by using TOEFL scores (the cumulative score for all sections except writing) as their criterion measure. Their participants were 254,435 TOEFL test takers who took the TOEFL computer-based test between 1998 and 2000. They divided the sample into a reference group of 132,941 NSs of Spanish, French, or German and a focal group of 121,494 NSs of Chinese, Japanese, or Korean. Their test takers had received a total of 81 prompts. They first entered the TOEFL scores into the regression equation, thereby obtaining expected essay scores, and computed the residual between the expected essay scores and the actual essay scores across all 81 prompts for the two groups separately. The expected score turned out to be nearly identical to the actual score, indicating that the TOEFL score is an extremely good predictor of the essay score and that differences in essay scores between the groups are almost certainly caused by proficiency differences. However, because an individual test taker would only be administered one essay, they then checked the residuals for the individual prompts, finding only effect sizes below 0.16, which can be considered a small effect (Cohen, 1988). They also entered group membership and an Ability-by-Group interaction into the regression equation to investigate on which items these factors had any impact. They found 27 items with significant group membership effects and 20 of those items also had significant Ability-by-Group interactions, indicating nonuniform DIF. However, the effect size in all cases was extremely small and far below the level that could be considered in any way relevant for practical purposes. So although L1 group membership has an effect on TOEFL essay scores, this effect is too small to warrant concern.

Kim (2001) in her study of the SPEAK test also used logistic regression in addition to IRT. She found that the contributions of group membership and the Group × Ability level interaction to the regression equation were significant, but their effect sizes were small.

Logistic regression is similar to the other DIF detection techniques discussed earlier, in that it focuses on DIF at the item level and is mostly applied to dichotomous items. However, there are also methods available for whole tests and tests with polytomous scoring, such as essays and speaking tests. Generalizability theory (G theory) can show the relative contributions of various factors to test scores (including test takers' L1 background), and multifaceted Rasch measurement can be used to show whether certain raters systematically rate certain test takers with undue harshness or leniency. We will consider these two approaches in turn.

4.8.3 Generalizability Theory

Generalizability theory (Brennan, 2001; Shavelson & Webb, 1991) is not a mainstream method for detecting DIF, but it can be used to expose interactions between facets of a testing situation. G theory uses analysis of variance to parcel out the variance associated with facets such as persons, items, and, where desired, such facets as ratings, topics, and occasions. Having determined variance components, a G coefficient is computed by dividing the desirable variance component (usually person variance) by the desirable variance component plus nondesirable variance components, such as variance due to raters, topics, interactions between facets, and simple measurement error. The coefficient that is obtained indicates to what extent test results are generalizable from the specific instance that was analyzed to the whole universe of observations. It is similar to the reliability coefficient of classical test theory (and is also expressed on a scale of 0 to 1), but G theory has the advantage that it can accommodate designs that involve small numbers of tasks, like on an essay or oral test, and ratings. It can also be used to predict fairly easily what G coefficient would be obtained with more or fewer tasks, more or fewer raters, and so on. In this regard, it resembles the Spearman-Brown prophecy formula of classical test theory.

As mentioned earlier, G theory is not a common approach for detecting bias, but because it shows interactions between facets, it can provide some indication of possible bias. For example, Lynch and McNamara (1998) conducted an analysis of the speaking module of an oral test. They found that the person facet was the largest component of overall variance (87%), which is desirable because the test was intended to distinguish between persons of different ability. The rater facet was the second largest (8.5%) but contributed less than one-tenth of the person facet's variance.

This is not desirable variance, as it indicates some fluctuations among raters, but this variance is simply due to random rater inconsistency rather than systematically different ratings, which would be indicative of bias. The third largest variance component at 3.2% was the interaction of persons and raters, which can be interpreted as bias, because it means that some raters rate some test takers higher or lower than others.[2] The other variance components in Lynch and McNamara's study were negligible in size: The portion of total variance for items, the interaction between items and persons, the interaction between raters and items, and the overall interaction among items, raters, persons, plus general measurement error.

In another G theory study, Brown (1999) looked at a TOEFL population of 15,000 test takers, equally distributed over 15 native languages. Similar to a general DIF concern, Brown investigated the effect of native language on TOEFL scores. He found a negligible effect for native language, which made up only 1% of the total variance. Similarly, the Language-by-Item interaction was below 1%, which shows that native language hardly had any effect on scores. By far the largest variance component (74.75%) was the Persons-by-Items interaction, which means that some items were easier for some test takers and other items were easier for other test takers. This is actually of concern, as it might indicate interactions between aspects of items and test-taker variables other than language, but, unfortunately, G theory does not provide more detailed information on this facet. Brown concluded with a calculation of the G coefficient, which, at 0.9576, is extremely high, indicating that scores from this test can be taken to a very large extent as representative of test takers' knowledge of the entire domain.

4.8.4 Multifaceted Rasch Measurement

Multifaceted Rasch measurement uses Rasch modeling (mathematically equivalent to 1-parameter IRT) to place various factors (also known as facets) on a common scale. These factors typically include task difficulty, rater harshness/leniency, and test-taker ability. It can also detect whether there are unexpected interactions between facets. This approach is mostly used for speaking or writing tests with limited subject populations. It can easily handle polytomous rating data and can expose differential functioning of raters or items for specific candidates.

Imagine three raters rating 50 candidates on two speaking tasks. Each candidate is rated by two of the raters and each candidate completes one of the two tasks, which are randomly assigned to them. Imagine further that (unknown to testers and candidates) one task is much easier than the other task and that the raters differ widely in their harshness, so that one rater rates very strictly, one very leniently, and one is in the middle. It is easy to see that two candidates of identical ability could end up with very different raw scores, depending on who is rating them and whether the task they draw is difficult or easy. If a candidate completes the difficult task, those scores will necessarily be lower than the scores of a candidate of equal ability taking the easy task. If the first candidate then also gets the strict and the moderate raters, those scores will be further depressed, compared with a candidate who is rated by the lenient and the moderate raters. Multifaceted Rasch measurement models the relationship among all the facets and takes task difficulty and rater strictness into account when estimating candidate ability. So in the case of the above apparently disadvantaged candidate, it would compensate for the difficult task and the strict raters when estimating ability.

Because Rasch modeling relies on explicit assumptions about the data, deviations from these assumptions can be detected and flagged for further analysis. For example, imagine that the lenient rater is much less lenient for certain candidates. In fact, for these candidates, the otherwise lenient rater is as strict as the strict rater. This uncharacteristic behavior leads to unexpectedly low scores from a rater who usually gives high scores, and this might indicate an interaction between the rater and some background factor among these candidates; for example, the rater might be reacting negatively to a specific accent. Such systematic deviations from expected scores are known as *bias terms* in a facet analysis, and they are obviously useful for detecting differential functioning of tasks or raters. Other interactions are possible too; for example, in a case in which candidates answer multiple tasks, some otherwise high-ability candidates might score poorly on a certain task, which indicates that this task is functioning differentially for these candidates. There can also be multiway interactions such that a specific rater might be more lenient than usual with certain candidates, but only on a certain task.

The outcome of a multifaceted analysis with the program FACETS (Linacre & Wright, 1993) includes a ruler—a graphic representation of the various facets, including test-taker ability, rater strictness, and task difficulty on a single scale. Statistical analyses show these estimates and their fit numerically and describe each unexpected interaction between facets (a "bias term" in FACETS terminology), which could be indicative of differential functioning. Multifaceted analysis is more useful for detecting specific instances of differential task or rater functioning than generalizability theory, which just shows the overall contribution of a facet to scores.

Elder et al. (2003) used a multifaceted analysis in their study of the test battery used at the University of Auckland. Their analysis included rater severity, item difficulty, item difficulty by score band, and NS status. They also investigated the interaction between NS status and item difficulty. They found some differences between NSs and NNSs on the fluency measure and strong differences on the accuracy measure, both in favor of NSs. They explained their findings by suggesting that NNS errors might be treated more strictly by raters, or alternatively that there might be fewer errors and better discourse structuring in the NS essays, so that the different ratings show true differences in ability.

In Lynch and McNamara's analysis (1998) of the ESL speaking test, the authors also conducted a FACETS analysis of their data. The findings in their FACETS analysis appeared quite strikingly different from their generalizability analysis: The FACETS analysis showed that 36% of rater-candidate interactions were biased in a FACETS sense. In other words, 36% of ratings were significantly higher or lower than the Rasch model expected. Even more strikingly, 48% of rater-item interactions showed significant bias, so raters were systematically stricter or more lenient when rating performance on some tasks than others. However, only 7% of interactions between candidates and items were biased, which indicates minor effects of item characteristics on candidates.

Lynch and McNamara (1998) explained the apparent differences between the generalizability analysis and the FACETS analysis in terms of level of detail: FACETS examines the data in minute detail and exposes every instance of deviation from the model's assumptions, whereas a generalizability analysis looks at aggregations, so that individual instances of unexpectedly high or low interactions even out. Clearly, a FACETS analysis is more useful when the goal is to make operational changes, including training raters to be more objective with respect to certain candidate groups, removing bias-inducing components from tasks, or understanding why raters react differently to different tasks. A generalizability study, on the other hand, gives an impression of the overall effect of various facets and the dependability of the test as a whole.

4.9 Problems with DIF Analyses

One issue with DIF analyses has already been mentioned: They are quite complex, not readily done with standard spreadsheet or statistical software, and not easy to interpret. They also require fairly large numbers of subjects.

Another set of issues is conceptual. For one, how are the reference and focal groups determined? Categorizations used in most studies are rough and not theoretically motivated, and it is fairly obvious that any category is just a proxy for other test-taker background variables. In fact, any characteristic (gender, race, native language) chosen for grouping has a multitude of covariates, which could also be responsible for the DIF effect found. Take a category like gender: Short of showing that there are differences in the way men and women use cognition, it is not really the test takers' gender that affects their performance. It is a host of other factors associated with gender, e.g., societal expectations about educational and personal choices that lead to exposure to certain kinds of experiences, so that boys/men have more exposure to science and sports topics, whereas girls/women have more exposure to humanities and social science topics. However, these explanations are usually ex post facto and ad hoc. In the absence of a principled theory about the effect of test-taker background characteristics on scores, DIF analyses are far from scientific hypothesis testing and amount to little more than fishing expeditions.

Similarly problematic are the categories of NS versus NNS. The categories have been questioned many times (see, e.g., Coulmas, 1981; Davies, 1991), and for most practical purposes, they represent crude dichotomous classifications of language proficiency. However, they ignore the fact that for many constructs and operational tests, many NNSs can be just as able as NSs.

When comparing NNSs of different L1 backgrounds, the case becomes even murkier. What accounts for DIF there? Again, certain topics being more familiar to members from certain cultures and vocabulary items being easier where they are true cognates (Chen & Henning, 1985; Schmitt, 1988) are the more obvious explanations. However, here, too, there is likely to be a host of socioeconomic, motivational, and educational factors, so it is not sufficient to state that test takers with different L1s score differently on a test. A theory that explains why that is the case is needed, and that theory must involve an explanation of how native language and its covariates affect scores in a construct-irrelevant manner.

An issue that is not at all integrated in DIF analyses is that people are simultaneously members of several groups. Perhaps an item in a test of ESL functions only differentially for Chinese-speaking women with intermediate English proficiency in comparison with Spanish-speaking men with upper-intermediate proficiency, but the item might not show DIF for male versus female comparisons, European versus non-European language comparison, or high versus low ESL proficiency comparisons. Such an item would simply not be detected because DIF analyses are not usually done for multiple focal groups. However, it is now technically possible to do this, as Penfield (2001) shows with a generalized version of the Mantel-Haenszel procedure and Drasgow and Probst (2005) demonstrate in their use of a technique developed by Kim, Cohen, and Park (1995) that is appropriate for comparing IRT-derived parameters. However, even if a sequence of DIF analyses was run where every group is compared to every other group and such an item was detected, it is unclear what to make of it. Should it be deleted? Should it only be given to test takers who are not members of these groups? Then how comparable are the test versions?

We also know far too little about how the interaction between an item and the test taker leads to DIF. Microanalytic studies like verbal protocols might shed light on this, or at least experimental designs that try to systematically induce DIF in some items. Most analyses of reasons for DIF are still far too speculative, and empirical research could be very illuminating.

4.10 Dealing With DIF and Bias: A Judgment Call

It is important to understand that any DIF analysis includes value judgments at many levels. The emphasis that is placed on DIF detection in many testing programs is in itself a value judgment and even shows a certain sense of humility among test makers: Even though they often appear like monolithic juggernauts to outsiders, many are in fact quite aware of their own fallibility in creating sound and fair tests. Whether their willingness to go the extra mile in detecting and avoiding DIF is due to a sense of ethical obligation or fear of legal exposure (as in the Golden Rule case) is unclear, but there is likely to be an element of enlightened self-interest involved. Biased tests are inferior in quality to unbiased ones, simply because they will lead to lower quality decisions: Unqualified applicants are admitted to a competitive program, whereas qualified ones are rejected. When users become aware of the shortcomings of such tests, the reputation of the tests and their general acceptability suffer. In other words, removing bias makes good business sense for test makers.

In terms of value judgments the first judgment concerns the assignment of reference and focal groups: What are the groups of interest? This will probably differ between language tests like TOEFL or IELTS and content tests like SAT and GRE. Traditionally, categorical background variables like gender, minority status, NS status, or L1 are used to split the population into groups, but these categories are by no means natural dichotomies. First, considering any of them dichotomous rather than continuous is a gross oversimplification of the real world. Being a NS is for all practical purposes not an all-or-nothing proposition: Very advanced NNSs are indistinguishable from NSs on most tests designed for large populations, with the exception of tests that specifically target extremely advanced groups. Even gender is now being retheorized as a performative achievement, rather than a biological given, which introduces a variability that the simple gender dichotomy does not adequately reflect (Butler, 1990; Cameron, 1999).

Second, the simple choice of variables to include in a DIF analysis is a value judgment: Why does it matter whether men or women perform better on a given item? Why compare NNSs of Indo-European and non-Indo-European language backgrounds? Why not compare those with highly inflecting languages with those with less inflecting languages (which would probably put English and Chinese in one category)? Why not compare test takers of high socioeconomic status with those of lower socioeconomic status? This might show tests to be "wealth-biased" and thereby maintaining the status quo of access to scarce resources, such as a high-quality education.

However, once bias is found, what should be done about it? To what extent is it incumbent on test makers to right social wrongs? What amount of impact on the construct is acceptable in the service of unbiasing tests: Can certain construct aspects be underemphasized because they are particularly prone to introduce bias? Which aspects of a construct are so central that they must be included, regardless of bias?

Once we start questioning constructs, the whole enterprise becomes much more far-reaching. Why do we measure certain skills or abilities but not others? For example, success in college is certainly dependent to some extent on intelligence, analytical ability, and knowledge of the language of instruction, but what about perseverance, discipline, emotional resilience, or social skills? In the language testing area, we never measure compensatory strategies that learners can use to overcome language knowledge deficits. Despite our much vaunted communicative orientation, we still focus primarily on the language code, and we do not look at learners' ability to make up deficits in that area through sociopragmatic skills, as Wes did so successfully (Schmidt, 1983).

Although many constructs are the consequence of theoretical armchair deliberations, even constructs based on empirical groundwork (like the extensive needs analyses that informed work on the most recent generation of the TOEFL) are not value-free, simply because the needs analyses are only models of the actual domain and they prioritize certain aspects over others. In practice, a further limitation is introduced by test makers' considerations of what is realistically testable without prohibitive expense. So the actual construct as it is operationalized through the test can be quite different from the ideal construct based on the needs analysis. Needless to say, what expense is considered prohibitive is yet another value judgment.

The technical process of DIF analysis is also full of value judgments. For example, even if an item shows DIF, it is a question of judgment whether DIF is considered high or low. The ETS categories of DIF described earlier are just as arbitrary as any other categorization of DIF values. The next arbitrary decision is what DIF level is acceptable. Zieky (1993) describes the ETS approach as one of preferences but with real-world constraints. Wherever

Type A items (no or low DIF) are available, they should be given preference over Type B or Type C items. If Type B items have to be used, those with smaller DIF values should be preferred to those with larger DIF values. Type C items should only be used if they can be shown to be fair and they must also be essential in terms of the test specifications. Any use of Type C items must be documented and reviewed. A less obvious constraint of significant operational importance is that different forms of the same test must be equivalent in their use of items from these categories. It would not be wise to use up all Type A items on the first few test versions and then assemble later versions from items with more and more DIF.

The other real-world constraint that Zieky (1993) mentions concerns the content specifications for the test, which is a technical operationalization of the content aspect of the construct. If differential functioning is judged to be due to construct-relevant differences on legitimate content, the item can be retained, but this is to a large extent a question of a developer advocating for an item. Also, what is or is not "legitimate content" is certainly open to discussion. For example, in Roever's (2005) test of interlanguage pragmatics, the Pope Q item ("Is the Pope Catholic?") was the only implicature item where L1 German test takers scored, on average, higher than L1 Japanese and Chinese test takers, although the Japanese test takers had, on average, higher scores. Roever argued that the Pope Q and its variations are legitimate components of the construct "knowledge of American English implicature" and should therefore be retained. At the same time, one could question the broader relevance of understanding the Pope Q for learners' communicative competence.

4.11 Conclusion

Fairness plays an important role in traditional psychometric work on testing, and a variety of approaches have been developed to detect unfair items and investigate unwanted influences of test-taker background factors. The motivation for such work appears as much guided by test makers' self-interest as by ethical concerns, but this is by no means negative: Strong and psychometrically innovative approaches arose out of dissatisfaction with the methods mandated through the Golden Rule settlement, which put DIF detection irrevocably on the agenda, at least in the United States.

There is still much development work to do, however. For example, most DIF detection procedures only work adequately for large samples or large amounts of DIF. Large sample sizes are not realistic in language testing, however, so procedures that can detect DIF in smaller samples would be a welcome development. Also, we still understand far too little about the Item-Test taker interaction that brings DIF about: Microanalytic work, possibly involving verbal protocols of people solving problems with artificially induced DIF, could help shed light on the factors that lead to differential functioning.

The methods outlined here can go a long way to ensuring equity and fairness in testing: Just as a good test must be a reliable and defensible measure of the construct, it must be unbiased to inform good decisions. At the same time, DIF detection only considers the test itself and does not look beyond the test booklet at the larger sociopolitical context. This is not its task, of course, but we are arguing that researchers need to go beyond the test booklet to understand fairness and bias in its social context. After all, DIF analyses only detect bias, but the factors that cause advantages and disadvantages for groups of test takers and bias their educational opportunities lie in the larger social context.

In chapter 5 we look at more politically inspired approaches to ensuring fairness: fairness reviews and codes of ethics.

Notes

[1] The scoring of the SPEAK test has since changed to a scale of 0–60.
[2] Note that a G theory analysis does not identify which raters and which test takers are involved, but it simply identifies the effect of such an interaction on scores.

CHAPTER FIVE

Fairness Reviews and Codes of Ethics

Although work on differential item functioning (DIF) is inspired by a concern for social fairness, it is done within the organizational structure of test developers and focuses on ensuring adequate psychometric properties of tests. In addition to this psychometric treatment of fairness, the testing profession has also implemented guidelines and policies to determine bias and assert a striving for fair testing. This has led to the implementation of fairness reviews and codes of ethics.

5.1 Preempting DIF: Fairness Reviews

Information on DIF can be used during test development if items are pretested, in which case, items showing DIF can be eliminated or rewritten before being included in the final test form or item bank. Sometimes, however, pretesting is not possible and items must be evaluated for DIF after the test. It is still possible to exclude items with high DIF when scoring the test, but only if scores are made available after a delay. This would obviously not work for computer-based tests that show scores immediately on completion of the test.

Some test makers work to reduce DIF in their items from the early stages of test creation. This is sometimes accomplished through a formal process called "sensitivity review" or "fairness review," and in other cases, it might be a part of the overall test development process. The former process is operated by Educational

Testing Service (ETS) and the latter by Cambridge ESOL. We will first briefly describe Cambridge's process and then ETS's process in some detail.

5.1.1 University of Cambridge ESOL Examinations

The review of test items and avoidance of bias for Cambridge ESOL examinations is integrated in Cambridge's larger Quality Management System (QMS). The QMS is anchored in the Association of Language Testers in Europe's Code of Practice (Association of Language Testers in Europe, 1994) and is intended to ensure a transparent and systematic approach to test development.[1] It views fairness as an overall characteristic of a well-constructed test, and there is no specific discussion of DIF. L. Taylor (personal communication, February 3, 2006) stated that an effort is made during the item-writing process to avoid potentially offensive or upsetting item content and that guidelines for item writers suggest avoiding material that is too specialized or technical. Once items are written, they are scrutinized for unsuitable content and other weaknesses at the pre-editing stage of test production.

Cambridge ESOL has not published any guidelines for fairness review, and it is unclear whether a formal and separate fairness review process exists. We turn now to an example of such a process, as it operates at ETS.

5.1.2 Educational Testing Service

Ramsey (1993) describes how the process operates at ETS, and the ETS Fairness Review Guidelines (Educational Testing Service, 2003) constitute the regulatory framework. Every test item, research report, or other material for use outside of ETS must be reviewed by a trained fairness reviewer. Training takes a day for all staff except test developers, who receive a day and a half. Training the developers intensively is intended to ensure that items are already created with the Fairness Review

Guidelines in mind, thereby reducing the number of items not in compliance with the Guidelines from the start.

Testing programs can elect to submit their items for a preliminary review, which is not part of the mandatory process but which might be useful to highlight potential problems early, particularly in cases where the detailed development of the item is time-intensive or cost-intensive. In all cases, once items are assembled, they are submitted to a fairness reviewer for assessment. The reviewer can suggest changes at the discretion of the developer where an item could use improvement but would pass the review as is, or reviewers can raise a challenge to an item, declaring it in breach of the Guidelines, and they must show which guideline the item infringes upon. The reviewer's comments are sent back to the item developer, who can either accept them and revise the item or initiate a dispute resolution process, which begins with a discussion between reviewer and item developer. If an agreement cannot be reached, a fairness review coordinator discusses the issue with the parties involved and suggests a solution. If that fails, a central fairness review office, which is part of the Office of the General Counsel, examines the issue and suggests a solution. If there is still no agreement, a higher level committee is involved and makes a suggestion, and failing that, ETS's general counsel makes a final, binding decision. It might seem somewhat curious that the review process is associated with the Office of the General Counsel, whose main task, after all, is to protect the organization from legal challenges, but this probably illustrates another identity of this process. It appears that it is not only intended to avoid DIF but also to protect ETS and its materials from litigation such as the Golden Rule case.

The review ostensibly centers on factors that might make a test less fair for certain predetermined groups by introducing construct-irrelevant variance. The ETS Fairness Review Guidelines (Educational Testing Service, 2003) identify construct-irrelevant knowledge and offensive content as the two main sources of such variance. The Guidelines give as an example the use of overly complex reading material in mathematics sections, which could impair the unidimensionality of the affected items and lead to the measurement of reading proficiency in addition to mathematical ability. A DIF study might identify such an item as being easier for test takers with high reading proficiency (e.g., native speakers [NSs]) than for test takers with low reading proficiency (e.g., second language [L2] learners).

Offensive content is a different matter. The Guidelines state:

> Offensive content may make it difficult for test takers to concentrate on the meaning of a reading passage or the answer to a test item, thus serving as a source of construct-irrelevant difficulty. Test takers may be distracted if they believe that a test advocates positions counter to their beliefs. Test takers may respond emotionally rather than logically to needlessly controversial material. The inclusion of such material may also have adverse effects on performance on subsequent items. Even if performance is not directly affected, the inclusion of inappropriate content or images may decrease the confidence of test takers and others in the fairness of ETS products. (Educational Testing Service, 2003, p. 5)

Offensive content is interpreted as leading to construct-irrelevant variance through test takers being distracted or responding emotionally rather than logically to test material. The subsequent section broadens this even further by referring to content that might "upset" test takers. This distraction or emotional response is thought to lower test takers' ability to answer items correctly and demonstrate the true extent of their knowledge. Two characteristics of material are identified that make it "offensive": if it conflicts with test takers' beliefs or if it is "needlessly controversial." This standard seems to require something that is practically or even theoretically impossible, as test makers cannot know all of the test takers' beliefs or what test takers might find controversial. However, the next section lowers the bar significantly by making it clear that only certain aspects of a test taker's identity matter in determining whether they might find content offensive. The Guidelines call for considering certain groups of test takers and they define these "groups of primary concern [...]

by age, disability, ethnicity, gender, national origin, race, religion, and sexual orientation" (Educational Testing Service, 2003, p. 5). To our knowledge, there is no DIF work comparing test takers grouped by their age, religion, or sexual orientation. In fact, the last sentence of the section on offensive content makes it clear that measurement precision or even fairness is not the only consideration in avoiding offensive content, but there is also concern that test takers or undefined "others" might have less confidence in ETS products; in other words, ETS's corporate image might suffer. Clearly, this is as much about excluding content that test takers might find offensive as it is about excluding content that the general public or specific pressure groups might find offensive. Ravitch (2003) describes the effect of political pressure from both ends of the spectrum on test makers and textbook publishers. She cites an unnamed ETS official as saying that "It is better to be bland than to be controversial" (p. 50) and claims that testing agencies simply delete items about which they receive complaints.

One could, of course, castigate test makers for their "wimpy" stance on societal issues and demand that they resist political pressure, but that does not change the fact that test makers and their tests do not exist in a sociopolitical vacuum. Although concern with public image is far removed from validity or DIF, test makers cannot afford to ignore societal pressures if they want to ensure the continued acceptance of their tests by stakeholders. It is also noteworthy that the Guidelines do not require that any potentially controversial content be avoided: If problematic content is important to the construct under assessment, it can be included. This means especially a distinction between tests measuring knowledge of specific subject matter (medicine, business, nursing) and general skills tests (TOEFL, SAT, SPEAK). Inclusion of possibly problematic material is less necessary to valid measurement in the latter, so it would be difficult to make a case for including material that the Guidelines discourage.

According to the Guidelines, fairness review assesses characterizations of social groups, ethnocentrism, underlying assumptions, sources of construct-irrelevant knowledge or skills, possibly

offensive material and terminology for groups of people, stereo-
types, and diversity. When items talk about groups of people
(by nationality, ethnicity, or other background variables), the
Guidelines require that characterizations not be denigrating,
stereotypical, or devaluing a group's beliefs or culture. Such mis-
characterizations can be expressed through underlying assumptions or an ethnocentric perspective. Ramsey (1993) gives the
following example of an underlying, ethnocentric assumption:
"The 3,000 Inuvialuit, what the Eskimos of Canada's western
Artic prefer that they themselves be called, live in the treeless
tundra around the Bering Sea" (p. 383). This statement implies
that the "real" name for the Inuvialuit is "Eskimos," simply because that is the name that is used for them in Anglo culture.
Also, cultural or religious beliefs should not be ridiculed or described as "wrong," although it is sometimes permissible to show
that there are conflicting views.

Similarly to the publication manual of the American Psychological Association (APA; American Psychological Association,
2002), the ETS Guidelines discuss at length what a group should
be called, and they also follow the APA guidelines in giving preference to the term that the group members themselves use. They
require that gendered and sexist language use be avoided, and
they strive for a balanced depiction of various groups' contributions to society. No group should be portrayed stereotypically as
needy or influential, but there should be a mix of roles throughout
the test.

The Guidelines contain a lengthy list of topics that should
not be used in tests or used only in unusual circumstances.
Among topics to avoid the Guidelines lists abortion, abuse of people or animals, hunting or trapping for sport, euthanasia, and
witchcraft. Extreme care is required for materials related to ac-
cidents, disasters, or death, which can be used but should not
dwell on graphic aspects of these topics. Evolution, which is rejected by some religious groups and is currently a hot political
topic in the United States, is allowed in test materials but should
not focus on the evolution of human beings. However, in content

tests dealing with biology, any aspect of evolution that is necessary for valid measurement is acceptable. Notably, this section of the Guidelines also urges test writers and reviewers to be sensitive to cross-cultural issues, particularly with regard to depictions of men and women in contact. The Guidelines, however, acknowledge that it is impossible to cater to all taboos operating in all cultures.

The part of the Guidelines summarized above deals mostly with potentially offensive content and is aimed at minimizing its offensive effect for test takers. Only one extensive section deals with material that has been shown to introduce construct-irrelevant variance—in other words, DIF. Again, it is important to remember that some of the material to be avoided is in fact necessary for the measurement of specific knowledge or skills, in which case its use is justified and any differences in performance between groups would be considered legitimate differences in proficiency/ability, rather than illegitimate DIF. The Guidelines require that visuals, such as charts and graphs, not be used unless they are essential to the item, and spatial skills should also not be engaged. The largest part of this section deals with topics and word choices that might induce DIF and gives as a general standard that overly complex words, idioms, or syntactic structures should be avoided. Of course, what is overly complex depends on the test-taker population in question. Specifically, military, sports-related, and religious topics and terminology should not be used, regionalisms should not be included, and other specialized words should also be avoided, including farm-related words, legal or political words, scientific or technical terminology, or terms associated with machinery, tools, or transportation. The section also warns against the use of words that might be felt to be elitist (*regatta*, *penthouse*) or business-related and goes so far as to suggest that depictions of people spending money on luxuries should not be included, which is probably more related to avoiding politically offensive content than actual DIF. The section also acknowledges that requiring specific knowledge of U.S. culture can introduce DIF and counsels the omission of such culture-specific items as product brands, geography, history, political system, units of measurement, and so on.

As the Guidelines recognize, what might be considered offensive or inducing DIF varies between cultures. ETS has developed the International Principles for Fairness Review in Assessments (Educational Testing Service, 2004), which are based on the Guidelines but outline a process for creating culture-specific fairness review guidelines to be used with tests developed by ETS for use in countries other than the United States. Because they only provide a general framework, the Principles are not as specific as the Guidelines with regard to topics that should be avoided, but it will be interesting to see how fairness review guidelines based on them differ from the U.S.-based Guidelines. It is also noteworthy that for tests used in a variety of countries, the Guidelines apply rather than the Principles. Although it is completely understandable from a practical perspective and for reasons of score comparability that ETS does not want to develop different versions of the TOEFL for every country where it is administered, it somewhat weakens the whole idea of cultural fairness, as the cross-cultural prescriptions in the Guidelines are somewhat vague and test takers might still encounter content that they find "offensive or upsetting" (Educational Testing Service, 2004, p. 3). A possible reason for the lesser concern in the case of tests administered worldwide (like TOEFL or GRE) might be that the score end users are located in the United States (e.g., university admission offices). Score users are more powerful than test takers, because users are in a position to mandate that test takers submit to the test. Thus, as long as the score users are satisfied with the test's fairness, the instrument's acceptability does not suffer and test makers can expect few repercussions, even if some content is problematic from the perspective of the test takers.

Despite its value-laden nature and the political contention around it, fairness review demonstrates that test makers are taking fair and equal assessment seriously. The testing profession as a whole has also declared its stance toward fairness and broader issues of appropriate professional conduct. Such policy statements are made as codes of ethics or codes of practice.

5.2 Fairness as a Professional Obligation: Codes of Ethics and Practice

The issue of ethics is not a recent concern in language testing, with the first papers appearing in the late seventies and early eighties (Davies, 1977a; Palmer & Spolsky, 1975; Spolsky, 1981; Stevenson, 1981). Work in this area gathered momentum with the publication of a special issue of *Language Testing*, edited by Alan Davies (1997a), followed more recently by a special issue of *Language Assessment Quarterly* (2004), also edited by Davies. This increase in interest in this area indicates an increasing awareness of the need to define professional conduct for language testers, and it is also a sign of language testing coming into its own as a profession rather than being a subordinate component of language teaching or general psychometrics.

There is quite clearly a need to discuss ethics in a language testing context because language tests can have a significant impact on test takers' lives: Test scores are used to make decisions about admission to a university or a profession, immigration and citizenship, and employment. There are very real consequences attached to such tests, and test takers and other stakeholders have a strong interest in knowing what guidelines testers follow in their professional conduct. This concerns technical aspects of tests as much as moral behavior, including fairness, equality, and best effort. Ethical questions can be asked with regard to a variety of areas, including test development, test administration, the use of scores, and even the defensibility of the whole testing enterprise (Lynch, 1997).

One approach to dealing with issues of ethics is to codify what ethical behavior means in a code of ethics. Such a codification of acceptable conduct allows an inside view of how researchers deal with issues of ethics and professional conduct.

Codifications of ethical and professional behavior can be published as "codes of ethics," "codes of practice," or, more generally, as "standards." We will consider work on ethics within and outside of language testing, and outline some directions for the future.

Boyd and Davies (2002) defined codes of ethics as "sets of principles that draw on moral philosophy and are intended to guide good professional conduct" (p. 304). In other words, such codes are based on views of what constitutes moral behavior by members of a profession, and they are intended to guide professionals in their decision-making and judgment of their colleagues' behavior. Codes often also serve a self-policing function, and members who violate them are sanctioned. In a sense, such codes are a unilateral promise of good conduct by a profession to its stakeholders: The profession obligates itself to follow certain rules and to punish those members who do not. It might appear strange that the profession takes on a unilateral obligation and gets nothing in return, but, in fact, it does get something in return: a perception of being concerned with the greater good and concomitant greater credibility. It might even avoid outside policing of its professional conduct, but, of course, only a code of ethics that is adopted in good faith really functions as such. If the primary function of the code is to make professionals look more moral and avoid questioning of their decisions by outsiders, such a code is no more than a fig leaf.

Codes of ethics are common in many professions, but the oldest and most well-known ethical self-obligation is the Hippocratic oath, traditionally taken by medical professionals and promising ethical professional conduct, including maintaining confidentiality and not to do intentional harm (for a modern version of the oath see http://www.pbs.org/wgbh/nova/doctors/oath_ modern.html). The promise to adhere to a profession's ethical rules is frequently a part of the initiation into that profession, and a member's promise to follow the rules constitutes the basis for sanctions in cases where members violate that promise. However, the issue of effective sanctions is a tricky one and differs between "weak" and "strong" professions (Boyd & Davies, 2002).

In the strong professions, like medicine, psychology, and law, admittance to the profession and continuing practice are contingent on adherence to an ethical code, and violations of the code can be met with effective sanctions, ranging from reprimands to exclusion from the profession. Such codes of ethics have "teeth" and are enforceable.

In a weak profession, like language testing, no professional association regulates the right to practice: Membership in a professional organization is voluntary, it is not a precondition for practice, and, consequently, there are no serious sanctions against members who violate codes of ethics. The association might exclude them, but they cannot be stopped from continuing to practice, ethically or unethically. Then why would a "weak" profession adopt a code of ethics if it cannot be effectively enforced? There are various good reasons why it might do so, apart from the cynical view that it makes the profession look better in the public eye. One function is that a code of ethics gives members a moral guideline for action and helps them to resolve ethical conflicts. It is also a recourse for members when they are asked by employers or other stakeholders to participate in work that violates ethical or professional standards. Basing their refusal to do such work on a code of ethics gives it a stronger foundation and makes it less likely to be construed as simple disobedience or stubbornness.

Even in cases where a member violates the code but cannot be effectively sanctioned, they can be exposed as acting unethically and might be informally punished through the disapproval of their peers, exclusion from professional networks, and other "human sanctions." Additionally, codes can also raise professional standards: detailed documents like the *Standards for Educational and Psychological Testing* or the quality management checklists developed by the Association of Language Testers in Europe (1994) (see section 5.3.2) require high levels of professional training to work with, and they implicitly define what it means to work in the profession. Such more detailed documents are often called codes of practice (or sometimes "standards") and they tend to be more detailed than ethical codes, which are often aspirational and somewhat vague. Codes of practice state more specifically the minimum requirements of professional practice, but whereas an ethics code might be too vague, a code of practice might be too specific and not cover all relevant situations.

A thorny issue is the universal applicability of ethical principles (Boyd & Davies, 2002; Davies, 1997c). Different cultures clearly have different views of what is moral and acceptable behavior. How can an international organization impose ethical standards on members from different cultural backgrounds? One possibility would be to only have local codes of ethics and practice, which is the case in professions like medicine, law, and psychology. However, in professions like language testing, this is not a very practicable approach, as there might not be a "critical mass" of language testers in many countries, and language testing itself is an example of globalization and often has international consequences: American test companies (like ETS) might conduct language tests (like TOEFL) in third countries (like China), possibly through local partners, with raters dispersed all over the globe. The test results might then be used for university admission in another English-speaking country (like Canada). Thus, if there were only local codes of ethics, which one would apply? Also, if all of them apply, what if they conflict? To avoid this problem, the International Language Testing Organization (ILTA) has developed a code of ethics for language testing, applicable worldwide.

5.3 Codes of Ethics and Practice in Language Testing

Two major internationally used codes exist in language testing: the International Language Testing Association's Code of Ethics (2000)[2] and draft Code of Practice (International Language Testing Association, 2005), as well as the Code of Practice and accompanying quality assurance framework from the Association of Language Testers in Europe (ALTE, 1994). The former applies to individual language testers and testing institutions, whereas the latter is designed for ALTE members, who are exclusively institutional.

5.3.1 *The ILTA Codes of Ethics and Practice*

The Code of Ethics consists of nine general principles that codify aspirational ethical goals and are elaborated and explained through annotations. The Code of Practice consists of seven sections, which describe minimum requirements for test design and use, as well as rights and responsibilities of testers and test takers.

5.3.1.1 *The ILTA Code of Ethics*

A fundamental concern of the Code of Ethics is the protection of test takers, who are necessarily in a less powerful position in the testing process. The Code of Ethics deals with the relationship between tester and test taker in the first three principles. It stipulates that testers must not discriminate against test takers or exploit the power that they hold over them and they must obtain test takers' informed consent for any test-related research, following standard consent procedures. Testers must also preserve the confidentiality of test takers' personal information and only relay it to others who are authorized to access this information and are bound by similar confidentiality rules.

Most of the remaining six principles of the Code discuss language testers' responsibilities in relation to their profession and the societies in which they practice. The Code requires language testers to maintain and update their skills and to educate others (colleagues or students) in the principles of good practice in language testing. Conversely, they must not use their skills to act in ways that are "inimical to their test takers' interests" (Boyd & Davies, 2002, p. 319). At the same time, the Code recognizes that testers' obligations to their society can conflict with their obligations to test takers, and the Code calls for allowing testers the option of individual conscientious objection to testing practices without repercussions. The Code also calls on testers to encourage ethical and professional conduct in their profession, improve the quality of language testing, and make it available as widely as possible.

5.3.1.2 The Code of Practice

At the time of writing, the third draft of the ILTA Code of Practice was available with plans to pass a final version by the middle of 2007. Following the Code of Good Testing Practice developed by the Japan Language Testing Association, the bulk of ILTA's Code is concerned with test design, administration, and score interpretation. For example, the Code requires test makers to state explicitly what construct is being tested, develop detailed item specifications, and ensure equality and fairness in test administration and scoring. In a brief section on the responsibilities of test users, the Code calls for a clear understanding of the strengths and limitations of the test, and under "special considerations," it very briefly outlines specific requirements for norm-referenced, criterion-referenced, and computer-adaptive tests. In its second, shorter part, the Code lists 10 rights of test takers, focusing not only on their right to be informed about the test and its consequences but also their right to be treated fairly and have their grievances heard. The Code also lists 10 responsibilities of test takers, including the responsibility to actively seek information about the test, be cooperative during test administration, and proactively arrange for test accommodations if necessary.

5.3.2 The ALTE Code of Practice and Quality Management Checklists

The second set of standards in language testing is the ALTE Code of Practice. The Code is divided into two parts, delineating the responsibilities of ALTE members and the responsibilities of score users. The responsibilities of ALTE members include the development of tests, the interpretation of test results, striving for fairness, and informing test takers. The responsibilities of score users include the selection of appropriate tests, correct interpretation of scores, fairness, and informing test takers. The ALTE code is very brief, encompassing about two to three printed pages. Although this is clearly insufficient to provide detailed guidance and the whole code has an air of ad hoc production to it, it is part of a larger quality management process, which attempts to master the Herculean task of ensuring comparable test quality for an association of 31 institutions representing 26 European languages (Association of Language Testers in Europe, 2006). The practical self-assessment exercises, contained on four Excel spreadsheets, encourage members to reflect on their assessment work and their adherence to the commonly agreed standards. An in-depth discussion of the issues involved in international harmonization of testing practices and standards exceeds the scope of this chapter, but such a discussion is provided by van Avermaet, Kujper, and Saville (2004).

5.4 Codes of Ethics in Related Areas

The most directly relevant code or set of standards outside of language testing are the *Standards for Educational and Psychological Tests*, published by the American Educational Research Association (1999) and produced jointly with the American Psychological Association and the National Council on Measurement in Education. Unlike the ILTA codes and the ALTE code, which are only a few pages long, the Standards are a book-length publication of almost 200 pages. Following an introduction and preceding a glossary of testing terms, the Standards are divided into three parts of roughly equal length, each containing four to six sections: a part on test construction and documentation, a part on fairness in testing, and a final part on testing applications, discussing specific areas of research and practice where educational and psychological tests might be used. Each section begins with summary of the "state of the art" and then contains between 11 and 27 standards, the vast majority followed by a comment of one to two paragraphs describing the intended meaning and operation of the standard and often giving examples. The entire book contains 264 standards, with the part on fairness the shortest (48 standards), followed by the part on testing applications (93 standards), and the part on test construction the largest (123 standards). The introduction states that all standards are of equal weight and are equally binding, but some standards are clearly limited to specific situations, and in most cases, only one or two sections of the part on testing applications apply to any given test maker.

The goal of the Standards is to help users evaluate tests by providing discussion of relevant issues, which also aids test developers in critically reviewing their instruments. Although the Standards provide a comprehensive framework to inform judgments of test quality, they are not a "recipe book" for test design, and they fundamentally rely on professional knowledge in their implementation. It is also important to note that the Standards are not devised as an ethical code: They are a code of practice, outlining minimum requirements for assessment.

The first part, on test construction, discusses and imposes standards for such fundamental psychometric concepts as validity and reliability, as well as for procedures such as scaling, equating, and norming, test development, and test administration. A whole section is devoted to documentation requirements. The fact that the section on test development has the most standards in the entire volume (27 standards) is testament to the technical slant of the Standards, whose creators seem to make the (arguably correct) assumption that good test construction is a necessary condition for a good test.

The second part, on fairness, encompasses standard fairness and antibias procedures like investigation of DIF, a section on rights and responsibilities of test takers, and sections on testing test takers with disabilities and from diverse linguistic backgrounds.

The final section, on testing applications, outlines responsibilities of test users and then covers in more detail such areas as psychological testing, educational testing, employment testing, and testing in program evaluation contexts.

Although the Standards are more of a code of practice than an ethical code, the Joint Committee on Testing Practices[3] has published a document that is a mix of an ethics code and a code of practice (or an ethical code with annotations): the Code of Fair Testing Practices in Education (Joint Committee on Fair Testing Practices, 2004). According to the Code's Web site (http://www.apa.org/science/fairtestcode.html), the Code is a condensation from the Standards, is aspirational in nature, and is intended to guide test developers and score users in employing tests. It consists of four sections, covering test development, test administration and scoring, score reporting and interpretation, and informing test takers. The first three sections cover the responsibilities of test developers and test users separately, whereas the final section combines them. All sections begin with a general statement, which is then elaborated through seven to nine annotations. As it states explicitly at the outset, the Code follows the Standards in content, and it is also quite similar to the ALTE Code of Practice, which was based on the 1988 version of the Code of Fair Testing Practices (van Avermaet et al., 2004).

In addition to the Standards discussed above, the American Psychological Association has published codes of ethics and practice, focusing on the more clinical aspects of psychologists' work (American Psychological Association, 2002). The document distinguishes between general principles of ethical conduct, which are aspirational in nature, and ethical standards, whose violation leads to sanctions. The general principles briefly describe "the very highest ethical ideals of the profession" (American Psychological Association, 2002, p. 3) in general terms and in one paragraph each: beneficence, responsibility, integrity, justice and fairness, and respect for people's dignity. The ethical standards are much more detailed, and describe the responsibilities and professional obligations of psychologists. They consist of 10 sections, dealing with the resolution of ethical issues, practitioners' competence, harassment and inappropriate relationships, privacy and confidentiality, advertising, record keeping and fees, education and teaching, research and publications, assessment, and therapy.

5.5 Future Directions

The passage of the ILTA Code of Ethics and the draft Code of Practice are important steps in ensuring the quality of language testing and ethical conduct among testers at a time when language tests are becoming ever more influential and increasingly affect test takers' lives. The ALTE Code of Practice and quality assurance program address the need for comparable standards for their membership of testing institutions.

From the point of view of professionalization, it is uncontroversial that language testers, like other professionals, need an awareness of the ethical dimension of their behavior, and codes of ethics are one component for raising ethical awareness. Ethical awareness also feeds into thinking about construct validation, as it focuses testers' attention on consequences, impact, and underlying values. Such codes can also help testers deal with outside pressures and provide a solid ground for rejecting political demands by stakeholders that would compromise fairness.

At the same time, codes of ethics and practice are no substitute for high-quality professional training. A bad test leads to bad decisions, is a waste of money for all stakeholders, and is, therefore, inherently unethical. To ensure that tests are useful to all stakeholders and used ethically, testers must be well trained in psychometrics and L2 acquisition and be aware of the larger sociopolitical context in which their test is going to be used. It does not help that codes of practice in language testing are brief and vague and that none even remotely approach the specificity of the American Educational Research Association's (1999) *Standards for Educational and Psychological Testing*. It is unclear why language testers do not simply adopt the Standards or at least its relevant portions. Why reinvent the wheel, particularly if there is an excellent wheel already?

Codes of ethics in language testing will also never have the same status as in psychology, medicine, or law. There simply is no way to give them the same "bite" that codes in "strong professions" have, and they will always fundamentally rely on members' conscience, which is influenced by their moral and ethical convictions, but also by the standards to which they hold themselves. The latter are fundamentally affected by training because only well-trained test developers and users can critically examine theirs and others' work.

Despite their weaknesses and shortcomings, codes of ethics and practice are important steps in strengthening the identity of language testing as a profession.

5.6 Summary

Both fairness review and codes of ethics highlight that tests exist in a social context and that there are diverse pressures on testing organizations and individual testers to serve the interests of a range of stakeholders. Fairness review constitutes a systematic process of identifying possibly biased items or items that might be so controversial that a test's acceptance might suffer. The implementation of fairness review processes is an acknowledgment of the political side of the test design process and a step away from purely psychometric procedures, which make an important contribution to test quality but are the least obviously socially oriented procedures.

Codes of ethics and practice go beyond individual test makers and provide guidelines for the entire language testing profession. They increase transparency of language testers' work, reassuring stakeholders of the ethical conduct of testers, and provide a moral framework for testers' work, although this framework is often vague and has no built-in mechanisms to deal with violations.

In chapter 6 we will shift our perspective to a broader consideration of the effects of language tests on individuals and societies. One important general way in which this occurs is their capacity to act as instruments for establishing, noticing, and even constructing social identities.

Notes

[1]For a detailed description, see Saville (2003, 2005).
[2]The Code of Ethics for ILTA was passed at the Language Testing Research Colloquium meeting in Vancouver in 2000.
[3]The Joint Committee on Testing Practices consists of the publishers of the Standards (AERA, NCME, and APA) together with the American Counseling Organization, the American Speech-Language-Hearing Association, the National Association of School Psychologists, and the National Association of Test Directors.

CHAPTER SIX

Language Tests and Social Identity

In earlier chapters we have examined to what extent and in what ways the social dimension of language testing has been understood in discussions of the validity of language tests, and we have considered procedures within the psychometric tradition intended to improve the relative fairness of tests. We have argued that the procedures for validation of test score inferences and for checking on bias can be seen as involving responsibility toward both candidates and test score users. We have also argued, however, that the discourse of psychometrics limits what can be said about the social dimension of language tests, as it lacks a theory of the social context in which tests have their function. More is needed. In this and the following chapter we will try to demonstrate some of what this "more" might be by studying test use. In this chapter we will consider the use of language tests to establish social identity, particularly within settings of competition and conflict among social groups. In the following chapter we will revisit a theme that has been the subject of discussion for over 2 centuries: the use of language tests to manage educational systems and to control the work of teachers and learners.

The language tests that we will discuss in this chapter are distinguished by the fact that their constructs are sociolinguistic in character, where test performance is significant primarily as an indicator of group membership. This is in contrast to the discussion of language test constructs in most treatments of validity theory, where the discussion generally centers around psycholinguistic constructs (i.e., constructs such as language proficiency [or various aspects of it] that are cognitive traits, possessed by individuals in measurable degrees). The lack of realization that language tests can act as tests of identity is, once you think about it, somewhat surprising given the way in which language offers cues to social category allocation in daily life: We routinely interpret obvious sociolinguistic cues to class, regional, ethnic, and national categorization in initial face-to-face encounters with strangers. Language acts socially as a marker of identity, and as linguistic identity is shared among members of a speech community, language tests can be used as a procedure for identification and classification of individuals in terms of relevant social categories. This function is particularly significant and useful in times of overt intergroup violence, where successful identification of the enemy (for attack or defense) is important, but it is also useful in any case where social identity of any kind (e.g., national, racial, or ethnic identity) is the basis for rights or claims to the protection of the law. This function of language tests is less salient in the literature on language testing on account, then, of its prevailing cognitive and individualist orientation.

6.1 Shibboleth Tests

In this first section we will consider what at first sight might appear to be an extreme example of the use of language tests: their function as tests of identification in contexts of violence. Examining such a consequential use of language tests has two advantages: It focuses us unambiguously on test use and it allows us to evaluate the relevance of psychometric considerations of validity in such circumstances.

The use of language tests within violent intergroup contact has been recorded since ancient times. The emblematic instance, the shibboleth test (Davies, 1997a; Lado, 1949; McNamara, 2005; Spolsky, 1995), is recorded in the Book of Judges in the Bible (Judges, 12, 4–6). This test was used to prevent defeated enemy soldiers from "passing." The neighboring groups at war had a minor but easily detectable difference in the way they pronounced words containing a particular consonant sound: One group pronounced such words with the palato-alveolar fricative /ʃ/, whereas others pronounced it with the sibilant /s/, so the test involved asking a person whose identity was in question to say the word *shibboleth*,[1] and depending on whether they said *shibboleth* or *sibboleth*, their identity would be revealed, and if they were found to be an enemy, they were killed. This linguistic test of identity involved the person's right to life.

The use of a shibboleth test in the context of violence occurs in many times and many cultures. For example, in response to the English peasants' rebellion led by Wat Tyler in 1381, Flemings living in London were used as scapegoats (in place of the more usual Jews, who had already been expelled from England by this time):

> The Flemmings or Dutch strangers, who since the Jews were banished [from London], suffer their part in every sedition, are fought for all the streets through, all of them massacred, no sanctuary could save them, thirteen Flemmings were drawn out of the Church of the Friers Hermits of Saint Augustine, and beheaded in the streets, and seventeen others pulled out of another parochial Church died in the same manner. They had a Shibboleth to discover them, he who pronounced Brot and Cawse, for Bread and Cheese had his lead lopt off. (Cleveland, 1658, p. 36)

A shibboleth is reported in medieval Yemen: in 1060, soldiers of King Al-Muharram Ahmed, in a vengeful slaughter in the city of Tihamah, used a shibboleth to distinguish their fellow Arabs of African descent from non-Arab African (Abyssinian) slaves, from whose hands the king had liberated his kidnapped mother:

> Al-Muharram's heralds now proclaimed his orders to unsheathe the sword against the people of the captured city. But he warned the army that the Arabs of Tihamah beget children by black concubines, and that a black skin was common to both slave and free. "But if you hear a person pronounce the word *aẓm*, *azm* (as if it were written with the letter z), know that he is an Abyssinian and slay him. If he pronounces it *aẓm* (with the letter ẓ), he is an Arab, and ye shall spare him." (Kay, 1892, p. 36)[2]

More than two centuries later, during the period of the early Mamluk sultans in Egypt, a shibboleth was again used, but this time against Arabs. The Mamluks (literally, "white slaves") were Caucasian and Turkish (i.e., non-Arab) slaves, used by Arab rulers to form loyal armies. As neutral outsiders to the intertribal rivalries of the Arab world, they were entrusted with more and more power; eventually, by the 13th century, they had actually taken control of the government of Egypt and its empire, creating Cairo as the cultural and economic capital. In 1302, the (Arab) Bedawi tribes in Upper Egypt rebelled against the authority of the Mamluk sultan. The revolt was put down very violently:

> The inhabitants were put to the sword, to the number of about 16,000 men, whose wives and children and property were seized. If a man claimed to be no Bedawi but a townsman [i.e. not an Arab], they bade him pronounce the word *dakīk* (which no Egyptian can say), and as soon as they heard the true Arab guttural, they cut off his head. The shibboleth disposed of a multitude of evaders. (Lane-Poole, 1901, p. 300)

In Japan, in the immediate aftermath of the Great Kanto earthquake of 1923, in which well over 100,000 people lost their lives, a shibboleth was also used (Gendaishi no kai, 1996; Yamagishi, 2002). Among those who were killed were around 6,000 Koreans living in Tokyo, including survivors of the earthquake who were accused of poisoning the water supply, looting, and other crimes. In order to escape detection, many tried to "pass" as Japanese; they were "outed" by the use of a shibboleth test: the phrase *jyugoen gojyussen* ("15 yen 50 sen," an amount of money), which Koreans would typically pronounce "chugo en kochussen." Hundreds, possibly thousands, were subsequently murdered.[3]

A shibboleth test was also used in violence against French and Kreyol-speaking Haitians in the Spanish-speaking Dominican Republic in October 1937, when between 15,000 and 35,000 Haitians were massacred by order of the Dominican dictator Rafael Trujillo:[4]

The soldiers applied a simple test. They would accost any person with dark skin. Holding up sprigs of parsley, Trujillo's men would query their prospective victims: "¿ Cómo se llama ésto?" What is this thing called? The terrified victim's fate lay in the pronunciation of the answer. For Haitians, whose Kreyol uses a wide, flat *r*, it is difficult to pronounce the trilled *r* in the Spanish word for parsley, *perejil*. If the word came out as the Haitian *pe'sil*, or a bastardized Spanish *pewehi*, the victim was condemned to die. (Wucker, 1999, p. 49)

Such terribly consequential shibboleth tests remain a feature of contemporary situations of violence, too; instances have been reported from Sri Lanka in 1983, between Tamils and Singhalese, involving the Sinhala word for "bucket," and in Lebanon during the war between Lebanese Christians and Palestinians, involving the word for "tomato"[5] (for details, see McNamara, 2005; see also Suleiman, 2004).

However, is right always on the side of the targets of shibboleth tests? Shibboleths have frequently been found in the context of violent, often extremely bloody, resistance to occupation or oppression. Apart from some legendary examples, such as the exploitation by the Saxons of the Danish pronunciation of the phrase "Chichester Church" with the sound /k/ (the Saxons had a softer palatal sound) during the St Brice's Day massacre of the invading Danes on November 13, 1002, there are many well-attested instances of this use of the shibboleth test historically. In Sicily, during the Sicilian Vespers, a 6-week-long uprising against the Norman rulers that began at an evening church service (Vespers) on Easter Monday, March 30, 1282, the word *ciciri* ("chickpeas"), which the Sicilians pronounced with a palato-alveolar affricate at the beginning, was used as a shibboleth to identify French speakers (who pronounced it /ʃiʃiri/) trying to "pass" (Calvet, 1987/1998; Crawford, 1900; Runciman, 1958), with the inevitable violent consequence:

The rioters broke into the Dominican and Franciscan convents; and all the foreign friars were dragged out and told to pronounce the word "ciciri," whose sound the French tongue could never accurately reproduce. Anyone who failed in the test was slain. (Runciman, 1958, p. 215[6])

Another example is from Friesland in what is today the Netherlands. In the period 1515–1517, the Frisian hero Grutte Pier assembled a guerrilla fleet that sailed the Southern Sea (what is now the Ijselmeer) where Dutch and Saxon ships were sailing toward Friesland with the intention of asserting their control over the territory. When Grutte Pier's ships encountered a suspicious vessel, in order to confirm that people aboard were in fact not Frisian, they were asked to repeat a shibboleth-like tongue-twister in Frisian: *"bûter, brea, en griene tsiis, wa't dat net sizze kin is gjin oprjochte Fries,"* which translates as "Butter, bread and green cheese—whoever cannot say this is no upright (true) Frisian." If they failed the test (being unable to repeat the phrase with a passable accent), their ship was plundered and the people aboard were drowned by keelhauling[7] (Rineke Brouwer, personal communication, October 6, 2005).

What these examples might obscure by their violence is that it is the context of use of shibboleth tests, rather than somehow the very practice of shibboleth testing itself, which appalls. This becomes clear with cases in which one might more readily endorse the use of such a test (e.g., in cases of legitimate self-defense). On the day that Nazi forces invaded the Netherlands in 1940, the password used in the Dutch navy was *schavuit* ("rascal"), one that potential German infiltrators would find difficult to pronounce. Czech resistance groups are said to have used the Czech word *řeřicha* ("watercress") as a shibboleth during the Nazi occupation. A further possible example are the anecdotal reports of the use of some variant of the word "lollapalooza" (= "a remarkable or wonderful person or thing") by American military intelligence in the Pacific theater of war during World War II to detect Japanese who posed as Chinese: Japanese hearing the "l" sound as "r," whereas Chinese realize "r" sounds as "l" (Jones, 2002). What these examples show is that it is not the test as such that is the issue, but our evaluation of the politics of its use. We will return to this point later in the chapter when considering discussions of the controversies over the use of language tests as part of immigration and citizenship procedures.

In summary, then, these examples illustrate the complex ethical issues involved when language tests determine the use of violence. Is the violence for offence or defense? In whose interests is it used? Do you support those interests? Is the violence excessive? Your own political stance and personal values (including your attitudes toward the use of violence in political contexts, in general, and in particular contexts) will determine your attitude toward the function of the test.

Obviously, such one-word tests are not psychometrically sound, but if they were, would this make their use more or less acceptable? Considerations of test quality, of the sort familiar from validity theory, might be relevant even in the case of classic shibboleth tests such as these. Consider the next example, from Botswana in southern Africa.[8] The principal language of Botswana is Setswana; there are several minority languages, including Kalanga, which is spoken by members of a speech community that straddles both sides of the border with Zimbabwe. Botswana is a prosperous country because of its great mineral wealth, especially from diamonds; Zimbabwe, in contrast, has experienced harsh economic circumstances, with a resulting pressure for Zimbabweans to seek to work illegally in Botswana. The Botswana authorities, when they encounter suspected illegal workers, informally use a shibboleth—a word such as *Makgekgenene* (a man's name), in which Kalanga speakers would tend to replace the difficult consonant cluster /kg/ with /kh/—to confirm whether the worker is a Setswana speaker and thus a Motswana or citizen of Botswana. (This practice has parallels in the attempt to detect illegal immigrant workers in the Netherlands: see McNamara, 2005.) However, the use of the test in this context is problematic because although the test might be successful in distinguishing Setswana from Kalanga speakers, it is not useful in distinguishing those Kalanga speakers who come from

Botswana (who, as Botswana citizens, enjoy full rights) from Kalanga speakers from Zimbabwe (who, as illegal immigrants, enjoy none), with the result that significant numbers of Botswana Kalanga speakers are rounded up and held in detention on the basis of this test. This confusion can, in turn, be exploited from the other side, so that Zimbabwean Kalanga speakers try to pass as Botswana Kalanga speakers simply by claiming that they are from Botswana. The adequacy of the sociolinguistic construct underlying this test is the source of the problem. In other words, we could argue, issues of validity are still relevant in considering issues of test use; this is the point of Kane's chain of inferences—the final inference step, involving test use, requires each of the other inference steps to be intact.[9] On the other hand, while improving the test quality reduces what we might call collateral unfairness, it leaves untouched the question of the use of the test in the first place.

One could proliferate examples of shibboleths in other times and places,[10] and the frequently dramatic circumstances of their use give them a compelling quality. What is most important about them from the point of view of the current discussion is the way they focus our attention on test use and the social contexts that generate it. Moreover, the enormity of the stakes involved in these examples of test use put the usual technical considerations into perspective.

Shibboleth-like language tests can be operationalized not only by a single word chosen in advance, as it were, but by any use at all of language associated with the social category that is the potential target of violence. We have such an instance in a shibboleth used in the immediate aftermath of the Battle of Worcester in 1651, the final and decisive battle of the English Civil War. Charles II, whose father had been executed by the Parliamentary forces led by Cromwell, had had himself crowned king in a ceremony in Scotland and subsequently led a Royalist army of 12,000 into England, the majority of the soldiers being Scots, mainly Highlanders, who at that time were Gaelic speakers. Charles's forces were defeated at Worcester by Cromwell. In the aftermath of the battle, according to a subsequent (indignant) Royalist account,

> The slaughter in the City was not less barbarous, the Citizens and Soldiers being promiscuously slain, all being filled with Rapine and Murther. There fell as well without, as within the Walls, where the Slaughter was greater, Three Thousand Five Hundred, and the Prisoners were above Six Thousand, most of the English escaping by the Benefit of their Tongue. (Manley, 1691, p. 247)

Here, no single word or phrase acted as the shibboleth; it seems that the simple fact that the Royalist English soldiers spoke English, not Gaelic, meant that they could pass as Republicans and hence escape, while the Gaelic speakers were identified and put to death.[11]

Nor need the use of the shibboleth test be restricted to a single event or occasion of violence such as this. The more general phenomenon of the use of language knowledge as a means of social identification can assume a particular significance in contexts of violence. A particularly acute and sustained example of this situation involves M, the mother of a Jewish friend. M, who was the sole survivor of her family during the Holocaust, was 14 and living in Lodz, Poland, when German forces occupied the country in 1939. The teenage M was fluent in both Yiddish and Polish and survived the war by passing as a non-Jewish Pole; while still in Poland, searching for food outside the Lodz ghetto, she had to disguise any trace of a Yiddish accent in her Polish, as Polish anti-Semitism threatened her discovery. She was eventually arrested by the Germans and sent as a presumed Polish non-Jew to work as a laborer on a farm in Germany where, because of her knowledge of Yiddish, a language that is related to German, she initially had to conceal her degree of comprehension of spoken German and the fact that she could understand much of what was contained in German newspapers or in newsreels shown at the local cinema, which included footage and reports of her family's fate in the Lodz ghetto. One false move would have led to discovery and its terrible consequences.

We might speak then of a regime of shibboleth conscious-ness: First, no single word or its pronunciation is involved, but speech in general; second, the relevance of the shibboleth is not limited to a particular moment, but is a sustained feature of so-cial relations; third, the threat of violence is pervasive, so that conformity with the regime must be sustained at all times, or the social and political consequences felt.

It is for this reason that consideration of tests used in con-texts of overt violence can help us understand what is involved in more familiar and apparently less contentious uses of tests. Even when the stakes are not so overt, or so painful, the pervasive phe-nomenon of monitoring the social significance of accent represents a form of what Jacoby calls *indigenous assessment* (Jacoby, 1998; Jacoby & McNamara, 1999), those naturally occurring moments in everyday interaction when we make assessments of individ-uals and their behavior. In other words, the notion of life being conducted in conformity with a pervasive regime of surveillance through language, where the details of language behavior offer opportunities for assessment and interpretation, extends beyond settings of intergroup violence to social relations in general. This idea is central to the work of Foucault, who in his book *Discipline and Punish* (Foucault, 1975/1977) saw modernity as involving regimes of truth accomplished through techniques of surveillance, primary among which was the examination.

We can thus understand formal language tests in intergroup settings as the crystallization of the regime of consciousness into a concrete, deliberate, "scientific" form. An example is the use of language tests designed to exclude homosexual recruits from the Royal Canadian Mounted Police in the 1950s (Kinsman, 2004). Recruits were given a battery of psychological tests, supported by electrophysiological measuring equipment that was designed to detect physiological responses to emotional stimuli, as in lie detection procedures. One set of stimuli consisted of an appar-ently innocuous vocabulary list, which included familiar words with a secondary meaning in homosexual slang: words such as *fruit* (= "homosexual"), *trade* (= "casual sexual partners"), *cruise*

(= "seek out casual sexual partners"), and so on—secondary meanings that at that time were presumed to be quite unfamiliar to the general population. Recognition of a series of words with secondary meanings in the list would alert the homosexual would-be recruit to the fact that an attempt was being made to screen for sexual orientation, which was known to be grounds for refusal and exposure to the harsh psychological, social, and even criminal sanctions of the era. The physiological response to the anxiety thereby provoked would be detected electrophysiologically. Recruits could attempt to "pass" by controlling their emotional responses, but this would obviously be difficult. The procedure came to be known as the "fruit machine," although it was never used, partly because of the difficulty of finding volunteers to test it![12]

The "fruit machine" is only one of many language tests that are deliberately targeted at the exclusion of unwanted outsiders. In many cases, the use of such tests will offend most ethical standards, and this will be unaffected by the psychometric qualities of the test. In other cases, the ethics of their use will be more complex; and psychometric considerations of quality and fairness of procedure will be relevant. Wherever such test use arises, its character and justification are deserving of the attention of researchers. For this purpose, conceptual tools beyond those normally available from the psychometric tradition might be needed.

6.2 Language Tests, Identity, and the Denial of Rights

Thus far, we have examined mainly how informal language assessments, either pervasive ones or those involving the deliberate choice of a word or phrase, are a means of establishing identity in settings of violent intergroup conflict. In this section we will extend the discussion to consider the ways in which linguistic tests of identity might be used to determine rights in settings of nonviolent intergroup conflict and competition. We will find that these instances frequently involve the use of formal language tests.

Language tests of identity may be used to determine the right of entry to a country. A particularly notorious example of the use of language tests in such contexts is the Dictation Test, used by the Australian Government in the early years of the 20th century (Davies, 1997a; Dutton, 1998; Jones, 1998; McNamara, 2005). The test was used for the exclusion from Australia of arrivals from Asia (for example) as part of an explicitly racist immigration policy known unashamedly as the White Australia Policy. The mechanism chosen to implement the policy of exclusion involved a language test (originally known as the Education Test and then as the Dictation Test) in which an undesirable applicant for residency on arrival in Australia could be administered a 50-word dictation in any European language or Japanese. Care was taken to ascertain which languages the person in question did know, and then a test was given in a language that the person did *not* know; the person would fail the test and then be excluded on that basis. Although the policy survived until the 1960s, the Dictation Test fell out of use after the 1930s, but in the period in which it was used, approximately 2,000 people were excluded from entry to Australia on their arrival at an Australian port. The test was also used to exclude others on political grounds. In the most famous case of this kind, a Czech Jewish communist, Egon Kisch, was subject to the Dictation Test; the authorities were perplexed because he knew many of the European languages in which they had dictation materials prepared. After being given and failing a test in Scots Gaelic, the reasonableness of which was successfully challenged in the High Court, he was finally refused entry on other grounds. Another undesirable visiting communist, an Irish New Zealander called Gerald Griffin, was deported after failing the Dictation Test in Dutch.

What is distinctive about this test is that it was used not to establish the identity of the individual concerned; the order was reversed—the individual's (problematic) identity was known in advance and was the basis for administering the test, which was then used as the grounds for exclusion. The test was not itself a test of identity, but a ritual of exclusion for individuals whose identity was already known and deemed to be unacceptable on a priori grounds. The test was also unusual in that this public ritual function prevailed over any real function of camouflaging the policy intent: It is significant that after a certain period of initial confusion, no one succeeded in passing the test. (In the first few years following its introduction, those administering the test treated it as a test that people might pass and sometimes offered dictation passages in languages that the applicants actually spoke; as a result, a few passed). Had there been a chance of passing the test, even if it was an extremely difficult one, its intent would have been made less clear; here, no need for any disguise of the political intent of the test can have been felt, as there was very little opposition to the policy that formed the basis for its use in Australia at the time. More usually, the political intent of language tests is often deliberately masked by using what appears to be an objective mechanism (a test). In fact, the authority of psychometrics acts as a kind of legitimation for the practice and makes its political character so much harder to identify and to challenge. This point will be considered further later.

The purely formal and ritualistic character of the Dictation Test is highlighted when it is compared with literacy tests for immigrants used in the United States at around the same time. In a climate of heightened xenophobia and racism at the turn of the 20th century, political pressure was strong for the compulsory literacy testing of the increasing numbers of immigrants entering the country (Wiley, 2005). After Congress passed a series of immigrant literacy test bills (in 1896, 1904, and 1916), each of which was vetoed by the president, a bill finally survived the veto and became law in 1917. Unlike the Australian Dictation Test, it required immigrants over the age of 16 to read a short passage from the Bible *in their own language*; that is, it was designed to be passable by those who met the (obviously restrictive) literacy criterion. At other periods and in other contexts, literacy tests have been used in the United States for purposes of disenfranchising voters: English-speaking Irish immigrants in the mid-19th-century, and African Americans in Southern states in the period following emancipation (Leibowitz, 1969). Wiley comments:

> There was considerable irony in the use of literacy require-
> ments against African Americans, because prior to the
> Civil War "compulsory ignorance laws" made it a crime
> for blacks to receive literacy instruction in most southern
> states (Weinberg, 1995). (Wiley, 2005, pp. 64–65)

This perverse situation whereby the likelihood of failure on the tests is raised by other linguistic and educational policies is paralleled in other contexts, three of which we will consider now. The first example comes from Germany, which in the period following the collapse of the Soviet Union was faced with applications for residency in Germany from ethnic Germans residing in the former Soviet republics, including Russia, Kazakhstan, Kyrgyzstan, Uzbekistan, and Ukraine. The absorption of these *Spätaussiedler*, as they are known, caused some political difficulty in Germany. The German government in 1996 sought a partial solution to the problem by introducing a language test. Applicants were required to prove their German ethnicity by demonstrating proficiency in the relevant regional form of German, with traditional pronunciation and lexical features (i.e., not the modern German that could be learned by language study). This requirement was difficult for many applicants, as in the postwar period the Soviet Union, following its bitter experience at the hands of the German armies during the Second World War, had encouraged the linguistic assimilation of German ethnic minorities in its territory. Whereas the test was intended to eliminate applicants making false claims to German ethnicity, it also ironically capitalized on this policy of assimilation. The introduction of the test led to a reduction by half in the number of successful applicants (McNamara, 2005). The (sociolinguistic) construct in this test, an obsolete form of German that many true ethnic Germans no longer knew, was clearly motivated by political considerations to reduce the number of successful applicants for residence in Germany.

A parallel example is found in Finland. It concerns the Ingrian Finns (*inkerinsuomalaiset*; Kolga, Tõnurist, Vaba, & Viikberg, 2002), the descendants of people who were encouraged from the 17th century by the mini-superpower Sweden (of which Finland was part) to move to an area near St. Petersburg to consolidate the Swedish possessions there. The Ingrian Finns suffered massive disruption and relocation during the political upheavals of the first half of the 20th century, particularly in the 1930s and 1940s, and in the postwar period. Russification efforts led to considerable language loss: By 1979, only 52% spoke Finnish, and this had fallen to 35% by 1989 (Kolga et al., 2002), with the result that the younger generation are less likely to know Finnish (Jasinskaja-Lahti & Liebkind, 1998). From the early 1990s, the Ingrian Finns were encouraged by the Finnish government to resettle in Finland. However, these "return-immigrants," as they are known, had difficulty in getting jobs and the younger people were accused of engaging in organized crime. As a response, since 2003 all intending return-immigrants have been required to take a test of Finnish. According to Sauli Takala (personal communication, January 11, 2005), the test is professionally developed[13] and administered,[14] with test specifications, professional test development teams, and interviewer and rater training. The test format includes a 30-min face-to-face test of speaking, and a 30-min test of the other three skills: some brief true/false item listening and reading tasks, and two short pragmatic writing tasks. The speaking test is conducted by an interviewer and independent rater, each of whom gives a rating, with the possibility of a third rating from tape when there is lack of agreement between the first two raters. A pass is required in the speaking test and in at least one of the other skills. The standard required is Level A2 on the Council of Europe Framework (Council of Europe, 2001) (the Framework and its levels are discussed later). The pass rate is about 65% and favors older people who are more likely to know and to have used the language.

In this example, we again see how language testing ironically capitalizes on a policy of linguistic assimilation to solve a complex social problem, and the instrument used to implement the policy is a language test. In terms of the test construct, although in a sense the construct of the test is psycholinguistic (it is a conventional test of proficiency in Finnish, unlike the test for the *Spätaussiedler*, in which knowledge of a dialect form was an important aspect of the test), it functions to determine identity and relies on sociolinguistic definitions of belonging that suited the political circumstances of the time.

A third example of language tests relying on earlier policies of linguistic assimilation in order to exclude people from exercising their rights comes from Australia. In the first two centuries of the colonization of Australia following the arrival of the British in 1788, a legal fiction that the land that was being colonized was empty of people (the doctrine of *terra nullius*) meant that no account was taken of the rights to the land of its indigenous occupants, who were systematically dispossessed without compensation. This doctrine was reversed in a famous decision of the High Court of Australia in the Mabo case of 1992, which recognized what was called native title or traditional ownership rights for indigenous groups who could establish that they had maintained their identity and customs in relation to a particular stretch of land, coast, or coastal waters. Evidence of such continuity, and hence the establishment of a legitimate claim, is heard at native title tribunals.

Linguistic tests of identity have sometimes featured in hearings on native title claims. In the hearing of the claim to the use of the sea around Croker Island,[15] linguistic evidence of the identity of the claimants was sought by those opposing the claim ("the respondents"):

> At various points in the claim the respondents produced posters showing a range of fish species and witnesses were asked to name them in detail. This procedure appeared to have two purposes. The first was to indicate only a limited number of fish species were recognized and taken (in fact it turned out that almost all were recognized and named by most witnesses, in a variety of languages). The second

purpose appears to have been to discredit the "traditional credentials" of witnesses who were younger or of mixed descent by showing, if possible, their ignorance of the language names of common fish. To this extent the fish posters functioned as a sort of informal vocabulary test designed to put the witnesses' fluency in traditional languages in the area to the test. (Evans, 2002, p. 57, n. 7)

In this case, as in the Finnish and German examples, a language test is used to determine access to rights, exploiting the results of a policy of linguistic assimilation working in favor of those opposing the granting of such rights. These three examples differ in the degree of psychometric sophistication involved. In the case of the German and Finnish tests, they are professionally developed and administered, but this sophistication only sharpens the instrument of a policy clearly intended to exclude. The kind of validation efforts discussed in chapter 2, which were presented there as guaranteeing fairness, do not touch the impact of the tests, except to make them more efficient. The following use of language tests, however, provides a clear counterexample.

6.3 Language Tests and the Claims of Asylum Seekers

A recent example of language tests used to determine rights on the basis of the linguistic verification of social identity involves the determination of the claims of asylum seekers. As earlier, sociolinguistic constructs are involved, and the politics and ethics of the use of these tests are complex. The procedures involved are widely used in Europe, Australia, and elsewhere in the processing of the claims of undocumented asylum seekers (Eades, 2005; Reath, 2004). In this case, however, the lack of validity considerations in their implementation leads to serious injustice, a situation that would be remedied in large part by attention to the quality of the testing procedure.

Under international refugee conventions, states are obliged to offer asylum to those who can establish grounds of a reasonable fear of persecution in their country of citizenship. Like all administrative procedures, this is open to abuse by individuals falsely claiming to be citizens of a country in which persecution is going on, particularly when they share ethnic group membership, but not nationality, with the group experiencing persecution, but are not subject to persecution themselves. The establishment of nationality is central to determining the rights of applicants in such cases, as refugee law involves agreements between nation-states, and the location of the persecution in terms of national boundaries and the identity of the claimant as a citizen or noncitizen of the country involved are central to such a determination. An individual's nationality is, of course, routinely established through documentation such as passports or other travel documents; but refugees and asylum seekers typically lack such documentation because of the circumstances that have led them to flee their countries in the first place.

As language and accent are associated in a certain sense with locality—for example, it is possible to tell which English-speaking country or even which part of the British Isles or the United States an English-speaking person might be from—governments have sought to use a form of language test as part of the procedure for investigating the validity of claims to refugee status of asylum seekers without formal documentation. In a procedure originally developed within the Swedish Ministry of Immigration and since adopted by a number of governments internationally, the asylum seeker is interviewed by an immigration officer either through an interpreter in their first language or sometimes in a second language such as English, where that language is used as a lingua franca. A tape recording is made of the interview, which is then sent off for language analysis to determine whether the features of the applicant's speech are consonant with their claims as to their region of residence and nationality. The report of the analysis is then used as part of the determination of the plausibility of the applicant's claims; although it can sometimes be crucial, it is not the only evidence used; for example, the applicant is also judged on knowledge of local foods, customs, festivals, and geographical features that are assumed to be within the general knowledge of anyone from the region concerned, and on the general coherence and consistency of the story of the journey to the point at which the applicant has claimed asylum.

The following example, which was reported in the Australian press in 2003,[16] illustrates several of the issues involved:

BURMESE SEX SLAVE GRANTED REFUGEE STATUS

A Burmese woman trafficked to Australia as a sex slave has finally been granted refugee status, despite Immigration Department claims that she was really a Thai national [...] although there was overwhelming evidence proving that she was from Burma's Shan state [...]

The Refugee Review Tribunal believed her story that she was raped and assaulted by the Burmese military as a child, a common scenario. The tribunal accepted she was trafficked to Thailand and forced into prostitution before being trafficked to Australia.

When the case was referred to the Immigration Department's Onshore Protection section, which makes the final decision on refugees, she was rejected on [a] language test, using the controversial voice testing method.

But tribunal member Paul White decided the language analysis was unreliable. In a decision published last week, he said the linguist who conducted the test had only used a few words of Burmese and had never been to Shan state [etc].[17]

The woman's application for refugee status in this case has many typical features.[18]

1. **Refugee status depends on nationality:** The question of her nationality is crucial, because Australia, as a signatory to the United Nations refugee convention, has an obligation to accept the woman if it can be shown that she is from Burma, where abuse of human rights under the current military regime is well attested (particularly

of minority populations such as those living in the Shan state in eastern Burma, which borders northern Thailand),[19] whereas no such obligation exists if she is from Thailand, where systematic abuse of this kind does not occur. (It is not enough that the woman is a "sex slave"; she must be a sex slave from Burma, where such abuse is systematic and involves the authorities, for her rights as a refugee to become relevant.)

2. **Lack of papers:** The circumstances of the woman's removal from Burma, her residence in Thailand, her entry to Australia, and her eventual release from the hands of her captors mean that she is not in a position to provide a Burmese passport or other identity papers by which the nationality issue could easily be determined (she arrived in Australia on a false passport). Thus, other means of establishing her nationality are required. Perhaps one could tell by the languages she knows or does not know or by regional or other accents in her speech?

3. **Linguistic evidence gathered during an interview is used in the adjudication of nationality:** The woman claimed to be able to read and write Burmese and to speak it, and to be able to speak Thai, but not to read and write it. She was interviewed a number of times, twice in Burmese and at least once in Thai. Her reading and writing abilities in Burmese were also tested in the form of questions written in Burmese to which she had to provide written answers. Tape recordings of the spoken interviews formed the primary linguistic evidence used in this case by the immigration authorities, which concluded on the basis of this evidence that the woman was Thai and thus not entitled to claim rights as a refugee.

4. **The sociolinguistic issues involved are complex:**
   a **The relevant sociolinguistic situation is poorly described**. Given that the construct in this form of language test is sociolinguistic, we would need to be

confident that up-to-date data were available on the sociolinguistic context relevant to determining the issue (the amount of code mixing, the influence of one variety on another at the lexical, phonological, and syntactic level, the extent of variability, etc). In fact, the sociolinguistic situations in which this woman successively found herself (the Shan area of Burma and the area of northern Thailand near the Burmese border) are not well described by linguists, for various reasons, including accessibility, not the least aspect of which is the decades of conflict in the relevant area that make the needed sociolinguistic research unlikely or difficult.

b **The applicant's sociolinguistic history is complex**. The woman involved in this case has a complex history of residence for sustained periods in different regions involving different linguistic communities, and this is reflected in her speech. She was raised in the Shan state of Burma; in adolescence she was taken to northern Thailand, where she lived for many years; she was then taken to Australia. The sociolinguistic histories of refugees can often be complex, reflecting the trajectory from place of origin to the place where refuge is sought (Blommaert, 2001; Maryns & Blommaert, 2001; McNamara & Eades, 2004).

5. **The administrative arrangements for language analysis are controversial:** The report of this case does not make clear where and by whom the analysis was conducted. It might have been done within the Department of Immigration itself or by an external agency (a number of companies in Sweden, in particular, specialize in providing this service). The qualifications of the analyst and the exact procedures used in the analysis have frequently been challenged (see details below for cases involving Afghan asylum seekers in Australia). In this case, the amount of data analyzed ("a few words"

in the case of the Burmese data) and the qualifications of the analyst were disputed and, in the end, found wanting on appeal: The analyst of Burmese was a native speaker of Burmese from Western Burma, but was not a speaker of Shan, the dialect of Burmese from eastern Burma (the variety in question) and had never been to the Shan region of Burma; the analyst of Thai was a native speaker of Thai, but this person's qualifications and linguistic expertise were in doubt.

6. **Initial decisions by the authorities might be subject to appeal:** The initial administrative decision that Australia owed no obligation to the woman was appealed at the Refugee Review Tribunal, at which she was legally represented for the first time, and further linguistic evidence was produced to support her case. This was a sworn statement from a native speaker of Shan Burmese that the woman spoke the Shan dialect "confidently and without hesitation." The woman's appeal was successful in this case, largely on the quality of the initial and new linguistic evidence.

This issue of the quality of the language testing procedures that arose in this individual case is far from unusual. This is clear from a study of appeals to the Refugee Review Tribunal by Afghan refugees seeking asylum in Australia in which linguistic evidence was an important determining factor in the initial decision to refuse the application for refugee status (Eades, Fraser, Siegel, McNamara, & Baker, 2003). In the few years prior to 2001, numbers of ethnic minority Hazaras fled the Taliban regime in Afghanistan and sought asylum in countries including Australia, many arriving without documentation in vessels that had embarked from Indonesia and landed in remote areas of Australia's northwestern coast. The Australian immigration authorities suspected that the refugees included Hazaras who were citizens of Iran or Pakistan, each of which has long-standing Hazara communities (e.g., in the city of Quetta located near the

Pakistan-Afghanistan border). There was also a political motivation to challenge the claims of the refugees, as the issue of "border protection" became a central issue in Australian politics in 2001. The immigration authorities applied the language test to these asylum seekers in the belief that the variety of Hazargi[20] that the applicant used could assist in the determination of whether the applicant was a resident of the Hazara communities of Pakistan or Iran or was, indeed, from Afghanistan. For example, it was assumed that Hazaras in contact with Urdu (the language of Pakistan) would show traces of Urdu influence in features of their speech such as lexical choice or pronunciation, which would be absent from the speech of those Hazaras from central Afghanistan who were presumed not to have been exposed to such influence. Similarly, Hazaras from communities resident on the Iranian side of the Iran-Afghanistan border might be expected to show traces of Farsi (a language closely related to Dari) in their speech, features which again were assumed to be absent from the speech of Afghan Hazaras.

In order for such analysis to be fairly conducted, what is required is that the sociolinguistic construct be clear and unambiguous and that the credentials of those carrying out the analysis and the details of the procedures used be capable of sustaining professional investigation.

First, as in the Burmese case, the sociolinguistic situation in Afghanistan is not at all clear at the level of detail required and is, in principle, likely to be complex, with considerable blurring of the relevant sociolinguistic boundaries. For example, Iranian teachers brought into Afghanistan to provide religious schooling for religious minorities banned from education under the Taliban in Afghanistan brought with them Iranian expressions that can be found in the speech of their students. Further, vocabulary from nonindigenous foodstuffs is typically borrowed. For example, the word "patata," related to the English word "potato," is in common use in many parts of Afghanistan. There is a tradition of movement between Hazara communities inside and outside of Afghanistan, and the influence of this on the speech of the Afghan

Hazaras is not clear. Finally, the journey between Afghanistan and Australia involved certain periods of residence in Pakistan, and the possible influence of this on details of speech is, again, not well understood.

Second, the methods used by the companies carrying out the analysis were crude, and the analysts clearly lacked appropriate linguistic training. The linguistic evidence used was often slight and easily open to dispute: The use of what were held to be "typical" Pakistani or Iranian words (e.g., the use of a single Urdu word, a single Iranian word, and two words [*Afghanistan* and *dollar*] spoken with an Urdu accent) was enough to conclude that one applicant was deemed to have lived some time in Iran and Pakistan, a fact that he had denied. In another case, the use of the English word "camp" with a Pakistani accent was held to be evidence that the applicant originated from Pakistan. (Of course, as the head of the Tribunal in this case pointed out, this word could have been easily picked up while in a Pakistani refugee camp in transit to Australia.) One analysis, referring to the use of Urdu words by the applicant, claimed, incorrectly, that Urdu is not spoken in Afghanistan.

The appeal process was successful in reversing the decisions against the applicants in almost all of the cases investigated in this study, showing again how unsafe the linguistic analysis procedures are. Given this, it is disturbing to learn that their use is spreading and has now become routine for asylum seekers in the United Kingdom. The efforts of the Australian linguists, applied linguists, and language testers involved in this investigation to alert the Australian government to their findings met with a blank response, an experience echoing that of Swedish linguists in 1998 who attempted to draw the attention of the Swedish government to similar concerns.[21]

Although some applied linguists and language testers have objected to the use of such procedures altogether, it is reasonable to think that the evidence that they provide, when that evidence is properly obtained and interpretable, might be as useful in supporting a valid claim to asylum as in denying an invalid one. In the Burmese case, for example, the evidence that the applicant was a fluent speaker of Shan was helpful in supporting her claim. Certainly, this is the view of certain linguists who have carried out such procedures carefully and, they would claim, responsibly and ethically on behalf of the Swiss and Dutch governments (Corcoran, 2003; Singler, 2003) and is the assumption on which a group of linguists and language testers have prepared a set of guidelines for the proper use of language analysis in relation to questions of national origin in refugee cases (Language and National Origin Group, 2004). The problem is that the procedures are currently too often being used unaccountably, with little regard for questions of validity and reliability. As with the use of the shibboleth tests discussed earlier, the broader question of the use of language tests in determining the rights of asylum seekers will depend on your view of the justice of international refugee law. What is also relevant to the broader argument of this volume is that critique of the use of the existing procedures and their execution can in any case often be challenged on traditional validity and reliability grounds, where (as in the cases discussed) they violate professional standards for carrying out assessments.

6.4 Language Tests and Immigration

The broader context in which the issue of how to handle the claims of asylum seekers arises is a situation of increasing transnational flows, inflamed intergroup relations between host and immigrant communities, and heightened debates about national identity, shared values, and belonging. In this context, there is a tendency for policy to exploit, covertly or overtly, the identity marking provided by language tests, although this motivation is sometimes hard to disentangle from the more familiar functionalist rationales for language testing in such contexts (in the case of asylum seekers, to detect those making false claims; in the case of immigration and citizenship more generally, that proficiency in the national language is required for effective participation in society).

Given this, language tests are bound to play a significant but potentially ambiguous role at all stages of the immigration process, right up to the granting of full citizenship. We have already seen the complexity of the issues involved in the processing of the claims of undocumented refugees. Language tests might not involve all aspects of a country's immigration program; for example, components of family reunion or the intake of documented refugees typically have not involved language tests at entry, whereas so-called skilled migration (i.e., for employment) often involves a language test. Thus, for example, candidates for skilled migration to Australia and Canada are awarded points under a number of categories, including age, health, type of employment sought (i.e., whether it is in demand in the destination country), education, and so on. Applicants need to achieve a certain level of points for their application for admission to be successful, the level being determined by the immigration policy at the time. One of the categories for which points are given is knowledge of the language of the country concerned. For example, in Canada, points are given for knowledge of English or French (in Québec, which maintains its own immigration policy, points are for French only), and in the United Kingdom, Australia, and New Zealand points are given for English; in Germany, a new points system gives points for knowledge of German. The means of determining proficiency for the allocation of points varies; it can involve a simple subjective assessment on the part of an immigration officer at interview, a self-assessment on the part of the applicant (without further check, in most cases), or a formal language test, either one designed specifically for the purpose (e.g., the Australian *access* test of the early 1990s; Brindley & Wigglesworth, 1997) or a widely available test of convenience such as IELTS or TOEFL iBT. In the case of immigrants applying to enter particular professional contexts, such as health professionals, there might be compulsory language tests such as (in the case of Australia) either the Occupational English Test (McNamara, 1996), a specific-purpose English language test for health professionals, or a general test such as IELTS; in the case of health professionals entering the United States, the Test of Spoken English (TSE) or the new TOEFL iBT, which contains a speaking subtest, might be required.

The policy arguments in favor of such tests usually stress the functional requirements of proficiency for successful participation in the workforce or, in the case of health professionals, the welfare of patients and the safety of professional colleagues. Questions of values, cultural identity, and the politics of immigration are also involved, however, as we will see.

In the context of skilled migration to Australia, Hawthorne (2005a, 2005b) discusses the rationale for and outcomes of the greater emphasis on pre-immigration language testing intro-duced within Australian immigration policy in 1999 (Department of Immigration and Multicultural Affairs, 1999). Prior to this change, according to Hawthorne (2005a),

> During most of the 1990s NESB [non-English speaking background] professionals in Australia faced serious bar-riers related to their English ability and recognition of overseas credentials: a product of minimal pre-migration screening. The impact of poor English skills on NESB pro-fessionals can hardly be over-estimated. (p. 675)

Data from a database known as the Longitudinal Survey of Immigrants to Australia (based on a representative sample of 5% of migrants/refugees from successive cohorts of 1990s mi-gration) confirmed the impact of language in terms of employ-ment outcomes. In the 1995 cohort, approximately only 40–50% of migrants for whom employment skills formed any basis for acceptance into the immigration program were in employment within 6 months of arrival in Australia (Richardson, Robertson, & Ilsley, 2001). An analysis of employment outcomes for non-English-speaking background (NESB) professionals from a va-riety of countries/regions of origin, based on 1996 census data (Birrell & Hawthorne, 1999), showed a similar picture.

The changes introduced in 1999 tightening up pre-entry screening made language tests mandatory not only for skilled migrants but for several other categories as well. Richardson et al. (2001) report dramatic changes in the English skill levels of those admitted and concomitant changes in employment rates, with now between 65% and 70% of skilled migrants in employment within 6 months of arrival. Hawthorne (2005b) also cites data linking English language skills and employment outcomes: In 1993–1995, of those who self-assessed as speaking English "well" or "very well" at application, only 45% succeeded in finding employment on arrival, whereas in 1999–2000, following the compulsory independent assessment of language skills, this figure had jumped to 73%.

To summarize, this policy change involved what Hawthorne (2005a) describes as "the exclusion at point of entry of NESB professionals perceived as at risk of delayed labor market entry" (p. 666) in the interest of "the more immediate employability of NESB professionals" (p. 684). Hawthorne describes this as "a shift from altruism to pragmatism" (p. 690), a policy that "has sharply contracted Australia's accessibility to NESB professionals, reversing the policy liberalizations of the previous decade" (p. 684). However, it is not clear in whose interests this policy of exclusion through language testing was introduced—that of the migrants, so that they might avoid the dangers of unrealistic expectations about entry to their professions on arrival and the demoralizing experience of unemployment, or that of the host community. Hawthorne reminds us of the wider social and political context within Australia of the introduction of the policy:

> Collectively, within both Australia and Canada, negative employment outcomes for NESB migrants were contributing to a growing community polarization on immigration, exacerbating dissatisfaction with the thrust of contemporary policy and reinforcing demand for justification of migration's economic value to the host community. In Australia, this pressure was resulting in growing demand for the introduction of pre-migration English language testing. (Hawthorne, 2005a, p. 675)

She characterized the change in policy in the following terms:

Following two decades of research confirming the comparative labor market disadvantage of NESB groups, the
Australian government had moved determinedly to reduce
these migrants' access at point of entry—a shift from altruism to pragmatism. Australia's determination to "select for success" among skill applicants is now leading
to a profound re-shaping of the migration program ... in
terms of the redefinition of "acceptable" human capital.
(Hawthorne, 2005a, p. 690)

In other words, the relationship of the host community and
the immigrants is involved in the policies involving language testing; and it is in this context that language tests are used for purposes of exclusion. Clearly, the merits of this policy are a matter
of debate, but the connection between the policy of language testing and the wider context of "growing community polarization on
immigration" is clear.

A further example of the complex combination of identity,
values, and language testing in the case of immigration is the policy of requiring a particular category of intending immigrants—
ministers of religion—to demonstrate knowledge of the language
of the country of immigration, which is being canvassed or
adopted in several countries. This requirement has been enacted
in the United Kingdom Nationality, Immigration and Asylum
Act, 2002. The response of the immigrant communities involved
underlines the complexity of the identity issues involved. A BBC
news report[22] claimed that a majority of British Muslims in a
sample survey supported the need for clerics to preach in English,
on the grounds that the majority of congregations consist of
younger, British-born Muslims for whom English is the principal
language and in order to "break down cultural divides between
Islam and mainstream society." The report added that Muslim
community leaders "also supported a Home Office move to impose language tests on all religious ministers coming to the UK,
saying they regarded it as key to imams being able to do their job."

In Australia, a similar call has been made, although, to
date, it has not been enshrined in legislation. A report by the

Australian Multicultural Foundation entitled *Religion, Cultural Diversity and Safeguarding Australia* (Cahill, Bouma, Dellal, & Leahy, 2004) recommended that "All arriving religious personnel, whether applying for permanent residency or a long term temporary visa, be given provisional visas for six months until they have achieved vocational proficiency in English" (p. 124). This is justified on the following grounds:

> Failure to speak adequate English, even after many years in Australia, implies [that religious leaders] cannot communicate adequately with second- and third-generation members of their immigrant and refugee communities. Equally importantly, it implies that such leaders cannot act as cultural and religious bridges or as mediators between their own community and the wider community. Australia is a community of communities. This capacity to build linkages between the communities is a key component of social capital. (Cahill et al., 2004, p. 123)

A newspaper article about the report[23] quotes a Muslim religious leader as supporting the recommendation on the grounds that "it was important to know enough English to deal with people and to follow the news on radio or TV."

The policy of exclusion by means of language tests in the case of religious leaders involves complex questions of values in a pluralist society, but also has to be understood in the context of intergroup tensions, as the reference to "safeguarding Australia" in the title of the Australian report makes clear. We will consider these issues further in discussions of language tests for citizenship.

In other contexts of immigration, the role of language tests as a mechanism of exclusion is simpler and more obvious. For example, under recent changes to Dutch immigration law (Marinelli, 2005), Dutch residents sponsoring prospective spouses for entry to the Netherlands face a new barrier: The intended spouses are required to take a proficiency test in spoken Dutch before being admitted to the Netherlands and must achieve a given level in order for their application to be successful. The test, which is technically very sophisticated, is administered over the telephone using an adaptation of the American PhonePass Spoken English Test technology (Ordinate, 2000). Given the lack of readily available tuition in Dutch as a foreign language in countries such as Morocco, where many of the intended spouses reside, the language requirement constitutes a particularly effective barrier.

6.5 Language Tests and Citizenship

The complex role of language tests within situations of intergroup tensions arises in the context of language tests for citizenship. Language requirements have been part of citizenship procedures in some countries for decades. For example, United States law states that

> No person . . . shall be naturalized as a citizen of the United States upon his own petition who cannot demonstrate— an understanding of the English language, including an ability to read, write and speak words in ordinary usage in the English language. (8 U.S.C. § 1423 [1964], cited in Leibowitz, 1969, p. 13)[24]

Until recently, the proficiency of intending U.S. citizens tends to have been assessed rather informally during the citizenship interview with an administrative officer and has not involved formal language tests:

> Not clearly operationalized, the English speaking and listening requirement is tested incidentally throughout the interview. The test of English writing is given in the form of a sentence dictation, and sentence selection is entirely at the interviewing officer's discretion. Applicants have the right to be dictated up to two sentences, and interviewing officers vary as to whether or not they will accept a minor spelling error. The English reading test entails reading aloud a sentence or short passage from the application for Naturalization, the list of one hundred US history and government questions, or a basal reader. (Winn, 2005, p. 266)

This leads to great variability in practice:

> Anecdotal information collected from citizenship applicants indicates the test may consist of any of the following: The applicant may be asked to write a sentence in English (such as "Today is a beautiful day"), read the civics questions aloud and answer the questions in English ("Who was the first President of the United States?"), or answer questions on everyday matters in English ("Where do you live?"). (Kunnan, 2005, p. 785)

The only study to have examined the procedures currently used in the United States from an applied linguistics perspective (Winn, 2005) found that 16% of the 67 interviewees that she observed failed the test, all on the basis of language proficiency, although the interview was administered sympathetically and applicants were given every chance to show what they could do. This, according to Winn, was typical of the wider population of applicants, where the national failure rate over an 8-year period in the 1990s varied between 5% and 18% annually, with language proficiency being the cause in approximately three-quarters of the cases. Given that there were over a million applicants annually in that period, the English proficiency requirement for citizenship is clearly a nontrivial issue.[25]

In Australia, too, there is a language requirement that intending citizens speak basic English, but it appears to be enforced very variably and informally. According to a recent newspaper report[26] entitled "MP Urges Tougher English Test for Migrants," Dr. Sharman Stone, a member of Parliament for a rural area with substantial immigrant communities, complained about the lack of enforcement, saying that in some areas:

> Language testing was conducted by the local postmaster on behalf of the Department of Immigration. She questioned whether they had proper training.
> Dr. Stone asked how officials could tell if people were committed to Australia and understood their rights and responsibilities if they could not speak English. She

claimed some people often brought an interpreter to the postmaster interview.

A spokeswoman for Australia Post was unable to say if postmasters received training, but said "borderline cases" were referred to the Department of Immigration for a decision about English-speaking abilities.

"The applicant needs to be able to understand the questions put to them in the interview without anybody interpreting for them," the spokeswoman said.

Note that the argument for requiring knowledge of English is presented in terms of both practicality ("understanding rights and responsibilities") and values ("commitment to Australia"). Both this and the previous example also raise the issue of the problem of the extreme informality of the test, a matter that can be addressed by introducing a psychometrically sounder procedure;[27] although this seems defensible in terms of fairness, it does not, of course, resolve the wider debate about the appropriateness of this test use.

In Europe, discussions about language testing and citizenship are taking place in the context of the inflamed intergroup relations between "host" and (long-standing) immigrant communities in many countries. Blackledge (2005) has shown how, in the heightened debate about national identity associated with urban disturbances in the United Kingdom, the role of language in national identity and rhetoric around language as a unifying force have led to the strict enforcement of long-standing requirements of language proficiency for citizenship, independently assessed through language tests. New legislation also has been introduced, so that, for example, the 2002 Nationality, Immigration and Asylum Act requires spouses of British citizens to demonstrate their proficiency in English when applying for British citizenship. The situation throughout Europe is complex, and the present discussion cannot do it full justice; the interested reader is referred to two forthcoming collections of papers (Extra & van Avermaet, 2007; McNamara & Shohamy, 2008). What is most relevant from the point of view of the present chapter is the ambiguous role that language tests play in these developments, acting as mechanisms of exclusion in the name of national inclusiveness. The situation in Germany is particularly interesting in this regard (Piller, 2001). The traditional basis for German citizenship, the principle of *ius sanguinis*, denied citizenship to those who could not show a bloodline connection to the country, thus excluding generations of immigrant workers and their children from full citizenship. This was changed in a historic reform, the Nationality Law of 2000, in which the principle of *ius solis* was adopted, under which residency became the basis for citizenship. In a little discussed clause in the new law, a test of German language was required as part of the procedures for citizenship. It is striking that among the German states that administer citizenship procedures under the new law, it was the most politically conservative, who had opposed the change in the law, who immediately sought the help of language testers in creating the language tests required (Rubeling, 2002).

The legislation on immigration and citizenship in several countries makes reference to levels on the Common European Framework of Reference for Languages (Council of Europe, 2001). There are only six levels, A 1&2, B 1&2, and C 1&2, spanning the whole range of language proficiency from beginner to fluent nativelike command; A1 is the lowest level. The levels required under this legislation differ by country, depending on the politics of the setting. Austria has recently increased from A1 to A2 the language requirement that immigrants need to demonstrate within 18 months of residency, and failure to achieve this level ultimately results in loss of the residence permit (König and Perchinig, 2005); the Netherlands requires new migrants to reach A2 (Marinelli, 2005); Finland requires A2 for returning Ingrian Finns (discussed earlier); the recent German citizenship law requires B1, and changes in immigration and citizenship law in Denmark also require B1. It is hard to see what justification there might be for the different levels on functional grounds and it is clear that the politics and cultural values of the setting in each case will be the decisive factor.

6.6 Canada: Language Tests and the Official Languages Policy[28]

In this section, we will examine a further example of the use of language tests as the instruments of policy in situations of intergroup tension: the implementation of the official Canadian policy of bilingualism by means of language tests for civil servants. These tests, known as the Second Language Evaluation/ Evaluation de langue second (SLE/ELS), have been controversial among some test takers, especially senior anglophone civil servants, with the test of speaking being a particular focus of complaint. The controversy surrounding the test provides an interesting test case for whether the use of the test in this context can be understood as a question of test validity as set out in chapter 2, including test use understood in those terms. It will be argued that although such an analysis goes a long way to helping us understand and even to suggest ways of resolving the controversy surrounding the tests, at a deeper level the issue involves larger questions of the ideology of Canadian bilingualism and the identities and subjectivities that the tests construct within this. For such an understanding, we need to move beyond validity theory to a broader social theory of the context in which the tests find their meaning.

It should be noted that the following discussion of the SLE/ELS is far from adequate as a full treatment of issues arising in relation to these tests. For one thing, we will only be discussing the speaking test, and concentrating at that on the experience of a small group of senior anglophone executives taking the test of spoken French. This should not be taken as privileging the experiences of this group or of endorsing the kinds of complaints that they have frequently made; in fact, there is a certain irony in the fact that this elite and, in other ways, highly privileged group of senior bureaucrats should be made so uncomfortable by the implementation of a government policy (the Official Languages Policy) that they are bound to support and in fact do, in principle, support. The discussion is not meant to imply any criticism of the Canadian policy of official bilingualism. Quite apart from the fact that as non-Canadians it is not appropriate for us to have a view on this complex policy, the point of the present discussion is not to evaluate the policy but to use the example of the SLE/ELS to consider the broader issues forming the argument of this volume. A complete evaluation of the tests and their role in the implementation of government policy would have to include, at the very least, examination of the experience of francophones taking the tests of English and the experience of civil servants, including those at lower levels, taking the whole battery of tests in each language.

Under the Official Languages Acts of 1969 and 1988, the federal government has a commitment to the provision of government services in both official languages: French and English. The policy also allows government employees to be supervised in the workplace in their own language. The policy of bilingualism has a complex history in Canada, located as it is in the sometimes difficult relations between the English-speaking majority and the French-speaking minority, which have seen periods of heightened tension at various times over the last 40 years. The bilingualism policy emerged partly as a response of the government of Pierre Trudeau to the separatist threats from in the 1960s and 1970s and specifically in response to language planning legislation to protect the status of French in Québec.[29] Its political significance has been renewed whenever the issue of separatism becomes acute in Canadian politics. In 1995, for example, a referendum in Québec on separation from the Canadian federation only narrowly failed, and in an attempt to be seen as not neglecting language issues, the federalists in the federal government strengthened the enforcement of its bilingual policy in its own workforce. In 1998, the authority responsible for the Official Languages Policy decided that "departments must ensure that the more rigorous language requirements of positions in bilingual regions were met by new [executive level appointees] within two years and by incumbents as of April 1, 2003" (Mitchell, 2005, p. 6).

Civil servants working for the federal government occupy positions that are classified at various levels of seniority, approximately 60% of which are designated as bilingual. Each bilingual position has a description of its language requirements, in terms of a classificatory system developed by the Public Service Commission of Canada (PSC), which administers the language tests that civil servants need to pass. These tests certify achievement at five proficiency levels, X (no proficiency), A (elementary), B (intermediate), C (advanced), and E (exempt from further testing) for three areas: oral skills (speaking and listening), reading, and writing. Bilingual positions may be classified as requiring advanced skills in all areas (CCC), a mix of advanced and intermediate skills (CBC), or intermediate skills only (BBB), and so on. These classifications are laid down by policy in some cases; for example, employees in Human Resources or in the Public Service Commission (which administers the test) require advanced skills in all areas; senior executives in other areas must have a CBC profile in reading, writing, and oral communication skills, respectively (Bessette, 2005). For other positions, the language requirements are determined by the manager at the level above the position concerned. Proof of the necessary language proficiency has to be shown either at the time of application for those positions classified as having "mandatory" language proficiency (known administratively as "imperative staffing") or within a certain period following appointment for those positions classified as having "required" language proficiency. If necessary, more senior executives are seconded from their position for as long as it takes to complete language training in order to pass the level successfully; the cost of this language training is borne by the government and frequently involves one-on-one tuition or home stays (e.g., with French-speaking families in the case of anglophones). For those applying for more junior positions, responsibility for language training falls on their own shoulders and is done at the individual's own cost, often well in advance of application for the position. Decisions about the degree of support for language training are made locally and result in considerable variability. Individuals need to be retested after 5 years, or earlier if they move positions. Retention of the language level achieved, especially in speaking, has been shown to be a problem, particularly for anglophones who do not frequently use French in the workplace (Edwards, 1977; Mitchell, 2005).

Two recent studies (Bessette, 2005; Mitchell, 2005) have shown that the administration of this policy is associated with considerable feeling among a small but elite group of those most directly affected by it: anglophones holding executive positions, particularly in relation to the test of spoken French.[30] One the one hand, the policy has widespread support in principle among the federalist employees affected (Mitchell, 2005) and bilingual proficiency is widely admired in the workforce. On the other hand, it is associated with a certain unreality or detachment at the personal level. Based on an interview study with 20 senior anglophone civil servants, Mitchell reported:

> There is [a] gap between the lofty goals of the O[fficial] L[anguages] A[ct] and the largely instrumental sense in which too many public servants view language training... Instead of regarding the acquisition of competency in French as a skill essential to their effectiveness as public servants and to their own career development, they focus on "passing the test," as if obtaining the certificate were simply an obstacle to be overcome. This lack of personal engagement with the language skills they are seeking to acquire can only be explained by a broader ethos in a Public Service in which French is not generally respected or used as a language of work, and in which the acquisition by anglophones of competency in French is seen as essentially the employer's responsibility. (p. 10)

Perceptions of the experience of preparation for the test, the standard required (especially given the perceived gap between that and the current reality of actual usage in the workplace), and the actual administration of the test are often very negative:

> Too many of those who exit language training quickly lose whatever fluency they had acquired. Too many come out with their attitude toward their second language soured by months of language training and successive failures on the test. (Mitchell, 2005, p. 5)

Mitchell (2005, p. 17) on the basis of an interview study with 20 senior anglophone civil servants, reports that these executives felt that:

- testing is much more rigorous than it was a few years ago (and unfairly so)

- testing is unfair and needlessly subjective

- people are being tested to a standard that bears no relation to their jobs

- the whole testing method is unnecessarily stressful and artificial. (Mitchell, 2005, p. 17)

Note that what is questioned in the current situation is not the policy directly—that is too large a question, and in any case is broadly, if notionally, accepted among the civil servants involved—but the policy as represented by the test, specifically the speaking test. We can consider the significance of the complaints of Mitchell's (2005) informants either using the language of validity and reliability or via the notion of the social construction of identities from social theory. Let us consider each in turn.

Clearly, if we are to take the complaints of the informants reported in what follows at face value,[31] there are a number of problems with the administration of the test that threaten its validity and reliability. These can all be considered in the light of Bachman and Palmer's (1996) concept of test usefulness, which involves consideration of the following aspects of the test: *reliability, construct validity, authenticity, interactiveness, impact*, and *practicality*. The test has problematic features in terms of each of these aspects.

Oral tests are conducted by a single interlocutor, which inevitably, and reasonably enough, raises questions of *reliability* and, hence, fairness.[32] According to one informant:

The variables that play in are the time of day, the personality of the tester, [and] the types of questions the tester wants to ask. [...] You'll always get a different tester every time you go to the testing facility [...and] so much depends on their personality. (Bessette, 2005, p. 61)

The fact that there is no standardization of oral test content in terms of choice of topics will be discussed later.

Questions over the test's *construct validity* involve doubt over the view of language taken in the test, particularly when it is different from that taken by teachers in the language training courses leading up to the test. The situation is made worse by the lack of explicitness of the construct. It is felt that communication between those responsible for the testing, on the one hand, and language trainers, on the other, is lacking, in terms of the evaluators' perceptions of the standard and what specifically they are looking for in a performance. Bessette (2005), in her study of the experience of senior civil servants undertaking language training in preparation for the test, quoted one of her informants as saying that:

> "You just don't know what their procedures are. [...] None of the information is ever shared.". . . She could not comprehend why it did "not seem to be shared with those who are tasked with the training so that they can help the students they have. . .. you never really know what the evaluator really wants from you." (pp. 48–49)

For example, the evaluators are perceived as having prescriptive views about language and test performance, insisting on formulaic requirements such as full sentences, full paragraphs, and the use of tenses not used in actual speech, so that the performance resembles giving a speech rather than the oral interaction more characteristic of the workplace.[33]

In terms of *authenticity*, we have already noted the gap between the assumptions of the test about the use of both official languages in workplace communication and the reality of the workplace itself. This leads to disputes about the appropriate target and focus of the test. The problem is accentuated by the structure of the measurement scale used, which, like most scales, is not an interval scale (i.e., it has unequal intervals). For example, in the case of oral skills, various aspects are defined: *ability to converse, ease in using the language,* and *clarity of communication.* Under *ease in using the language,* the three levels are defined in the following terms:

A delivery may be slow

B speaks with some spontaneity

C has a natural delivery

Under *ability to converse*, the levels are as follows:

A can sustain a simple question and answer exchange

B can sustain an informal conversation on concrete topics

C can participate effectively in discussions on a broad range of topics

There thus seems to be a consistently larger gap between levels B and C than between levels A and B. This is significant for those required to achieve level C in speaking, such as the senior executives, as the standard required seems a big leap. There is also a perception that the standard required at level C is now being interpreted more strictly, although the PSC, which is responsible for test administration, denies this.

Mitchell (2005) summarized the "widely differing views" on what standards and expectation of performance are appropriate among the senior civil servants and policy advisers that he interviewed:

> Some feel there is too high an expectation of what is implied by C-level competency in French. They see colleagues and subordinates who, as far as they are concerned, are certainly bilingual enough for the purposes of effective management and communication, going off to be tested and failing repeatedly.
>
> Others believe our expectations of linguistic competency are too low. They see people coming back from training with a "C" who are far from functionally bilingual, and who can neither manage nor communicate effectively in their second language. (p. 14)

He pointed out that decisions about the definition of an appropriate level of bilingual proficiency in senior management positions are political ones, which will need to be decided by Ministers. In this case, we see that an important dimension of the construct of the test is essentially political, an important point for validity theory that we will discuss further in chapter 7.

At a more detailed level, a further problem with test authenticity arises in relation to test content, which, as we have noted earlier, is not standardized. In the warm-up section, which is not marked but which might be perceived as setting the tone of the interaction, one frequently asked topic is about hobbies. Anecdotal evidence[34] suggests that instead of focusing on the actual hobbies of the candidate or about familiar hobbies such as, say, basketball or motor sports, candidates might be required to discuss things with which they are not familiar: An example given was fly-fishing, which the candidate concerned struggle to discuss, as he might have even in his first language. This led the candidate to question not only the choice of topic but also the fundamental relevance of the test to the workplace and, hence, the whole policy. It is hard to evaluate to what extent the administration of the test warrants this criticism; obviously all tests will suffer in terms of quality of administration at times. The policy in relation to the test states that candidates will be given a choice of broad topics on which to converse in the warm-up stage, and at least in the other, work-related, sections of the test, they can indicate whether they lack familiarity with a topic or procedure, in which case, the interviewer will change it without penalty to the candidate.

For *interactiveness*, we have seen from the above quotations that candidates feel frustrated by the lack of opportunity to engage naturally with the interlocutor in the oral test, and the levels of anxiety experienced also depress performance. In terms of *impact* and *practicality*, the test has significant impact both on the lives of those who take it and the work setting from which they are removed, often for months, to undergo intensive one-on-one language training and also, one must say, for the Canadian taxpayer who is funding these periods of leave on full salary and the expensive individualized language training. It is routine for people to fail the test numerous times, even after extensive language training; this can result in the candidate's confidence plummeting and is counterproductive of an improved performance on the next attempt. Bessette's (2005) study of executive level civil servants who took the test reported that a number of the senior executives she studied had had to take the test several times ("5," "7," and "several") before succeeding; this was after between 9 and 12 months of language study. According to one candidate (who in fact managed to pass on the first attempt):

> There has to be a better way. [...] The process [is] set up for failure. .... In a way, it's set up [so that] you go through, boom, [and] you pass or you fail and most people fail, [...] more than fifty percent fail; [...and] that's hard personally. Some incredibly brilliant people I know have taken eight times to actually pass. (Bessette, 2005, p. 58)

Those candidates who experience repeated failure have referred to the experience of taking the test as a "ritual of humiliation."[35] The reference to the test as "ritual" leads us into a second kind of understanding of the issues raised by test participants—this time not from the point of view of validity theory, but from social theory. The test is the point of insertion of power (the policy) in the lives of those to whom it is directed. In Foucault's (1975/1977) brilliant analysis of the relationship between tests and power, he showed us how tests can be experienced as exercises in subjection to power:

> The examination ... is ... a surveillance that makes it possible to qualify, to classify and to punish. It establishes over individuals a visibility through which one differentiates and judges them. That is why ... the examination is highly ritualized. In it are combined the ceremony of power and the form of the experiment, the deployment of force and the establishment of truth. (pp. 184–185)

The power manifest in tests is seen as productive of individuality:

> The examination as the fixing, at once ritual and "scientific," of individual differences, as the pinning down of each individual in his own particularity ... clearly indicates the appearance of a new modality of power in which

> each individual receives as his status his own individu-
> ality, and in which he is linked by his status to the fea-
> tures, the measurements, the gaps, the "marks" that char-
> acterize him and make him a "case." (Foucault, 1975/1977,
> p. 192)

The elements of the executives' complaints are illuminated
by such texts. The experience of failure is a "ritual of humiliation";
the anonymity and impersonality of the interviewer's behavior
are disconcerting:

> [One] evaluator that I had was somebody who has a rep-
> utation within the testing community <laughs> [and...]
> I associated this individual with what I thought the out-
> come would be [and] that might have some bearing on [not
> passing]. [Another] evaluator refused to look me in the
> eye when I was speaking, [...] and consequently trying
> to build a rapport, and eye-to-eye contact was impossible.
> (Bessette, 2005, p. 49)

The francophone testers are seen as unsympathetic to the
anglophone candidates, who are mostly in midcareer. Another informant in Bessette's (2005) study described

> her feelings of anxiety and uneasiness that were present
> during the oral evaluations: "We can't in any way show
> that we're vulnerable or that we have our weaknesses
> or whatever. It's like you have to be perfect [....] if you
> auto-correct yourself in an exam, it's the wrong thing to
> do... [there's] this attitude that seems to impose on us that
> we have to be so perfect." (p. 49)

One informant expressed the view that "individuals were clearly
frustrated [...and] emotionally damaged by their experience,
depending on the number of years that they'd been there."
(p. 69).

In contrast, for those who have succeeded on the test, the
subjection to the test is rewarded with a subjectivity— a sense of
self—that is conferred by the test as the expression of the ideology
of Canadian identity represented by the Official Languages Policy.
In the following case, it is significant that the person who passed

is a member of a "visible minority" who might otherwise struggle to identify and be identified as Canadian:

> On the whole, this participant "surrendered himself"....
> He felt that this experience has given him a fuller sense of himself as "someone who represents the new Canada: visible minority person who speaks both official languages."
> (Bessette, 2005, p. 55)

What is at stake in this examination is particularly striking given that those required to take the test are senior executives responsible for the administration of the policies of the government that requires them to go through what is, for many, plainly a watershed personal experience —"by far the most stressful thing I've ever done in my life" (Bessette, 2005, p. 57), "harder than having kids <laughs>" (Bessette, 2005, p. 63). One effect of the technical improvements emerging in the above discussion of the validity of the test is that the social and political functions of the test in constituting an aspect of the identity of the participants would become less visible. For Foucault (1975/1977), one of the key features of the use of tests as instruments of power is that they conceal the exercise of power by focusing on the subject of that power:

> Disciplinary power ... is exercised through its invisibility; at the same time it imposes on those whom it subjects a principle of compulsory visibility. In discipline, it is the subjects who have to be seen. Their visibility assures the hold of the power that is exercised over them.... The examination is the technique by which power ... holds [its subjects] in a mechanism of objectification. (p. 187)

Herein lies one of the most important aspects of tests as instruments of public policy: Because tests represent the point of insertion of a policy into individual lives, a "good" test (in terms of the quality of test administration, perceived fairness of content and judgment, and so on) can lead to acceptance of the policy, not judged in terms of the fairness of the *policy itself* but as seen in the degree of fairness of the *test* that implements it. In the case of an unfair policy, a good test can lead to political quietism. On the other hand, a "bad" test (one that is perceived as unreliable or arbitrary in some other way) leads to resentment of the entire policy context in which it is imposed, particularly if that policy rests (as most policies inevitably do) on contested foundations. Part of the power of tests lies in their technical qualities. The success of a policy as implemented by tests rests on issues that language testers tend to see as purely technical. (Of course, policies that one might wish to defend as "good" and that are implemented by fair tests might not thereby be immune from criticism.)

There is another side to this as well: The social and political functions of language tests are served by the kind of disguise represented by the test itself, with its potentially impressive formality and impersonality and association with science and authority. In fact, in all testing, the emphasis on the cognitive and psychological in measurement is part of the means through which the social construction of subjectivity and, hence, the social function of the test are rendered invisible. The way in which the social is rendered invisible within a discourse of individual cognition has been addressed in discussions within feminism and queer theory. For example, the queer theorist Judith Butler makes a distinction between two different ways of understanding gender identity: the expressive and the performative (Butler, 1990; see also discussion in McNamara, 2006). She argues that our inner, private, psychological experience of gender as an "interior essence" is not anything essential to our natures but is in fact a result of social actions, which she sees as performative, extending the notion of linguistic performativity proposed by Austin (1962). Conventionally, gendered behavior is held to be expressive of our inner (masculine or feminine) "natures." Instead, Butler argued that we are socialized into such behaviors, but instead of recognizing them as the product of social forces, we attribute them to an inner essence of masculinity or femininity. Butler distinguished *performativity* (the construction of a sense of something inner by certain acts) from *expression* (the external manifestation of something "inner"). Expression goes from the inside to the outside; some "inner essence" is expressed. Performativity goes from outer to inner: Actions construct a belief in the existence of an inner essence, which is only a fiction, an effect.

> If gender attributes, however, are not expressive but per-formative, then these attributes effectively constitute the identity they are said to express or reveal. The distinction between the expression and performativeness is crucial. (Butler, 1990, p. 141)

Moreover, the tendency for the social origins of gender iden-tity to disappear inside our sense of an interior essence is conve-nient, as it means that the social construction of gender is thus made invisible.

> If the "cause" of desire, gesture and act can be localized within the "self" of the actor, then the political regulatory and disciplinary practices which produce that ostensibly coherent gender are effectively displaced from view. The displacement of a political and discursive origin of gender identity onto a psychological "core" precludes an analy-sis of the political constitution of the gendered subject. (Butler, 1990, p. 136)

In the same way, discussion of test qualities within a cognitively based discourse of psychometrics might have the effect of disguis-ing their social character.

In summary, the discussion of the SLE/ELS has contrasted two ways of considering the social dimension of the test. The first is to understand test use in the terms set by the test itself (i.e., as a test of workplace communication serving functions of personnel selection and training in a bilingual environment) and to interpret the issues implicit in the comments (fair or otherwise) of the test takers as essentially questions of validity and reliability, given that stated use. The second is to attempt to understand the ex-perience of the test takers in terms of notions of social subjection and subjectivity deriving from social theory. We have tried to show what is gained by each kind of discussion. We would also argue, however, that if we are to understand fully the social dimension of this and other language tests, the conceptual tools of validity theory are not enough. We need other, complementary sources of theoretical insight if we are to appreciate what is at stake for the participants and the questions this raises.

6.7 Conclusion: Language Tests and Subjectivity

We will conclude this chapter by considering in more detail the relationship of language tests to social identity implied in the work of Foucault. In the examples discussed in this chapter, language tests are seen as weapons within situations of inter-group competition and conflict. In the cases discussed earlier in the chapter, the group identities involved appeared to be given a priori and the tests reinforced those identities, both on the part of the excluders and on the part of the excluded, who were reminded of the salience of their identity by the fact of exclusion, punishment, or the denial of rights. For Foucault, however, tests are seen as mechanisms for the very construction of the identities that they police. Within this perspective, the test taker is understood as a social being whose subjectivity is a function of subject positions realized in the test itself. From this perspective, tests become technologies of subjectivity. They act as mechanisms both for the definition of subject positions and for the recognition of subjects. Tests create the identities that they measure. In the Canadian case, for example, although the test involved arises from inter-group competition between long-established groups, the bilingual identity promoted through the Official Languages Act is conferred through the test itself. The tests in immigrant contexts operate in the same way: Certain kinds of "acceptable" identities are defined by the test and the test is a procedure for conferring those identities—for recognizing the individual in terms of the qualities identified by the test. In order to consider further how we might understand this, we will examine one more example: the identities defined within the sphere of modern medical clinical practice, within which a test of communicative skill for immigrant health professionals such as the Occupational English Test (McNamara, 1996) takes its place (see chapter 2).

Subject positions are articulated within discourses ("big D" discourses, to use the term adopted by Pennycook, 1994, and Gee, 2003). The subjectivities defined within the discourse of modern clinical practice are discussed at length in Foucault's *The Archaeology of Knowledge* (1969/1972). Foucault defined the discourse of clinical medicine as consisting of a system of elements that include *speaker status*, *site of speaking*, and *subject positions* of speakers:

> Clinical medicine must ... be regarded as the establish-
> ment of a relation, in medical discourse, between a number
> of distinct elements, some of which concerned the status
> of doctors, others the institutional and technical site from
> which they spoke, others their position as subjects perceiv-
> ing, observing, describing, teaching, etc. It can be said that
> this relation between different elements ... is effected by
> clinical discourse: it is this, as a practice, that establishes
> between them all a system of relations. (p. 50)

Of particular interest are the *subject positions* defined within medical discourse, and particularly the role of language involved:

> The positions of the subject are also defined by the sit-
> uation that it is possible for him to occupy...: according
> to a certain grid of explicit or implicit interrogations, he
> is the questioning subject and, according to a certain pro-
> gramme of information, he is the listening subject; accord-
> ing to a table of characteristic features, he is the seeing
> subject, and, according to a descriptive type, the observ-
> ing subject; ... To these perceptual situations should be
> added the positions that the subject can occupy in the in-
> formation networks (in theoretical teaching or in hospital
> training; in the system of oral communication or of written
> document: as emitter and receiver of observations, case-
> histories, statistical data, general theoretical propositions,
> projects, and decisions). (p. 52)

Such subjectivities are implicated in relations of power; thus Foucault's analysis is not an exercise in pragmatism but a social critique. This is what makes this different from the job analy-sis stage in the development of specific-purpose language tests, which it superficially resembles. The function of a test of English for immigrant health professionals such as the Occupational English Test (OET) in such a discourse is clear: It is a technology for recognizing (i.e., publicly confirming and certifying) individuals as suitable occupants of such subject positions. In this sense, the OET, like other tests, is a test of identity. Like all tests, it represents a site of social recognition and control.

The perspective adopted in this chapter on the social and political functions of language tests means that we cannot afford to be merely naïve players in the discursively constructed world in which language tests are located. Appropriate intellectual and analytical tools enable us to recognize the roles that tests will play in the operation of power and of systems of social control. We will be less inclined to seek shelter in the impersonality of the purely technical aspects of our work. We need critical self-awareness in order for us to first recognize and then to decide whether to accept or to resist our own subject position in the system of social control in which tests play such a part. Research conferences in language testing, such as the annual Language Testing Research Colloquium, should be occasions for us to reflect on our subject positions—our identities—as language testers, rather than simply reinforcing them.

A more adequate theorization of the social context of testing will help us to understand the discourses in which the demands of our sponsors and clients are shaped. This will better prepare us to expect, to recognize, and to deal as constructively as we can with various kinds of pressure on tests as a result of their function as sites of social control. We should expect that our sponsors would want to retain control of the setting of cut scores in the interests of policy objectives. Moreover, we will not expect the subjectivities located in any discourse to be stable, but to be superseded given the right circumstances. For example, the discourse of rural decline in Australia means that immigrant health professionals are suddenly being welcomed and testing regimes such as the OET, which are strenuously maintained as legitimate in terms of patient welfare, at one moment, are seen as unnecessarily obstructive and unfair, at another moment.

A deeper engagement with the theory of the social context in one sense confirms the position of Messick (1989) that all language tests imply values, a position set out in the discussion of validity in chapter 2. However, neither Messick nor those who have followed him have provided us with the tools that we need to recognize the full extent of this or the way in which the language test developer might not have any power to influence the values that a test expresses, although this is an assumption of current versions of validity theory. Such values are necessarily political and social and can be understood most fruitfully in terms of the discourses within which language tests have their meaning. We need different theoretical perspectives to enable us to recognize this fact and its significance.

Notes

[1] The meaning of this word is disputed; it is usually understood to mean "ear of wheat," but an alternative translation is "stream."

[2] Arabic has a voiced alveolar (pharyngealized) fricative that is written in Romanized form as z and is transcribed as $[z^{\varsigma}]$ in the International Phonetic Alphabet. /z/ and /z$^{\varsigma}$/ are contrastive in Arabic.

[3] We are grateful to Kana Shirai, a student in the Masters in Applied Linguistics program at Melbourne, for drawing our attention to the relevance of this tragic event.

[4] Different versions of the details of the shibboleth in this case are given in Calvet (1987/1998), who mentioned the pronunciation of the dictator's name, with the jota in Trujillo being the focus of the shibboleth, or the r sound in perro ("dog" in Spanish).

[5] "In Lebanon during the civil war (1975–1992)... [the] pronunciation of the Levantine word for 'tomatoes,' a modern-day shibboleth, served as a clue to one's ethnic/national identity in a war situation. As a boundary-setter, a person's rendering of this shibboleth sometimes signaled the difference between life and death" (p. 5).

[6] Compare Crawford, 1900, Vol. 2, p. 321:

> No Frenchman who met [the Sicilian rebels] lived to turn back, and when they were in doubt as to any man's nation, they held him with the knife at his throat and made him say the one word 'Ciceri,' which no Frenchman could or can pronounce. It was dusk when the killing began in Palermo, and when the dawn stole through the blood-stained streets, not one of the French was left alive, neither man, nor woman, nor child.

[7]Keelhauling was a severe form of corporal punishment to sailors at sea. The sailor was tied to a rope that looped beneath the vessel, thrown overboard on one side of the ship, dragged under the keel, and then up the other side. Alternatively, the sailor was dragged from bow to stern. Keelhauling along the length of the hull was generally a death sentence because it could take as long as 3 min, and perhaps longer, to walk the ropes all the way back to the stern, resulting in death by drowning. (Retrieved October 7, 2005, from http://en.wikipedia.org/wiki/Keelhauling.)

[8]We are grateful to Leonard Nkosana for this example and to Daniel McNamara for pointing out aspects of its significance.

[9]Further examples of the failure of the shibboleth test to effectively distinguish friend from enemy are given in Horowitz (2001), this time in the context of violent riots in Sri Lanka in 1958 and again in 1983. In the 1958 riots, "a Sinhalese mob sought to distinguish Sinhalese from Tamil victims by requiring a prospective victim to recite Buddhist stanzas in Pali. Most Sinhalese are Buddhists. Tamils are not. As it happened, however, the particular Sinhalese being questioned was a Christian. Unable to oblige the crowd with the recitation, he was murdered" (p. 129).

[10]A shibboleth test has been reported from Algeria (Shell, 2001) and was a feature of the Bruges massacre on March 24, 1302.

[11]See also Heath (1663, p.123): "There were slain [at Worcester] in Field and in Town, and in pursuit some 3,000, and some 8,000, taken prisoners in several places, most of the English escaping by their Shiboleth" (cited in Shell, 2001, p. 2, note 11).

[12]The machine used, known as Mathison's Electropsychometer, is displayed in the Canadian War Museum in Ottawa. An image can be found at http://collections.civilization.ca/public/pages/cmccpublic/emupublic/Display.php?irn=1304464&QueryPage=%2Fpublic%2Fpages%2Fcmccpublic%2Femupublic%2FQuery.php&SearchTerms=cold%20war&lang=0, retrieved June10, 2005.

[13]By the Center for Applied Language Studies at the University of Jyväskylä, on behalf of the Finnish Ministry of Labor.

[14]Tests are conducted at two places in Russia (St. Petersburg and Petrozavodsk) and at Tartu in Estonia.

[15]Croker Island is a small island 225 km northeast of Darwin and 6.5 km by boat from the Cobourg Peninsula. The waters surrounding it were the subject of the first Australian claim to exclusive native rights over the sea, led by plaintiff Mary Yarmirr against the Government of the Northern Territory. The claim was heard in the Federal Court of Australia (NT District Registry, General Division) by Justice Olney: Yarmirr *v* The Northern Territory of Australia [1998] 771 FCA (6 July 1998). Retrieved November 19, 2005 from http://www.austlii.edu.au/.

[16]*The Australian*, April 28, 2003.

[17]The Shan state of Burma borders northern Thailand [authors' note].

[18]Details are available from the Refugee Review Tribunal, RRT Reference: N03/45573 (24 February 2003). Retrieved November 20, 2005 from http://www.austlii.edu.au/au/cases/cth/rrt/N0345573.html.

[19]The Tribunal report of this case states:

> The Shan state in Burma has been in a state of conflict for decades. The World Directory of Minorities describes the "very existence" of the Shan ethnic group as "precarious" and mentions that reports from various internal agencies reveal a consistent pattern of gross violation of human rights by the military authorities, with enslavement and torture manifested in several forms. Document CX66321 in the CISNET data base draws attention to a recent report highlighting the current incidence of rape of Shan women and girls by the Burmese military.

[20]The Hazara ethnolect of Dari, one of Afghanistan's two main languages.

[21]In a letter dated January 5, 1998, written to the Director-General of the Swedish Aliens Appeals Board and the Director-General of the Swedish Migration Board, Professor Kenneth Hyltenstam, Professor of Research on Bilingualism at Stockholm University, and Professor Tore Janson, Professor of African Languages at Göteborg University, wrote:

> We maintain that these "analyses" lack any value whatsoever, inter alia because of the complex linguistic situation that exists in the linguistic regions in question. In addition, it is obvious that those who have done the work do not havesufficient qualifications to conduct a reliable linguistic analysis.

[22]Retrieved August 11, 2005, from http://news.bbc.co.uk/go/pr/fr/-/2/hi/uk_news/4139594.stm.

[23]"English Test Plan for Religious Leaders," *The Age* (Melbourne), December 28, 2004, p.3.

[24]This wording was first used in the Nationality Act of 1940 (Act of October 14, 1940, ch. 876, § 304, 54 Stat. 1140), although according to Winn (2005) the requirement was first introduced between 1906 and 1917.

[25]Plans are well advanced for the introduction of more formal procedures for language assessment as part of citizenship procedures in the United States beginning in 2007.

[26]*The Age* (Melbourne), September 18, 2005. Retrieved November 23, 2005, from http://www.theage.com.au/articles/2005/09/17/1126750170142.html#.

[27]The Australian government has recently announced plans for the introduction of more formal procedures. Retrieved June 4, 2006, from http://www.abc.net.au/news/newsitems/200604/s1625588.htm.

[28]I am grateful to Janna Fox and Guillaume Gentil of Carleton University, Ottawa and Mari Wesche of Ottawa University for their lively comments on an earlier version of this section, which has been substantially revised in the light of their feedback.

[29]The passage of first Official Languages Act in 1969 coincided with the passage of Bill 63 in Québec; Bill 22 (1974) and Bill 101 (1977) prompted the federal government to enact the Canadian Charter of Rights and Freedoms in 1982 (with sections pertaining to the rights of language minorities), the Official Languages Act (1988), and the Multiculturalism Act (1988): cf. Martel (1999). I am grateful to Guillaume Gentil of Carleton University, Ottawa for pointing out these parallels.

[30]Information about the spoken component of the test can be found at http://www.psc-cfp.gc.ca/ppc/sle_pg_01c_e.htm, retrieved June 4, 2006. Useful information about the test and its approach to oral assessment can also be found in Colby (2001), a study of prompt type and elicited discourse in the (English) version of the test taken by francophones.

[31]The issue of the representativeness or justice of aspects of the informants' complaints will be noted at various points in what follows, but the point for the present discussion is made even if we use as data the candidates' subjective, and possibly unfair, perceptions of the test.

[32]Note, however, that all oral interactions are recorded for remarking if candidates wish to contest the level they have been given.

[33]It is not clear how typical this might be. Guillaume Gentil (personal communication April 10, 2006) reports a counter case: "The examiner specifically asked for a simulation where the test taker had to use informal language as if conversing with a friend or colleague (including the use of the 'tu' form, contractions, etc.). This seems to contradict claims about prescriptivism."

[34]Information on which this part of the discussion is based was provided by two civil servant informants in interviews in Ottawa in July 2005 on condition of anonymity.

[35]This was the phrase used in an interview by an anonymous senior executive on December 7, 2005. In practical terms, this circumstance appears to be changing, as the number of people still needing testing is declining: The main "bulge" of executives is now through, and dissatisfaction is reported to be declining as a result.

CHAPTER SEVEN

Language Assessments at School: Social Values and Policy

In this chapter, we will examine a different aspect of test use: the assessment of language in school settings. We will examine how the use of such assessments can be understood in social and political terms, through considering both the cultural values implicit in such assessments as well as their role in the service of overt political goals. Such values and goals influence both the view of what it is important to assess (the construct) and the means for gathering information about it (the assessment procedures). Our argument in this chapter is intended to illuminate two aspects of the social dimension of tests present in Messick's discussion of validity (chapter 2): the social and cultural values present in test constructs and the consequences of test use—both the manipulation of test consequences in the service of political goals, such as accountability or systemic reform, and the unintended fallout from tests. We will again, as with chapter 6, find that we need a range of social theoretical tools to explore the social and political meanings of assessment.

The discussion and critique presented here of the deliberate use of tests to intervene in school systems and to influence the work of teachers and learners is nothing new: The issue has been discussed for centuries, although for a period from the 1950s until relatively recently, it was somewhat obscured within the "scientific" discourse of modern measurement theory. Madaus and Kellaghan (1992), in a useful discussion of the history of the use of tests for this purpose, cite examples from as far back as the 15th century of attempts to influence educational outcomes through payment of teachers according to the success of their students on a public examination. They commented about such examples that

> Testing... was accorded bureaucratic sponsorship as an administrative device to ensure that certain educational outcomes were obtained. Much of the testing that goes on today (particularly mandated, high-stakes testing), its sponsorship, financial base, character, and use, is also essentially bureaucratic and only secondarily educational, or if it is educational, it is educational as conceived by policymakers. (Madaus and Kellaghan, 1992, p. 121)

They also reported a tradition of vigorous criticism of such interventions—for example, the opposition of the eminent figure Matthew Arnold to the Payment by Results schemes in England in the 19th century. As the intervention of policy makers becomes more and more evident and explicit in contemporary education, it is not surprising that critical discussions of the overt and covert purposes of educational tests is again coming to the fore.

Educational systems necessarily reflect the values and aspirations of the societies that they serve, and assessments, which serve the purpose of managing the system, will also reflect those values. Often, however, the social and cultural values that underlie assessment regimes remain inexplicit and only become clear at moments when they are contested (e.g., when there is a proposal for reform of an existing assessment). We will begin the chapter with an example of this from a proposed reform of a key high-stakes test of English language in the Japanese secondary school system. Increasingly, however, the link between assessment and social and cultural values is made explicit in the mandating of assessment as a tool for the achievement of specific political goals. One way in which this has occurred has been the obligation on educational systems to report the outcomes of education to their sponsors against standards that are worded to reflect particular social and political values. These standards thus dictate the construct to be assessed and strongly influence the form of the assessment. In this chapter we will examine in detail the emergence of standards-driven assessment in educational systems in a number of countries as governments pay greater attention to accountability within the management of educational systems.

The focus in this chapter on assessment in the context of school language learning has been chosen in part because the impact of policy on language assessment in the education of adults has been written about more extensively (e.g., Brindley, 1998, 2001). We will begin our discussion by considering two contrasting examples: one, from Japan, in which the values and policy issues within language assessment remain relatively implicit, and the other, from Europe, in which an assessment system, the Common European Framework of Reference for Languages, has been developed and is being implemented as an explicit vehicle of social and educational policies. This will be followed by an examination of the movement to align assessment with standards and the use of tests to monitor outcomes of policies in relation to language education at school. This will be illustrated by an extended discussion of one well-known version of such an intervention: the No Child Left Behind Act of 2001 in the United States.

7.1 Values and Policy Dimensions of Test Constructs

7.1.1 The Japanese Senior High School Entrance Examination in English

We will begin the chapter by examining the issues of values and consequences implicit in the proposal for, and resistance to, the reform of a high-stakes English language examination within Japanese secondary education.[1] We examine differences among the various stakeholders in what the examination represents for them. The proposal to change the examination is revealed as a site of contestation over competing social, cultural, and educational values.

Students in Japan spend 6 years in elementary education, from the age of 6 or 7 to the age of 12 or 13, before moving first to junior high school for 3 years and then to senior high school for an additional 3 years. Entry to preferred senior high schools, which can be very competitive, is controlled by an examination, the senior high school entrance examination, set by the regional Education Board; the format across regions is similar. It consists of five 50-min tests in each of five subjects (Japanese, English, social studies, science, and mathematics). This high-stakes examination continues to have a great impact on students, their parents, and junior high school teachers (Hood, 2001; Sugimoto, 1997; Yoneyama, 1999).

One of the content areas tested is English language. English language education in Japan is provided for students for at least 10 years from junior high school to the university. The style of teaching and what is taught and assessed are laid out in guidelines established by the Ministry of Education, Culture and Science. In the latest guidelines for the teaching of English to junior and senior high school students, the importance of oral language skills is stressed (Ministry of Education, Culture, Sports, Science and Technology, 1998, 1999), in line with government policy to emphasize the importance of speaking skills in the global environment and acknowledging the lack of spoken English skills in Japan (Ministry of Education, Culture, Sports, Science and Technology, 2003). Routinely, English language teaching professionals and leaders of industry in Japan have expressed concern that students who learn English for 10 years from junior high school to the university cannot, in fact, effectively communicate orally in English (e.g., Akashi, 2000; Koike, 2000; Tanabe, 1997). A possible explanation for this failure is the structure of the tests controlling entry to senior high school and to the university in Japan, in neither of which are spoken language skills included. This has the further consequence of hampering the teaching of oral skills in the junior high school, given the importance of preparing students for the senior high school entrance examination. What is at stake, then, in reforming the examination to include the assessment of spoken language skills?

A study by Akiyama (2004) investigated the views of a number of stakeholders on reform of the examination, both those responsible for test policy and test design, on the one hand, and those affected directly by the test as classroom teachers and learners, on the other. In the former category were Ministry of Education officials, academics, and members of the education board responsible for test development; representatives of each of these groups were interviewed in depth. In the latter category were teachers and students in the junior high school preparing for the test and teachers in the senior high school who implement the senior high school curriculum and who would be involved in the administration of any new test of speaking; the opinions of these groups were surveyed by means of a questionnaire.

Broadly, Akiyama (2004) found strong support for the reform among junior high school teachers and their students, who felt that the inclusion of a speaking test would support the goals of the curriculum, but found broad opposition among senior high school teachers, partly on grounds of practicality (a speaking test would be time-consuming and complex to administer and might not be reliable) and partly because they saw speaking skills as irrelevant to the actual content of English teaching in the senior high school. In their own teaching, they paid little attention to speaking, as it was not included in the highly competitive university admissions tests that formed a primary goal of teaching at the senior high school. Moreover, and most relevantly for this discussion, senior high school teachers devalued speaking skills as such altogether. Such opposition was in large part a reflection of deeply held social and cultural values.

Among policy makers and test developers, there was a mixture of support in general terms but widespread practical opposition to the reform. This was partly on administrative grounds and reflected skepticism about the reliability of such a test. Akiyama (2004) demonstrated in his study that the practical concerns about administrative feasibility and reliability could be overcome; what remained, however, were deeper objections reflecting deeply held cultural values in relation to education. It is helpful in understanding this clash of views on reform of the test to locate the culture of examinations in Japan within the broader context of Japanese social, cultural, and educational values.

Japanese cultural values of meritocracy and egalitarian-ism originating in Confucianism are expressed in a merit-based system of competitive examinations: Candidates are differenti-ated purely according to test scores. Moreover, the nature of the examinations is such that in order to score highly, candidates need to demonstrate diligence and the capacity for hard work, along with ability in the subject area. In other words, the un-derlying construct is not communicative proficiency in English, which would represent a functionalist, contemporary value in the era of globalization (see the discussion toward the end of this chapter on implicit cultural values in the PISA reading tests), but, rather, diligence and hard work—attributes valued highly in Japanese society. Knowledge-based examinations play a role in building character through emphasizing the importance of these attributes, which are seen as the basis for selecting on merit (Horio, 1988; Law, 1995). Amano (2000) states that en-trance examinations have played a role in building the character of candidates, so that the elite are selected for attributes that will maintain the status quo. Thus, the actual content of the test and its validity in terms of conformity with the curriculum guidelines (which stress spoken communication skills) are not the central is-sue; what matters is that the test should be difficult and play the role of selecting for character attributes of diligence and effort. In this, we have another striking example of the broader social disci-plinary role of tests as described by Foucault (1975/1977), which was discussed in chapter 6.

These ideological issues are played out at the high school level in the contrasting attitudes of junior and senior high school teachers to the teaching and assessment of spoken communica-tive skills. As we have seen, senior high school teachers reject the focus on speaking, despite the fact that they are supposed to follow curriculum guidelines favoring the development of speak-ing skills in both junior and senior high school. According to Law (1995) and McVeigh (2002), within the cultural context of exam-ination outlined earlier, these teachers prefer to view English as an academic subject at school and its examination as properly noncommunicative, stressing, instead, the memorization of complex rules. Because oral communicative skills in a foreign language are less certainly evidence of academic skills (e.g., they could have been developed by residence in an English-speaking country), a test of *oral* skills does not conform to the traditional notion of a cognitively demanding academic subject.

In summary, we have seen that there are competing values among stakeholders, largely associated with their different roles. For the education board, the introduction of speaking tests constitutes a challenge to the cultural, educational, and administrative values embodied in existing testing practice. Senior high school teachers are constrained by the influence of the university entrance examinations, which reinforce important cultural values very effectively and control senior and junior high school teaching practice; in addition, they might have to change their teaching styles and their teaching values, undermining traditional teaching practice. It seems that the voices of test takers and their teachers are not being heeded in the debate over possible changes to the entrance examination. In effect, the existing entrance examination has been developed by those who are powerful in decision-making, and it reflects their values and interests, although those most affected by it have few avenues to influence the decision-making. The Ministry of Education, whose guidelines make the case for reform, is itself ambivalent, as the values expressed in the guidelines—the emphasis they place on practical communicative competence—cannot be implemented in the classroom because of the effect of other, contradictory policies instituted by the Ministry itself to reduce the amount of time available for the teaching of English in schools. In other words, the guidelines also embody conflicting values: practical and administrative values in the reality, and ideological and political values in the desire.

If we are to understand the feasibility of such a test reform, then we need to consider the social and cultural values and social consequences implicit in the existing and proposed test constructs and to recognize that test constructs can act (as in this case) as a site of social, cultural, and political struggle. Test constructs, as Messick (1996) argued, embody values and, hence, are the site of potential value conflict, as this example clearly demonstrates. If the values and interests of test developers or administrators are expressed in the construct at the expense of the values of other stakeholders more immediately concerned with teaching and learning, this will have negative (potentially quite negative) washback effects on teaching and assessment practices. The fate of the reform in this context is not a question of presenting convincing psychometric arguments and evidence around test use, as envisaged by Kane and Bachman (see chapter 2), but will be the outcome of the political struggle among stakeholders to have their values and interests expressed and supported by the test.

Before concluding this section, it should be stated that the issue discussed here is by no means unique to Japan. Elder (1997a, 1997b) investigated the use of scores from language examinations in the final year of high school in Australia as the basis for decisions about selection for highly competitive university places. She showed how communicative ability in languages is discounted by university admissions authorities if it seems that this ability has come about through naturalistic exposure to the language (e.g., among candidates with any sort of home background in the language) and is only considered relevant if it is the product of hard work and application among "true" second language learners. The underlying construct of the examination, in other words, is not its ostensible construct—communicative language proficiency—but intellectual ability and industriousness. In this, it resembles the Japanese context closely.

7.1.2 The Common European Framework of Reference for Languages

The political goal of introducing a more communicative orientation to foreign language teaching and assessment, which has involved deep questions of social and cultural values in Japan, has been approached in a different way in Europe: through the formulation of a set of standards or goals for language education known as the Common European Framework of Reference for Languages (CEFR) (Council of Europe, 2001).

The CEFR was developed by the Council of Europe, an educational and cultural policy organization that counts as members most of the countries of Eastern and Western Europe (and is independent of the European Union, a more limited grouping of countries). Since the early 1970s, the Council has been involved in the development of policies and materials for teaching the languages of member states as second or foreign languages. It was responsible for the groundbreaking development of the notional/functional syllabus in the early 1970s (Wilkins, 1973), ushering in the European version of communicative language teaching. Further work defined key benchmarks of second language communicative competence along a continuum of development; these included Waystage (Van Ek & Trim, 1998), Threshold (Van Ek, 1975), and Vantage (Van Ek & Trim, 1996), all defined in functionalist terms. These developments reached their culmination in the Common European Framework of Reference for Languages (Council of Europe, 2001). The CEFR defines six levels of proficiency, representing the three levels defined in the earlier work: Waystage, now renamed A2, Threshold (B1), and Vantage (B2); a lower level (A1, Breakthrough, or formulaic proficiency); and two further advanced levels (C1, Effective operational proficiency and C2, Mastery). The two lowest levels (A1 and A2) define the proficiency of the "Basic user"; the next two levels (B1 and B2) define the proficiency of the "Independent user"; the final two levels (C1 and C2) define the "Proficient user." The actual formulation of the wording of the levels of the CEFR involved a complex empirical project of repeated sorting of elements of possible level descriptors in the light of the experience of teachers at various levels (North, 2000; North & Schneider, 1998), using sophisticated statistical procedures (Rasch measurement). The descriptor elements were short, detailed statements of aspects of functional communicative competence, often in the form of "can-do" statements, drawn from a large number of existing scales. These functional descriptors used as the basic building blocks of the scale development faithfully reflect the fundamental underlying construct of the assessment, a 1970s notional/functionalism that was given its clearest expression in the work of Van Ek and Trim.

The initial motivation of the work of the Council of Europe in this area was to permit the transfer of credentialing for language proficiency across national and linguistic boundaries—to allow recognition to be given outside of particular national settings for standards of language proficiency among immigrant workers and professionals. The cultural context of globalization is obvious and accords with the political goals of the organization.[2] According to its Web site,[3]

> The Council of Europe is the continent's oldest political organisation, founded in 1949 ... [It] was set up to ... develop continent-wide agreements to standardise member countries' social and legal practices [and] promote awareness of a European identity based on shared values and cutting across different cultures.

Within the area of education, its mission involves

> Carrying out major projects on education policy, content and methods in and out of school ... Special importance is attached to ... the mutual recognition of competences to improve mobility and employment prospects, and lifelong learning for participation in an international society.

These policy goals are in fact now dominating language education at every level in Europe, in the most comprehensive example of policy-driven assessment yet seen. Its influence is being felt beyond Europe (e.g., in South America), and testing organizations wishing to operate in Europe (e.g., the U.S.-based Educational Testing Service and its Test of English as a Foreign Language [TOEFL]) have had to align their assessments with levels of the CEFR, despite radically different constructs, as a pure political necessity. Funding for reform of school language syllabi even for young children is tied to conformity to the CEFR in more than one European country. The impact of the CEFR and discussion of the adequacy of its underlying construct is one of the most pressing issues in language testing research currently, but discussion has barely begun (Fulcher, 2004).

7.2 Policy Implementation Through Standards

The CEFR reflects certain features of the management of contemporary educational systems. One is the requirement on educational systems by their sponsors that they report the achievement of students using the language of a specified framework of performance standards, which thereby act as the dominant influence on both curriculum and assessment. Another is the definition of those standards in terms that reflect the goal of preparation of a workforce for participation in a globalized and flexible system of production. There is a tendency for governments to use assessment as part of a general climate of greater accountability in education and, more specifically, as a means for the achievement of particular political goals. The politicization of assessment in these ways is perhaps the most striking feature of current developments in language assessment.

In the sections that follow, we will examine detailed examples of language assessments that illustrate these issues. We will begin with an examination of the general character of standards frameworks for guiding language assessment in schools. Standards-based assessments have emerged strongly in the last decade and more in educational systems in the United States, the United Kingdom, Canada, and Australia, where the growth of a managerial culture in education has seen the establishment of measuring systems for monitoring the achievement or nonachievement of educational outcomes as a priority. Funding is often tied to the achievement of agreed goals. Examples of such standards are given in Table 7.1. In the next sections, we will look at the following:

Table 7.1

Examples of policy-based assessment standards relevant to school language learning

Country	Name	Target	Organization	Reference
United Kingdom	National Curriculum for England	School learners, English as mother tongue, and EAL	Department for Education and Employment	DfEE–QCA (2000)
Europe	Common European Framework of Reference for Languages	School and adult learning of languages in Europe	Council of Europe	Council of Europe (2001)
Australia	ESL Bandscales	School learners of ESL	National Languages and Literacy Institute of Australia (NLLIA)	Commonwealth of Australia (1994)
Australia	ESL Scales	School learners of ESL	Australian Education Council, Curriculum and Assessment Committee	Curriculum Corporation (1994)
Australia (Victoria)	Curriculum and Standards Framework (CSF)	School learners, English as mother tongue, and ESL, P-10	Board of Studies, Victoria	Board of Studies, Victoria (1996)

Table 7.1

Continued

Country	Name	Target	Organization	Reference
Australia (South Australia)	ESL Scope and Scales	School ESL learners, P-10	S.A. Department of Education, Training and Employment	South Australia (2002)
Canada	Toronto Benchmarks	School language learners	Toronto Board of Education	Toronto Board of Education (1988)
United States	ESL standards	Pre-K–12 learners of ESL	TESOL	TESOL (1998)

- the format and structure of statements of standards

- the conceptual organization of standards (the construct)

- the process of their development

- the processes by which evidence of achievement against the standards is gathered.

7.3 Standards: Format and Structure

Standards are typically formulated as an ordered series of statements about levels of achievement or stages of development. (There might be multiple sets of ordered statements for different aspects of language development.) Usually, the statements at each level or stage will have more and less condensed versions, depending on the specific function of the assessment information, which might include, in addition to accountability, helping teachers with planning and assisting in their professional development by mapping the typical progress of learning over time (McKay, 2000). Program administrators in educational bureaucracies using standards for *accountability* need *summative* information (e.g., the number of students at a given level in a particular school at any one time), and in this case, the standard need only be expressed quantitatively. For this purpose, levels of achievement are given a simple code, usually a number. For purposes of reporting to parents or other members of the school community, short summary statements for each level, usually no more than one or two sentences long, might be most appropriate. For teachers and learners, more detailed statements of the strands in the description of each level (defining various aspects of language development such as discourse forms, formal linguistic features, range of vocabulary) are necessary, particularly where the assessment is *formative* (e.g., where it is used for diagnostic purposes). With learners from diverse backgrounds and for very young learners in the early stages of learning, additional contextual information might be given (level of support, cultural background of the learner, mother tongue language skills in bilingual learners, etc). At a more detailed level still, specific lesson-related assessment contexts might be suggested in which particular types of behavior relevant to the standard are likely to be observed (see, e.g., Lumley, Mincham, & Raso, 1994). Thus, standards often have a pyramidal format, a kind of Russian dolls solution, with the innermost doll being the most condensed and most general, as in Figure 7.1; claims are formulated at different grain size levels for the different audiences for whom the assessment is designed to provide information. A major challenge for a system of assessment is to balance the competing interests of different audiences in the formulation of standards.

7.4 Standards: Conceptual Organization (the Construct)

In standards-based assessment, the wording of the standards is determined by and is expressive of the policy goals that they are intended to serve. As we saw in the chapter on validity, the construct of an assessment can be understood as the claims we wish to make about learners and the general nature of the evidence required in order to support those claims. The standards

LEVELS

SHORT SUMMARIES

COMPLETE SUMMARIES

SUMMARIES WITH COMMENTARY

SUMMARIES WITH COMMENTARY AND EXAMPLES

CONTEXTUALIZED ASSESSMENT ACTIVITIES AND CRITERIA

Figure 7.1. The assessment pyramid.

constitute the terms in which claims about learners will be made; hence, they represent the construct of the assessment. Despite this, the relationship of the wording of standards to the political goals that they serve is complex and not fully explicit, and it only becomes clear in the light of conceptual analysis of the standards and their organization and how this relates to policy.

A clear example of this comes from adult language education in Australia in the form of the Certificate of Spoken and Written English (CSWE) (Hagan et al., 1993), the standards framework used within the Adult Migrant Education Service. In the 1980s, as part of a vocational training reform known as the competency movement, brought about by the demands of the rapidly changing workplace, the Australian federal government introduced a national certification framework for the recognition of training that stressed the demonstration of observable performance outcomes. All federal government funding for vocational education, including that of adult migrants, was tied to reporting of outcomes of training in terms of this framework, the organization and components of which were rigidly prescribed in accordance with the underlying competency-based philosophy. Until that time, the Adult Migrant Education Service had used a proficiency-based assessment scheme: the Australian Second Language Proficiency Ratings (ASLPR; Ingram & Wylie, 1979), which assumed an underlying psycholinguistic construct of proficiency; neither this construct nor the organization of its description of proficiency levels reflected the competency-based philosophy, and it was abandoned in favor of the CSWE, which reflects the prescribed organization very closely. Intellectual objections to the competency-based philosophy as it applied to language were dismissed because the construct underlying the new assessment scheme was mandated by government policy.

Within the school context, standards will reflect views of the relationship of language to the school context, particularly the curriculum context. For example, within the English subject in the former Curriculum and Standards Framework (Board of Studies, Victoria, 2000), the following aspects of performance were described separately for each macroskill: texts, contextual understanding, linguistic structures and features, and strategies. The first two of these imply a social orientation to language and the need to define its relationship to the curriculum. The TESOL ESL Standards (Teachers of English to Speakers of Other Languages, 1998) deal separately with three types of functional goal: to use English to communicate in social settings, to use English to achieve academically in all content areas, and to use English in socially and culturally appropriate ways. The choice between competing views of language will often reflect policy considerations ahead of general educational ones, as the following discussion will show.

Academic research into language and literacy is only one, and not necessarily the most important, source of input into language and literacy standards. Nevertheless, current theoretical understandings of the skills involved are important for a number of reasons. Some theoretical positions are more amenable to policy imperatives in relation to assessment than others and might be favored for that reason. In the best cases, up-to-date understandings are used to formulate standards that may have a progressive and beneficial impact on the work of teachers and learners.

7.4.1 Competing Views of the Construct: Literacy

Policy-based assessment has often focused on literacy standards, and these reflect views of the development of literacy in the context of schooling. This development is the subject of ongoing academic debate, of which Freebody and Gilbert (1999) and de Lemos (2002) provided useful summaries. De Lemos contrasts sociocultural and cognitive-psychological approaches. The former sees literacy as developing "through exposure to literacy practices within a particular environment" so that it "cannot be separated from its social and cultural context" (p. 3) (as in the well-known ethnographic study by Heath, 1982, 1983, on the different English literacy practices of three very different sociocultural communities within the United States). This yields what de Lemos

describes as a broader definition of literacy. Associated developments have been the work on the social development of mind inspired by Vygotsky (Assink, 1994; Gee, 2003; Olson, 1994), which
links literacy development and cognitive development, and the
movement known as critical literacy (cf. Hammond & Macken-
Horarik, 1999; Luke, 1993, 1996; Luke, Comber, & Grant, 2003;
Street, 1995), which draws its inspiration from critical theory and
aims to develop in students an ability to evaluate critically the
social function of texts.

Of particular interest here is the attempt to define the literacy demands of school subjects. One relatively successful attempt to do this has been the work of the Sydney genre school,
which draws on the socially and contextually oriented linguistics
of Michael Halliday (Christie, 1998; Halliday & Martin, 1993;
Martin, 1989, 2000; Painter, 1996). Significant advances have
been made in understanding the demands of various academic
genres at school, both spoken and written, at the primary school
and at the secondary level. One appealing feature of the work of
the Sydney school is that the linguistic demands of schooling are
defined in terms that are common to both first (L1) and second
(L2 or additional) language learners.

The narrower definition of literacy, according to de Lemos
(2002), views literacy as the ability to read and write and focuses
on "the specific processes that underlie the acquisition of reading
and writing, and the ways in which these processes can be en-
hanced by specific teaching" (p. 3). These processes include the development of phonemic (phonological) awareness and recognition
of spelling/sound correspondences, and they are seen as crucial in
the development of reading and writing. The most comprehensive
source for this view is the lengthy report of the National Reading
Panel (2000) in the United States.

The assessment implications of the two approaches are strikingly different, not only in the content of what will be assessed
but also the method of assessment. The sociocultural approach
defines the domain of reading achievement broadly, and stresses

the culture-specific nature of classroom literacy practices, and the relation of literacy to the broader curriculum. It also stresses the origins of writing in speech and emphasizes oral language development as part of its definition of literacy. This is particularly important for learners who are meeting the school language as a second or additional language, as oral language development will be particularly important for them; oral language development is an underdeveloped side of most approaches to mother-tongue language education. More progressive frameworks will include relevant oral genres for both L1 and L2/additional language learners (Leung & Teasdale, 1997). In terms of assessment method, this approach suggests observational methods sensitive to context and judgment of performances in context. This is not to say that such an approach automatically guarantees validity—far from it. The approach has recently been the basis for a standards-based curriculum and assessment scheme in schools in South Australia (South Australia, 2002; see also Matthiessen, Slade, & Macken, 1992; Mincham, 1995). (It is worth commenting in passing that a weakness of this work has been a tendency to claim "objectivity" for the assessment as a matter of principle rather than of empirical investigation [McNamara, 1997], ignoring the necessary element of judgment and subjectivity that teachers bring to the assessment, and which must be acknowledged in order to control for unreliability.)

The cognitive-psychological approach is more consonant with earlier work within the psychometric tradition and emphasizes objective tests of the discrete underlying components of reading skills. This approach is more commonly reflected in some of the standardized tests used for systemic monitoring and control in the current managerial emphasis on outcomes in education systems. The administrative convenience and reliability of these measurement methods thus determine the choice of construct to be measured, rather than that choice being determined by evidence and argument alone. This is a particularly important issue in the literacy assessments mandated under the

U.S. No Child Left Behind Act of 2001, to be discussed in detail in section 7.7. Only quantitative measures of achievement from standardized tests are permitted as evidence of achievement under that policy.

7.4.2 Catering for Second/Additional Language Learners in Policy-Driven Literacy Assessments

Another major conceptual and policy issue in the formulation of standards is the question of whether there is a need for separate assessments for learners of the language of schooling as an L2 or additional language. Some educational systems make no provision in standards frameworks for L2/additional language learners because of complex administrative and policy reasons. The resulting difficulty for teachers of subjects across the curriculum in responding to the needs of such learners in a system that is officially blind to them and the way in which teachers working with national curriculum documents can be made more aware of the needs of these learners have been studied in England by Leung (1999, 2005) and Rea-Dickins (2001). In England and Wales,[4] the authorities responsible for curriculum and assessment—the Qualifications and Curriculum Authority (QCA) and the Department for Education and Skills (DfES)—until recently refused to acknowledge that learners of English as an additional language (EAL learners) should be assessed differently from English as a first language (EFL) learners. Officially, at present, all EAL learners are assessed in common with mother-tongue learners for purposes of national assessments. However, different local education authorities (LEAs) have introduced local systems of dealing with EAL learners for their own purposes, leading to a plethora of different descriptive frameworks used across the country, none of which is recognized by the government. The most important independent development of this kind is a national scheme run by the Northern Association of Support Services for Equality and Achievement (NASSEA) (Northern Association of Support Services for Equality and Achievement, 2001), which has produced a scale relevant to EAL learners.

A further issue is the need to match assessments to the level of cognitive maturity of EAL learners independently of their proficiency levels. In 2000, a new policy, set out in a document entitled *A Language in Common* (Qualifications and Curriculum Authority, 2000), introduced two levels for EAL learners below the lowest level at which mother-tongue learners are assessed. Note that this is not an appropriate solution for new arrivals at the secondary level, who have a different level of cognitive and emotional maturity. Cognitive maturity needs to be taken into account in the definition of standards, particularly where contextual information is provided; the complicating factor is that we cannot make assumptions about the cognitive maturity of beginning learners, as new arrivals in a country might be beginner learners of the L2/additional language at any age, depending on when they arrive. Thus, there is a need for different scales for learners who begin learning at different ages: Ingenious solutions have been found to this problem in some settings (e.g., as reflected in the standards developed within Victoria, Australia; Board of Studies, Victoria, 2000).

In Australia, the situation with regard to L2 learners is complex, with some state policies defining separate standards for L1 and L2 learners and other federal policies resisting this. At the state level (e.g., in Victoria), curriculum pathways for both groups of learners were defined, as was the point at which L2/additional language learners were ready to be assessed in common with L1 learners (e.g., in the work of the curriculum and assessment authorities in Victoria, Australia; Board of Studies, Victoria, 2000), although this framework has now been replaced by a different set of standards required under a further change in policy (Victorian Curriculum and Assessment Authority, 2005). Moore (2005a, 2005b) has examined the policy conflict underlying the federally funded development of two opposing sets of standards for English as a second language (ESL) learners in Australian schools in the 1990s. One set recognized the special needs of ESL learners and drew on teachers' insights into the characteristics of learner language and skill at various developmental levels; the other emphasized equality of outcome regardless of learner background (L1 or L2) and opposed the construction of ESL learners as having special needs. The differing assumptions behind the two projects were associated with markedly differing methodologies for the development of standards, their conceptual organization, and the terms in which they were expressed. The latter set of standards prevailed for political reasons against the advice of the most senior members of the ESL profession in Australia. This case illustrates well the way in which constructs in standards-based assessments are expressions of values, and the battle over whose values will prevail is determined not essentially by the intellectual merits or academic currency of the constructs involved, but on political grounds. The case parallels in certain respects the Japanese example at the beginning of this chapter, in which test constructs were the site of struggle over values, a struggle that was not resolvable by validity research, but through normal political processes.

The issue of L1 and L2 learners being assessed in common has become important in the United States in the standardized testing required under the No Child Left Behind policy (Kunnan, 2005). Various accommodations have been tried by school systems to deal with learners of ESL who are required to take part in assessments designed for L1 speakers (Butler & Stevens, 2001). Although more appropriate assessments for L2 learners are required to be conducted and instruments for this purpose have been developed as a complement to this, the fundamental problem of how to deal with L2 learners remains. We will consider the impact of this policy in detail in section 7.7.

7.5 Standards: The Process of Formulation

The most comprehensive survey of the formulation of standards is provided by North (in press). Standards are formulated by a variety of methods and often lack an empirical basis. Although academic input into the conceptualization of standards is possible, crucial decisions about the content and form of assessments and issues of construct validity are not, in the end, determined on the basis of research, but of policy. We might call all such approaches in which policy determines the wording of standards on a priori grounds "top-down" approaches to scale development, varying in degree of politicization. The formulation of many language and literacy standards is explicitly political in character (academics played little role, for example, in the formulation of the standards that are the basis for the No Child Left Behind policy, to be discussed in a later section). Language test validation research in such cases might have an impact through the sheer power of its reasoning but only to the extent that it is useful, or is itself politicized. Standards are often formulated by committees representing the most important players or by researchers sensitive to the policy context on behalf of such committees. These researchers might subsequently be required to negotiate the acceptability of the proposed standards on behalf of the commissioning interests (cf. Trim, 1997, on the negotiation of the wording of the Council of Europe framework [Council of Europe, 2001] to relevant stakeholders).

In contrast to this are a variety of "bottom-up" approaches, which use empirical data of varying kinds as the basis for the construction of scales. Data from test performances in reading were used to validate a theoretically well-informed reading scale in the important work of Kirsch and Mosenthal (1990) on the assessment of adult literacy in the United States. Data from teachers formed the basis of North and Schneider's (1998) scaling of descriptors that informed the development of the Common European Framework of Reference for Languages, although as we have seen the assumptions of earlier work of the Council of Europe acted as a powerful constraint on the methodology used in the development of the framework.

7.6 Standards: Gathering Evidence—Teacher Assessment and Formal Tests

How can evidence of learner achievement in relation to policy goals be gathered? Many policy-driven assessments use teachers as agents for this purpose; others use standardized tests; still others use a combination of the two, with varying degrees of co-ordination and conflict between the two practices.

7.6.1 Teacher Assessment

Many standards-based systems rely on teacher assessment as one source of data for reporting on achievement at the level of the individual, class, school, region, or system. Teacher assessment is also the central focus of what is sometimes called assessment for learning (Black, Harrison, Lee, Marshal, & Wiliam, 2003), which standards frameworks also support in many (but not all) educational systems. Rea-Dickins (2004) provides evidence on the way in which teachers act as agents for assessment. The difficulty of reconciling the needs of accountability with the needs of teachers and learners in classrooms is documented by Brindley (1995) and Breen et al. (1997) in Australia and by Rea-Dickins, Gardner, and Clayton (1998), Gardner and Rea-Dickins (1999) and Teasdale and Leung (2000) in England. Problems include (a) the tendency of teachers to teach to outcomes at the expense of proper curriculum planning, (b) failure to take into account relevant contextual information in interpreting performance against the standards, (c) the wide range of interpretation and use of standards, and (d) difficulty in achieving psychometrically reliable assessments from aggregated teacher assessments. Teasdale and Leung framed this last point in terms of a paradigm clash between the conflicting demands of psychometric measurement theory and constructivist approaches to assessment, known generally as alternative assessment. The very notion of generalizability of assessment inferences, seen as so fundamental to validity, can paradoxically hamper the potential of assessment to serve the needs of teachers and learners. The need for assessments to be comparable—the basis for reliability—places constraints on classroom assessment, particularly in the area of communicative skill (speaking and writing), which most teachers cannot meet (Brindley, 2000). Moreover, any attempt to meet such demands constrains the possibilities of assessment in the classroom. Nevertheless, most of the above-cited authors stressed the benefits to teachers of the articulation of teaching targets and the detailed advice about assessment that at its best, accompanies curriculum and standards frameworks (Board of Studies, Victoria, 2000; Office for Standards in Education, 2003a, 2003b). We urgently need to explore ways in which assessment concepts can be better used in classrooms to benefit learning and teaching (Leung, 2005; McNamara, 2001). Important advances have been made in England through the work of the Assessment Reform Group[5], particularly in the work of Paul Black and Dylan Wiliam (Black & Wiliam, 1998; Black et al., 2003).

7.6.2 Formal Tests

As an alternative or supplement to teacher assessments, educational systems use a variety of formal tests of language and literacy development at key points in schooling to monitor the extent to which standards are being met. Often, a single psychometric agency at the provincial or national level has the responsibility for devising new tests specifically targeted at the standards—for example, the Qualifications and Curriculum Authority (QCA) and the National Foundation for Educational Research (NFER) in England, the Australian Council for Educational Research in Australia, and Educational Testing Service or private testing companies in the United States. At other times, educational authorities will resort to the use of existing, commercially available off-the-shelf tests whose validity for the purpose is often unclear. The relationship of these externally imposed standardized tests to teacher assessment within the curriculum is a matter of heated debate in virtually every setting in which such an arrangement has been established (for treatment of the extensive controversy in the Australian context, see Dilena & van Kraayenoord, 1995, 1996). The issue is acute in the early years of learning. Antagonism toward formal testing is a feature of many primary school teachers in Britain and Australia, at least: in the words of Teasdale and Leung (2000): "at primary level ... the culture of objective testing is inimical to the beliefs about primary teaching held by many teachers" (p. 175). The desirability of external standardized testing is also highly controversial where there are learners for whom the language of the school is an L2/additional language and/or when it is done with school populations in socially deprived areas (e.g., for the controversies in the United States, see Heubert & Hauser, 1999; Linn, Baker, & Betebenner, 2002).

In this section, a short summary will be given of some of the standardized tests used in various settings.

In the United States, the National Assessment of Educational Progress (NAEP) has carried out systemwide monitoring for some years. However, this testing involves sampling from populations of interest, rather than universal testing, and is not meant to identify the strengths and weaknesses of individual learners. In fact, it has for a long time been associated with progressive developments in standardized testing, including a greater range of test tasks, an emphasis on performance assessment, and the use of advanced psychometric techniques to give greater interpretability and transparency of test scores in terms of curriculum goals. The situation changed radically in 2001 with the passing of the No Child Left Behind (NCLB) Act, mandating statewide annual testing of (among other things) English language reading for grades 3–8. All students are tested. The impact of this policy will be discussed in detail at the end of this chapter.

In Canada, the province of Ontario has introduced standardized assessments operated by the Education Quality and Accountability Office (EQAO) to yield a report card on educational progress. Curriculum-based tests used include the Ontario Secondary School Literacy Test (OSSLT) for literacy in the secondary school (grades 9–11).

In England and Wales, the National Curriculum defines four Key Stages of learning (1–4). At each stage, there are standardized national assessments: Key Stage 1: levels 1 and 2; Key Stage 2: levels 3 and 4, and so on, up to level 8. In Key Stages 1 and 2, the assessments are in the core subjects: English, Mathematics, and Science. The assessments are called SATs (Standard Attainment Tests). By age 7, the predicted average level is 2; by age 11, the predicted average level is 4. In addition to these tests, a wide variety of standardized tests is used for other purposes. For example, the British Picture Vocabulary Scale (BPVS), based on the American Peabody Picture Vocabulary Test, is a standardized measure of receptive vocabulary that has been empirically tested on both English L1 and additional language speakers by the NFER (National Foundation for Educational Research). It is used to monitor progress of EAL learners in some areas, the data being used in the bidding process for grants to support EAL learners in the early years.

In Australia, assessments are made against Literacy Benchmarks at national (Curriculum Corporation, 2000; Masters & Foster, 1997) and state levels. Various kinds of standardized assessments are used. In Queensland, for example, information from the Year 2 Net "is used to determine whether students participate in Reading Recovery or receive support through other withdrawal and in-class programs, or are grouped or streamed for instruction" (van Kraayenoord, 2003, p. 281). Evaluation of this program is available in van Kraayenoord, Luke, Elkins, and Land (1999) and Young and Fletcher (2000). The controversial public reception of a test used in Victoria, the Learning Assessment Project, is discussed by Lynch (1997). The Australian Council for Educational Research carries out the Western Australian Monitoring of Standards in Education (WAMSE) on behalf of the government of that state.

7.6.3 Formal Tests and the Evaluation of Policy Initiatives

In the rest of this chapter we will consider in detail three further aspects of the role of formal language tests in the delivery and evaluation of educational policy. We will begin with an example of the integration of formal testing and teacher-based assessment in the evaluation of the success of a national initiative in language education: the National Asian Languages Strategy in Australian Schools (NALSAS) evaluation project. We will then examine the cultural and political assumptions behind an international comparative survey of L1 literacy achievement (the Program of International Student Assessment [PISA]), conducted on behalf of the Organisation for Economic Co-operation and Development (OECD). We will conclude with an examination of the impact of the assessment of literacy under the U.S. government's initiative on school achievement, the No Child Left Behind Act of 2001.

7.6.4 The NALSAS Evaluation Project

Language assessment might play a variety of roles in the execution of school language policy (Hill & McNamara, 2003). In many cases (e.g., the No Child Left Behind policy and the National Curriculum Key Stage assessments in England and Wales), tests operate as the "stick" used to ensure conformity with government policy goals. In the following example, tests play a slightly different role, as the means of evaluation of the success or otherwise of a policy initiative: the promotion of the learning of Asian languages in Australian schools. In the evaluation project, an attempt was made to integrate teacher assessment and formal testing in the measurement of proficiency outcomes in two of the Asian languages concerned (Hill, Iwashita, McNamara, Scarino, & Scrimgeour, 2003). The project also shows how teacher views can be fully incorporated into language assessment policy development.

Given its geographical location, the Australian government's policy since at least 1990 has promoted the study of Asian languages at school, to the point where Japanese and Indonesian for a number of years have rivaled traditional European languages such as French and German as the most popular languages learned in school. In some parts of the country, the study of these languages is commenced in primary schools (covering the first 7 years of education, from kindergarten to year 6). As part of the evaluation of its policy promoting the study of Asian languages in schools, the Australian government wanted to establish whether the considerable expenditure in support of the policy had yielded measurable achievements in terms of learner proficiency. A complicating factor is that educational provision is not the responsibility of the federal government itself but of the eight states and territories of Australia, each of which has three distinct educational systems (government, Catholic, and independent non-Catholic). There was a need then for coordination between these many different educational systems to agree on a single nationally agreed set of measures to evaluate the outcomes of student learning. The project therefore aimed to develop nationally agreed Key Performance Measures (KPMs):

- for two Asian languages: Indonesian and Japanese

- at two transition points: the end of primary schooling (years 6/7) and the end of compulsory foreign language learning (year 10).

Given the diversity of provision (three different education systems in each of eight states and territories), each with its own curriculum and assessment frameworks, it was decided to use Mislevy's framework (Mislevy, 1996; Mislevy, Steinberg, & Almond, 2002, 2003; see a discussion of this framework in chapter 2 of this volume) to organize the discussion of existing commonalities and possibilities for agreement across systems (Figure 7.2).

Through an intensive series of consultations and workshops, administrators and teachers were engaged in discussions of how claims were to be formulated, the kinds of evidence that would support these claims, and the way that evidence would be captured in task design. The KPMs are the claims. The project went beyond claims, however, to evidence and broad task design, and in the discussions of the latter, opportunities for this evaluation project to serve the needs of teachers and learners were built in. It was agreed that there would be a mix of external standardized

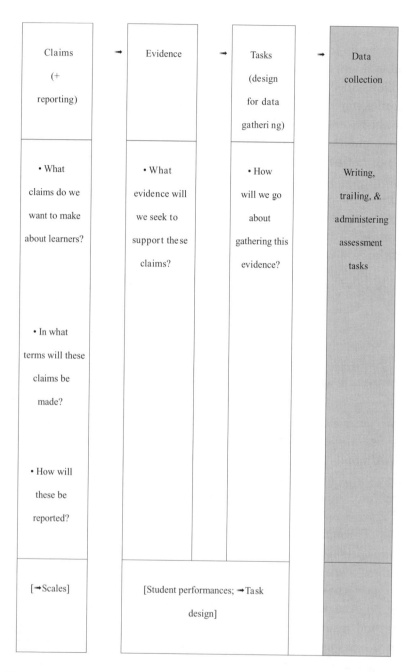

Figure 7.2. Key Performance Measures for the Asian Languages Project.

test measures for the skills of listening, reading, and writing, but that these would be supplemented by further writing and speaking tasks that would be more locally relevant and delivered by teachers, but assessed externally using an agreed common set of scoring criteria. In addition, student training in self-assessment would be a feature of any data gathering, as aggregated self-assessments have been shown to be sufficiently reliable to constitute further evidence of system-level (not individual-level) achievement. In this way, in addition to this assessment serving external management purposes, it had the potential to be of lasting benefit to teachers and learners. It was found that those participating in the project related easily to this broad framework, and the project was completed successfully. The project did not require the actual development, trialing, and administration of the tests to be used (the shaded section of Figure 7.2), but the blueprint for their development had been agreed.

7.6.5 *Policy-Related International Comparative Assessments: PISA*

In addition to the national or regional assessment schemes discussed so far in this chapter, a series of international comparative evaluations of educational achievement (e.g., studies carried out for the International Evaluation Association [IEA]) have involved the development of standardized assessments of school literacy. The most important of these is the Program for International Student Assessment (PISA), developed for the OECD (Organisation for Economic Co-operation and Development, 1999, 2000, 2002).

The thinking about the test construct in PISA is set out in the form of a framework document, *Measuring Student Knowledge and Skills: A New Framework for Assessment* (Organisation for Economic Co-operation and Development, 1999), which provides a basis for detailed content specifications for formal tests intended to yield measures of the construct. In line with the broader goals of the organization, a "forum where the governments of 30 market democracies work together to address the economic, social and governance challenges of globalization as well as to exploit its opportunities" (Organisation for Economic Co-operation and Development, 2005, p. 7), the intention of the PISA literacy survey is to consider readiness for work and ability to handle work-related literacy tasks. This is done in the interests of promoting a competency-based approach to education, part of a larger OECD policy. Taking this as a policy "given," the theoretical treatment of the cultural dimension of reading is sparse in the framework document; instead cultural issues are treated as practical and administrative "problems" that need resolution. The aim of the project was to enable cross-national comparisons of reading performance; thus, the performances had to be comparable and the solution was to use identical (translated) texts. The process for text selection was as follows: National teams from the participating countries could suggest texts for inclusion in the reading measures, which, if chosen, were then translated into the languages of the participating countries for administration in those countries (McQueen & Mendelovits, 2003). Because none of the texts could be so culturally specific as to render them unsuitable for assessment of literacy in another cultural context, the texts chosen had to occupy a supposedly culturally "neutral" space, independent, in particular, of local curricula. In fact, this meant that texts chosen reflected the literacy practices of the emerging global monoculture of industrially and technologically advanced urbanized societies. The project committed itself to the use of authentic texts, but, obviously, given the international scope of the project, this would mean the rejection of texts that were culturally specific in content or genre. Whereas 45% of items used in the reading test were contributed from non-English language sources, fewer than 4% were contributed from non-European language sources (McNamara, 2000). The project has had a huge impact on educational systems in participating countries. For example, the performance of German students reading in German ranked relatively low. It has been suggested by those familiar with the German education system (M. Clyne, personal communication, May 5, 2004) that the relatively poor results for

Germany might be an artifact of the test, as the kinds of functionalist, pragmatically focused text used in the assessment were untypical of those used in reading tests within the German education system, which have a more literary bias. Nevertheless, the results caused consternation in Germany and triggered efforts to reform the teaching of reading in Germany (Ehlich, 2005), in readiness for a future assessment.

7.7 Standards and Impact: The No Child Left Behind Act and ESL Learners

Whereas policy-related language tests are obviously intended to achieve the educational and social outcomes targeted by the policy, it is important to consider actual outcomes independently of the policy makers' intentions. It is possible that the tests might have both intended and unintended outcomes. As we saw in chapter 2, investigating the consequences of test use is a fundamental requirement of Messick's approach to validity (Messick, 1989). Writers have made a distinction between two sorts of consequence: the effect on the language teaching and learning leading up to the test, which is termed *washback* (Alderson & Wall, 1993, 1996; Bailey, 1996; Cheng, 1997; Cheng, Watanabe, & Curtis, 2004; Messick, 1996; Watanabe, 1996), and effects beyond the immediate language learning situation, which is termed *impact* (Hamp-Lyons, 1997; Wall, 1997). (Note that although these terms are of recent currency in the language testing literature, in particular following the publication of the important article by Alderson and Wall, the concepts, as we noted at the beginning of this chapter, are of venerable ancestry.) Both washback and impact can involve intended and unintended consequences; the unintended consequences can be positive or negative (intended consequences are naturally framed in positive terms). Research into test impact has to consider both. In what follows, we will consider some aspects of the impact of the U.S. government's policy of literacy testing in schools known as No Child Left Behind (NCLB).

In 2001, the U.S. government enacted the No Child Left Behind Act, a comprehensive legislative framework requiring states to define instructional standards, monitor the quality of school education through statewide assessments, report findings publicly, and improve schools that perform below standard. Although the effects of NCLB reverberated throughout many aspects of each state's educational system, we will focus here on the impact on ESL students of the implementation of this policy.

7.7.1 The NCLB Itself[6]

The main thrust of the NCLB is the establishment of academic standards, standardized assessments, and accountability measures including sanctions for schools not performing to standard. The implementation of the NCLB is the responsibility of the states, and states have a great deal of leeway in setting standards and designing assessments. However, the NCLB mandates certain benchmarks, which are obligatory for all states, school districts, and individual schools.[7]

The law currently focuses on two *content* areas: reading combined with English language arts, on the one hand, and mathematics, on the other. Science is to be added as a third content area. The accountability provisions in the NCLB require yearly, statewide tests in grades 3–8 and one test for grades 10–12 (Yell & Drasgow, 2005) in the content areas of reading/English language arts and mathematics. Results are to be reported at the school, district, and state levels for the entire population of students at each grade level tested. Results are also disaggregated for students of lower economic status, major ethnic groups, students with disabilities, and ESL learners. It is important to note that ESL learners must be included in the reading/English language arts and mathematics assessments, and although "reasonable" accommodations can be made for their limited English proficiency, they cannot be excluded. In fact, all public schools in a state must test 95% of their students using the state-mandated tests, including 95% of students in the disaggregated subgroups.

Test accommodations for ESL students could consist of more time, instructions in students' native language, or testing in the native language (although students who have attended U.S. schools for more than 3 years must be tested in English in reading/English language arts). Butler and Stevens, 2001, discuss the kinds of accommodation that are currently used. There is additional, separate monitoring of progress in ESL proficiency whereby states also have to develop specific proficiency standards for ESL learners together with appropriate ESL assessment instruments by which they must report learner progress annually, but this does not affect the involvement of the learners in the *content* assessments and the requirements for ESL learners as a group to show progress in content domains.

Test content is to be tied to state-developed standards and performance objectives, and sanctions come into effect if these objectives are not met in the two focal areas of reading/English language arts and mathematics. States can develop tests for other areas, but performance in those areas does not lead to sanctions. Importantly, a school is subject to sanctions even if just *one* of the four disaggregated subgroups performs below standard.

Performance standards are set from a statewide baseline in the 2001/2002 school year. Each subsequent year, the number of students meeting proficiency standards must increase by a set amount, so that by the school year 2013/2014, all students have reached proficiency. For example, if in a given state, 40% of students reached a "proficient" designation in reading/English language arts as a baseline in 2001, these numbers must increase, on average, by 5% every year for the following 12 years, so that by 2013, 100% of students in the state are designated proficient. Therefore, 1 year after the baseline testing, at least 45% of students in every school, district, and the entire state, as well as in every disaggregated subgroup, must reach proficiency. In the following year, 50% must reach proficiency, and so forth. In addition, the state imposes a "second indicator" of academic performance: This can be determined locally at the elementary level (e.g., attendance), but graduation rates are mandated as the indicator at the secondary level.[8] If a school reaches the yearly proficiency quota for its entire student body and all disaggregated subgroups and meets the state requirements on the second indicator, it is considered to make Adequate Yearly Progress (AYP).

Adequate Yearly Progress is an all-or-nothing proposition, and if a school does not make AYP in either reading/English language arts, mathematics, or the second indicator for 2 consecutive years, an escalating series of sanctions takes effect. As a first step, the school is identified as a "needs improvement" school, and parents are given the option of transferring their children to a better performing school in the same district. The school must also develop an improvement plan. If the school does not meet the standard for another year, it must arrange free tutoring for students. If the school fails to meet standards again the following year, it must take major corrective action (e.g., replace staff, extend the school day or year, or appoint an outside adviser). Upon not meeting standards for a subsequent year, the school must develop a plan to restructure its governance arrangements (i.e., become a charter school, turn itself over to a private management company, or plan some similar, drastic change, which basically means that it would no longer exist in its original form). Finally, if it fails to meet standards yet again the next year, it has to implement the restructuring plan.

Monitoring is also obligatory for ESL assessments, but direct consequences are much less grave: If a school district fails to make adequate progress with its ESL students for 4 years, the state must initiate curriculum reform or changes in instructional approaches in that district. Of course, as we will discuss in the following subsection, the indirect consequences of less-than-effective ESL instruction can be very serious, because students with little *language* competence are likely to score low on the *content* assessments, thereby endangering a school's AYP.

7.7.2 The Law's Impact: Consequences Intended and Unintended

It is easy to see the dramatic effect that assessment has in the accountability-driven world of NCLB. Although the ESL assessments do not lead to serious sanctions, the mandatory inclusion of ESL learners in the test populations that determine the AYP has powerful effects and poses some serious practical problems.

For one thing, the classification of a student as an ESL learner is quite unclear in the NCLB itself, so that operational definitions are at the discretion of the states and even individual school districts. As Abedi (2004) showed, the correlation of students' classification with their scores on the standardized Language Assessment Scales (LAS) is low, accounting for less than 5% of the variance. In addition, the educational background of a student's parents tends to be a stronger predictor of English proficiency than classification by native/nonnative speaker status: In a study by Abedi, Leon, and Mirocha (2003), ESL students whose parents had postgraduate degrees outperformed native English-speaking students whose parents had less than a high school education. This reflects a great deal of heterogeneity in the ESL population, which, in turn, exacerbates a problem specific to this population: transitory group membership.

Of all the subgroups whose performance impacts a school's AYP rating, the ESL population is the one whose group membership is most in flux. Although it is quite unlikely that large numbers of students would cease to be classified as "low income" from one year to the next and while it is nearly impossible to move out of populations defined by disability and race, a given student can cease to be a member of the ESL population if that student passes an ESL proficiency test at a level of "proficient." This means that the students with the highest English proficiency leave the group, and it is likely that these students would also score high on content assessments, simply because they have less trouble following classroom instruction. Their absence depresses the average scores of the ESL group on the content assessments, and these scores are further lowered because new students joining the population are likely to be recent immigrants, whose language proficiency is low and who, consequently, are also more likely to receive low scores on content assessments. Abedi (2004) demonstrated this effect statistically and showed a widening score gap on a reading and mathematics assessment between the population classified as ESL and students who have "tested out" of the ESL group. Some states have tried to solve this problem by including former ESL students in the scores for the ESL population for 2 more years after these students have reached proficiency in English and are no longer receiving ESL services.

At the same time, measures that would identify "proficient" students are notoriously difficult to develop and operationalize. Different states have taken different pathways to deal with the requirements of NCLB in this regard—some using standardized, norm-oriented tests and others commissioning the development of new tests.

The test used in New York State, the New York State English as a Second Language Test (NYSESLAT), illustrates the difficulty of defining exit criteria from ESL programs. In 2005, a stark contrast emerged between satisfactory exit proficiency as defined by NYSESLAT (achieved by 7% of learners) and a supposedly comparable criterion on the English Language portion of the State's Regents exam, governing university admission (achieved by over 50% of the same learners). This led to protests when students who passed the Regents exam and had been offered places at universities were still unable to pass the NYSESLAT at a level of "proficient". While there may be good reasons for this discrepancy from a measurement perspective, it is difficult to explain to those impacted by the tests.

7.7.3 ESL Learners in the Larger Student Population

Given the importance of ESL learners' performance for the AYP, a potentially serious problem is the possible lack of suitability of content assessments for ESL populations. Abedi (2004), using data from a population of nearly 300,000 students, showed that Cronbach's α reliability for the mathematics, language, science, and social science sections of the Stanford 9 test is between .1 and .2 lower for ESL students than for English-only students.

Only for the mathematics section is the ESL students' reliability above .8, and it is lowest on the social science section, at a worrying .53. This indicates that standardized assessments, which are usually developed and normed with native-speaker populations, are not equally appropriate for ESL learners and measure their content knowledge imprecisely. However, NCLB forces states to use the same assessments for every population and leaves it to the states' discretion to what extent they accommodate ESL learners.

Because schools are dependent on the ESL group for making the AYP, a paradoxical situation can arise at the school level with regard to graduation rates (Losen, 2005). Because graduation rates are not disaggregated by subgroup, a school at risk of not meeting the AYP in one of the subgroups (e.g., ESL) could try to reduce its population of very low-scoring ESL students by encouraging them to drop out. Graduation rates would decline only negligibly, but scores for the remainder of the subgroup would thereby rise, allowing the school to make the AYP, but this approach, of course, would terribly disadvantage the ESL students who left and would in fact reward a school for shedding learners who need instruction the most, whereas a school that tried to serve its ESL population regardless of scores might be placed in the "needs improvement" category.

In addition to these direct and unenvisioned consequences of NCLB, it has also impacted other content areas (e.g., foreign language teaching). Based on a survey of 1,000 public school principals in four states, Rosenbusch (2005) shows a marked decline in time devoted to foreign language instruction in schools with large populations of minority students and a concomitant increase in class time focused on reading/English language arts and mathematics.

Evans & Hornberger (2005) similarly document the impact of NCLB on federally funded bilingual education programs. Their view is stark:

> All of this changed dramatically with the introduction of the *No Child Left Behind Act* in 2002. Current policy implicitly repeals the Bilingual Education Act and

emphasizes the need for schools to quickly develop students' English language proficiency and move them to
English-only classrooms. (p. 88)

They argue that *"No Child Left Behind* is likely to have only
a negative impact on the education of language minority students,
given its failure to incorporate research-based understanding of
the necessary and optimal conditions for English language learners' language and literacy development" (Evans & Hornberger,
2005, p. 103), particularly its neglect of, even tacit opposition to,
any role for support for the child's L1 in language and literacy
development in the L2.

Despite this, Evans and Hornberger (2005) do concede the
potential of NCLB to impact positively on language minority students, even though they are pessimistic on the most likely actual
outcome:

In the final analysis, the inclusion of language minority
students in overall educational accountability requirements might have potential dividends for their academic
achievement, if adequate provision were made for facilitating and assessing their language acquisition and bilit-
eracy learning. (p. 103)

As Freeman and Riley (2005) pointed out, NCLB has produced some beneficial effects for ESL learners and has the potential to lead to a marked improvement in ESL services. Prior
to the rigorous accountability provisions that NCLB introduced,
school districts tended to focus on monitoring compliance with
regulations rather than ensuring that actual learning took place.
Under NCLB, the stakes have risen significantly, and it is now
in the best interest of all education providers to increase students' ESL proficiency rapidly without isolating them from content teaching. At the very least, this has thrown a spotlight on
the ESL group, which previously often subsisted in the darker re-
cesses of the educational landscape. Additionally, states now have
to become serious about designing ESL standards, implementing

suitable assessments, and training teachers to assist ESL students effectively.

As Evans and Hornberger (2005) put it:

> ESL teachers are likely to have conflicting thoughts about *No Child Left Behind*. On the one hand added attention paid to English language learners, the added support that ESL teachers may receive, and the additional funds, however small, dedicated to services for English language learners may be seen as beneficial. (p. 100)

Data from interviews with a small number of teachers and program administrators in southern Oregon confirmed this:

> The ESL coordinators and the Migrant Education/ESL staff were happy about the increased attention paid to English language learners in the area's schools. Money that previously would have gone into the general fund is now dedicated to materials and services for students with limited English proficiency, and ESL teachers and associated personnel are receiving more support. District superintendents and school principals have become more concerned about students' increased English proficiency and academic achievement and are supporting professional development activities, unseen in the past, in relation to teaching English language learners. (p. 101)

At the time of writing, it seems as if political opposition to NCLB is growing in some quarters; it is the subject of critique from state education systems and has attracted much negative media. It is significant that the fate of this reform is determined through policy processes, rather than academic critique. Ironically, Evans and Hornberger (2005) express some regret over this:

> Inhibiting factors to the *No Child Left Behind Act's* achieving favourable outcomes include the recent backlash against the law from many agents at the institutional level—state departments of education, state legislatures and news media in particular. (p. 103)

If NCLB were to have an impact, it would be because of the increased visibility of ESL learners through their identification by means of tests, an issue that, as we have seen, emerges in the different context of Australia in the work of Moore (2005a, 2005b). The use of tests as means of identification and Foucault's analysis of the role of tests in the construction of identities in modern systems of government return as a relevant theme in this case, too.

7.8 Conclusion

This chapter has examined the way in which language assessments in educational systems serve social, cultural, and political goals. Often, the social and political character of language assessments is implicit; however, increasingly, governments and other agencies are using assessment in the furtherance of explicit policies of social engineering. This might take the form of educational standards against which student achievement is assessed as part of a method of ongoing monitoring of the performance of systems in delivering desired outcomes. Language assessments can serve additional purposes of evaluating the success of specific initiatives in language education designed to meet national social, educational, and political goals. The impact of politicized language assessment systems can be profound and involve unintended as well as intended consequences. The politicization of assessment has implications for validity theory, because the political imposition of test constructs means that they are not amenable to or subject to influence by the validation processes fundamental to discussions of test validity. On the other hand, they confirm Messick's view of the importance of social context in assessment, both in terms of the values embodied in assessment schemes and in the need to attend to the social consequences of their implementation. Yet, even here, discussions within the scope of validity theory need to be supplemented by social analysis of a different kind: the sort of cultural critique that is the subject matter of contemporary social theory. In particular, the work of

Foucault continues to have great relevance to understanding the social dimension of language testing.

Notes

[1]This section is based on research conducted for the Ph.D. thesis of Akiyama (2004), which is gratefully acknowledged.

[2]A clear parallel can be seen in a language assessment project known as PISA, developed on behalf of the Organisation for Economic Co-operation and Development (OECD) and which will be discussed later.

[3]Retrieved January 10, 2006, from http://www.coe.int/T/e/Com/about_coe/.

[4]I am grateful for the help of Pauline Rea-Dickins for the material on England and Wales in this section.

[5]Retrieved June 8, 2006, from http://arg.educ.cam.ac.uk/.

[6]Our overview of the NCLB is necessarily abbreviated. For a thorough and highly readable account, see Yell and Drasgow (2005).

[7]From the beginning, the NCLB has been controversial because it is perceived by many as an unprecedented expansion of federal influence in the educational domain (Sunderman, Kim, & Orfield, 2005), which has always been within the control of the states.

[8]However, graduation rates are only computed for a school's entire student population, not by subgroup.

CHAPTER EIGHT

Where to From Here? Implications for Research and Training

The broad argument of this book suggests that language testing is at a difficult juncture. A discipline whose intellectual sources are fundamentally asocial, in measurement, psychology and a linguistics that focused on individual cognition, has found itself lacking effective tools to conceptualize, acknowledge, and confront the social dimension of assessment either at the microlevel (of face-to-face interaction) or at the macrolevel, the social context in which test use occurs. Although the social dimension of assessment might not be such a pressing issue in the measurement of other areas (although we have shown the general function of assessment, not only language assessment, as crucial to the subjectivity of individuals in contemporary society), the fact that language is so inextricably part of the fabric of, indeed constitutive of, social and cultural life, and of face-to-face interaction has meant that the paradigmatic one-sidedness of conventional approaches to assessment comes into particularly sharp focus in language testing.

In chapter 2, we set out these issues in general terms in a discussion of validity theory in educational measurement generally and how this has been taken up in language testing. We noted there the way in which early versions of validity theory (e.g, in Cronbach's work on educational measurement) set out certain grounds for the social responsibility of testers by emphasizing that tests were inferential procedures and thus could never be objective; hence, they were inherently potentially unfair. In general theoretical terms, this took up a concern that had long been practically recognized—for example, in Edgeworth's study of the unreliability of written examinations (Edgeworth, 1888) and the extensive work on this subject in Hartog and Rhodes (1936). Validity theory set out a general approach to conceiving of threats to fairness and empirically investigating the extent of their impact on scores. There was a belief not in the perfectibility of the fairness of tests, but that recognition of the "inevitable uncertainty" of tests (Edgeworth, 1890, p. 660) would lead to efforts to reduce it to manageable proportions, or at least to alert test users to the degree of uncertainty associated with any scores. Such a view was unlikely to be reflected in the public reception of tests, where, as Spolsky (1995) in particular has reminded us, enthusiasm for their use as managerial tools on the part of those wishing to control the process and goals of education has triggered concern about the social function of tests ever since their appearance in Europe in the 15th century and particularly in the 19th and 20th centuries, when they were universally taken up as a means of "guard[ing] the gates that lead from elementary to intermediate and secondary education, from secondary education to the Universities, the professions, and many business careers, from the elementary and middle stages of professional education to professional life" (Hartog & Rhodes, 1936, p. vii). Although validity theory investigated the technical qualities of tests in the interests of fairness, it did not address the wider social function of tests, and as procedures for understanding and, to a certain extent, controlling the unreliability of tests became more sophisticated, the broader question of their use became less and less salient. A concern for test use reemerged from a different source: the study of the evaluation of educational programs, particularly in the work of Cronbach, and this eventually became grafted onto the theory of validity, particularly in the hugely influential work of Messick. However, despite Messick's efforts to build a unitary approach to validity that acknowledged the social meaning of tests, validity theory has remained an inadequate conceptual source for understanding the social function of tests.

The general structure of the argument of the volume derives from the discussion in chapter 2. In the first part of the volume (chapters 3–5), we looked at the social dimension of testing from within the psychometric tradition, in order to demonstrate its capacities and its limitations. In chapter 3, we examined test constructs, looking at challenges to language testing presented by formulations of the social dimension of language proficiency, represented most clearly by the communicative movement. We considered theoretical and practical difficulties in the testing of spoken language in face-to-face interaction and the assessment of pragmatic competence. In chapter 4 we surveyed a range of methods within psychometrics for addressing group-related sources of unfairness in tests, through investigation of bias, differential item functioning, and the impact of variables associated with the rating process in performance assessments. In chapter 5 we considered other processes addressing issues of social fairness in tests, including fairness review, and the formulation of codes of ethics and codes of practice for test developers and test users, again within the general constraints of validity theory as currently developed.

In the second part of the volume (chapters 6 and 7), we broadened the focus to examine test use within its social context. In chapter 6 we considered an extreme use of language tests: to determine who will be the object of violence. We did this not only in order to dramatize the consequential nature of language test use but also because the use of tests for purposes of identification and boundary maintenance is enduring and widespread and only recently acknowledged in the language testing literature. We examined such uses in the contemporary contexts of debates over immigration, refugee flows, and citizenship. In order to understand the role of language tests in defining the subjectivity of those to whom they are directed, we turned to the work of Foucault on the role of examinations in modernity. In chapter 7 we returned to test constructs, showing their essentially political character. We did so by considering the way in which test constructs can represent a site of struggle over social values (e.g., when test reform is proposed). We then examined the challenges to validity theory presented by the increasingly explicit politicization of language testing and language test constructs, with particular reference to schooling contexts. We examined the way in which control over reporting, in the form of performance standards and assessment frameworks, yields effective control of educational systems: a recent example of a centuries-old tradition of the control of education through tests.

Whereas the aim of the volume has been to begin to sketch the nature of the dilemma facing language testing research, it raises the question, Where to from here? In the following sections, we summarize the implications of our discussion for research in the field and for the training of the next generation of those wishing to carry out research in language testing.

8.1 Directions for Research

The work of defining the social dimension of language assessment from within the existing psychometric tradition that we have sketched here is only a beginning. Although the volume has stressed the limitations in principle of conventional approaches to measurement, that is not to say that much that is valuable in practice can not be done within the existing paradigm. At the most general level, language testing research will continue to monitor and contribute to the discussion of validity in educational assessment. The very rootedness of language in social and cultural life and the role of language assessments in implementing policies on education, immigration, employment, and citizenship, which we have seen as a challenge to current work from within validity theory, also mean, ironically, that language testing has much to contribute to validity debates—for example, in response to recent moves to strip validity theory of its concern for values and consequences and to take the field back 80 years to the view that a test is valid if it measures what it purports to measure (Borsboom, Mellenbergh, & van Heerden, 2004). The relatively recently established journal *Measurement*, which does not report empirical work but publishes agenda-setting articles followed by a series of commentaries by leading figures in measurement in different fields, offers scope and a forum for debates of this kind.

There is, of course, also ample scope for empirical work within a conventional measurement framework. For example, there is a need for more work on test bias. Very little has actually been done in language testing to investigate bias in language tests, and we also know far too little about what induces bias: How does the interaction between test taker and item lead to differential functioning of items? Verbal protocols of test takers answering items could be useful in investigating this. Which groups of test takers are truly disadvantaged in terms of the construct? Our usual binary divisions by gender or first language (L1) family are not motivated by research and are, in any case, the subject of critique in contemporary theories of gender; we need greater insight into the role of gendered and other socially constructed identities on test performance. Additionally, how can existing bias detection methods be adapted for small samples, as we are usually dealing with in language testing?

Further, there are a number of emerging research areas that fall within the general rubric of the social dimension of assessment. We will list two that we have not so far discussed but that represent a cutting edge of research issues in the field. The first is the measurement of learning potential in terms of eventual attainment and rate of development. For example, language tests for entry to educational or employment settings often focus on tasks with which the candidate might not always be expected to be familiar, particularly when they occur in a new cultural setting. Assessments that are more sensitive to the issue of readiness to develop would have great appeal in such settings. The issue of potential for growth in language ability is a central concept in language aptitude testing, but its social aspects have been underemphasized and little attention has been paid to aptitude for discoursal aspects of cross-cultural communication and to the ability to learn from interactions. It is, indeed, the latter that is fundamental to language learning, as a great deal of opportunity for language learning occurs in socially interactive settings—most notably through conversations with native speakers or other learners—and learners' ability to learn from others through modeling, perceiving recasts, and noticing the gap is a crucial predictor of language learning success. Little work exists on identifying aptitude for learning from interaction, and some of it is still fundamentally individualistic-cognitivist, focusing on the learner and deemphasizing the social setting (Robinson, 2002a, 2002b; Skehan, 2002). Another strand is informed by Vygotskyan cultural-historical psychology or sociocultural theory (Lantolf & Thorne, 2006) and explores the potential of dynamic assessment (Lantolf & Poehner, 2004; Sternberg & Grigorenko, 2002), which explicitly measures a learner's ability to profit from intervention. The potential of this approach has been explored for many years in special education (Feuerstein, 1979), where it has helped identify differing potentials for growth in children with apparently similar levels of disability. However, work on learners' ability to profit from interaction and different kinds of intervention is still in its earliest stages and deserves ongoing attention.

The second topic under the heading of emerging issues in the social dimension of language assessment is the status of the native speaker norm and, in particular, the testing of English as a lingua franca (Canagarajah, 2005; Davies, Hamp-Lyons, & Kemp, 2003; Elder & Davies, in press; Jenkins 2000, 2006; Seidlhofer, 2001, 2004; Taylor, 2006). As the use of English in international communication increasingly involves only nonnative speakers in many settings, the relevance to this communication of relatively distant native speaker norms is increasingly questioned. The topic raises complex sociolinguistic, policy, cultural, and political issues that are only beginning to be explored; we can expect to hear much more on this important topic.

Work on testing language use in social context could use an infusion of testing experts with a strong knowledge of discourse analysis. There is a simultaneous need for research on performance-oriented tests that measure *ability for* social language use and knowledge-oriented tests that measure *knowledge about* social language use. Especially pressing is the need to understand better the relationship between the two. However, even within those two areas, we still know relatively little about the strengths and limits of role-plays and oral proficiency interviews, especially how to make the latter actual measures of conversational ability rather than spoken language samples. We also need more research on testing of sociopragmatic knowledge and design of discourse completion tests for testing purposes.

We are relatively less convinced of the beneficial impact of codes of ethics in language testing. The whole testing enterprise is too scattered and diversified in this increasingly global and mobile world economy to respond to the same ethical prescriptions. The lack of enforceability for any code in a profession like language testing makes codes of ethics or practice little more than broad aspirational documents. We are not suggesting that work on ethics be abandoned in language testing—far from it—but we are uncertain whether the codification of ethical principle will have any measurable impact on the field.

Moving beyond the parameters laid out within current theories of validity, even progressive ones such as those of Messick and Kane, to investigate the social meaning of tests and their social impact takes us into relatively uncharted waters theoretically. The problem here is that we need an adequate social theory to frame the issues that we wish to investigate. The most productive and relevant of these theories are not only relatively unfamiliar to language testers but in fact challenge many of the fundamental epistemological and ontological assumptions of the field and thus require intellectual stamina and confidence to negotiate. However, as the true social impact of language tests slowly dawns on us, this research becomes more and more urgent and significant. Current work on language testing in relation to immigration and citizenship needs to be more and more informed by relevant social and policy theories. In the context of inflamed international tensions (e.g., in the recruitment of language testers within defense establishments) the involvement of language testers in the implementation of language policy is a subject ripe for debate and deeper understanding.

What this means is that language testing will become a broader and more diverse field because it will be unlikely that any single researcher or group of researchers will be able to be sufficiently on top of the range of relevant intellectual fields. Although this will lead to less coherence, it will make the field more socially and intellectually responsive and less isolated from other areas of applied linguistics and the humanities. This is important, as language testers are in a position to offer informed, detailed reports and analyses from crucial sites of institutional power and to produce work that has the potential to inform debate in wide areas of the humanities. Because language has become more central to social theory and because language testing is a prime disciplinary site within contemporary society, this renewed and broadened research within language testing is likely to be of interest well beyond the immediate field in which it is conducted.

8.2 Implications for Training

The argument we have made here so far implies that the relatively narrow intellectual climate of language testing research will need to be broadened, with openness to input from such diverse fields as sociology, policy analysis, philosophy, cultural studies, social theory, and the like, in addition to the traditional source fields. This will mean that efforts will have to be made to break down the disciplinary walls between language testing researchers and those working within other areas of applied linguistics, social science, and the humanities generally. For example, the current practice of holding workshops prior to major international research conferences on language testing that focus exclusively on technical issues will have to be supplemented by, if not replaced with, workshops on a host of sources of ideas relevant to the new perspectives that we are emphasizing. More socially oriented fields within linguistics and applied linguistics will also have a particularly important role, especially various schools of discourse and analysis, particularly Conversation Analysis, as argued in Brown and McNamara (2004).

In terms of academic training, we stress the importance of a well-rounded training for language testers that goes beyond applied psychometrics. We are in no way advocating the abandonment of training in psychometrics and second language acquisition, as we do believe that testers have to be well versed in psychometric theory, quantitative research methods, research on second language learning, and test construction and analysis. However, we are also advocating a training that includes a critical view of testing and social consequences, whether those effects concern the educational sector (college admission, school graduation) or society at large (immigration, citizenship, security, access to employment). All of this would mean that language testing professionals have a broader training than psychometricians but one that is not as deep in the psychometric aspects of testing. We see this as unproblematic, however, and indeed unavoidable: Language testing is not simply applied psychometrics, but, rather, a central area of applied linguistics. The increasingly important social roles of language tests that we have outlined in this volume mean that understanding language tests and their effects involves understanding some of the central issues and processes of the contemporary world.

References

Abedi, J. (2004). The No Child Left Behind Act and English language learners: Assessment and accountability issues. *Educational Researcher*, *33*(1), 4–14.

Abedi, J., Leon, S., & Mirocha, J. (2003). *Impact of student language background on content-based performance: Analyses of extant data* (CSE Tech. Rep. No. 603). Los Angeles: University of California, National Center for Research on Evaluation, Standards and Student Testing.

Akashi, Y. (2000). Language and peace. In AILA '99 Tokyo Organizing Committee (Ed.), *Selected Papers from AILA '99 Tokyo* (pp. 27–31). Tokyo: Waseda University Press.

Akiyama, T. (2004). *Introducing speaking tests into a Japanese Senior High School entrance examination*. Unpublished doctoral dissertation, The University of Melbourne.

Alderson, J. C. (1981). Report of the discussion on General Language Proficiency. In J. C. Alderson & A. Hughes (Eds.), *Issues in language testing. ELT Documents 111* (pp. 187–194). London: British Council.

Alderson, J. C. (2000). *Assessing reading*. Cambridge: Cambridge University Press.

Alderson, J. C., & Wall, D. (1993). Does washback exist? *Applied Linguistics*, *14*, 115–29.

Alderson, J. C., & Wall, D. (Eds.). (1996). *Washback* [Special issue]. *Language Testing*, *13*(3).

Amano, I. (2000). Admission policies in Japanese universities. *JLTA Journal*, *3*, 30–45.

American Educational Research Association. (1999). *Standards for educational and psychological testing*. Washington, DC: Author.

American Psychological Association. (2002). *Ethical principles of psychologists and code of conduct*. Retrieved February 22, 2006, from http://www.apa.org/ethics/code2002.html

Angoff, W. H. (1982). Use of difficulty and discrimination indices for detecting item bias. In R. A. Berk (Ed.), *Handbook of methods for detecting test bias* (pp. 96–116). Baltimore: Johns Hopkins University Press.

Angoff, W. H. (1993). Perspectives on differential item functioning methodology. In P. W. Holland & H. Wainer (Eds.), *Differential item functioning* (pp. 3–24). Hillsdale, NJ: Lawrence Erlbaum Associates.

Anrig, G. R. (1987). ETS on "Golden Rule." *Educational Measurement: Issues and Practice, 6,* 24–27.

Assink, E. M. H. (Ed). (1994). *Literacy acquisition and social context.* Hemel Hempstead, UK: Prentice Hall Harvest Wheatsheaf.

Association of Language Testers in Europe. (1994). *The ALTE code of practice.* Retrieved March 26, 2006, from http://www.alte.org/quality_assurance/index.cfm

Association of Language Testers in Europe. (2006). *Introduction to ALTE.* Retrieved April 5, 2006, from http://www.alte.org/about_alte/index.cfm

Austin, J. L. (1962). *How to do things with words.* Oxford: Oxford University Press.

Bachman, L. F. (1990). *Fundamental considerations in language testing.* Oxford: Oxford University Press.

Bachman, L. F. (2004). *Statistical analyses for language testing.* Cambridge: Cambridge University Press.

Bachman, L. F. (2005). Building and supporting a case for test use. *Language Assessment Quarterly, 2,* 1–34.

Bachman, L. F., Davidson, F., Ryan, K., & Choi, I. C. (1993). *An investigation into the comparability of two tests of English as a foreign language: The Cambridge-TOEFL comparability study.* Cambridge: Cambridge University Press.

Bachman, L. F., & Palmer, A. S. (1996). *Language testing in practice: Designing and developing useful language tests.* Oxford: Oxford University Press.

Bailey, K. (1996). Working for washback: A review of the washback concept in language testing. *Language Testing, 13*(3), 257–279.

Baker, F. B. (1981). A criticism of Scheuneman's item bias technique. *Journal of Educational Measurement, 18,* 59–62.

Bessette, J. (2005). *Government French language training programs: Statutory Civil Servants' experiences.* Unpublished master's thesis, University of Ottawa, Canada.

Billig, M. (1999a). Conversation Analysis and the claims of naivety. *Discourse and Society, 10*(4), 572–587.

Billig, M. (1999b). Whose terms? Whose ordinariness? Rhetoric and ideology. *Discourse and Society, 10*(4), 543–558.

Binet, A., & Simon, T. (1916). *The development of intelligence in children.* Baltimore: Williams & Wilkins.

Birrell, R., & Hawthorne, L. (1999). *Skilled migration outcomes as of 1996: A contribution to the review of the independent and skilled-Australian linked categories being conducted by the Department of Immigration and Multicultural Affairs.* Canberra: Department of Immigration and Multicultural Affairs.

Black, P., Harrison, C., Lee, C., Marshall, B., & Wiliam, D. (2003). *Assessment for learning: Putting it into practice.* Maidenhead: Open University Press.

Black, P., & Wiliam, D. (1998). Assessment and classroom learning. *Assessment in Education, 5*(1), 7–74.

Blackledge, A. (2005). *Discourse and power in a multilingual world.* Amsterdam: John Benjamins.

Blommaert, J. (2001). Investigating narrative inequality: African asylum seekers' stories in Belgium. *Discourse and Society, 12*(4), 413–449.

Blum-Kulka, S., House, J., & Kasper, G. (Eds.). (1989). *Cross-cultural pragmatics: Requests and apologies.* Norwood, NJ: Ablex.

Board of Studies (Victoria). (1996). *Using the CSF: Assessment and reporting.* Carlton, Victoria, Australia: Author.

Board of Studies (Victoria). (2000). *The ESL companion to the English CSF.* Retrieved March 15, 2006, from http://www.eduweb.vic.gov.au/curriculumatwork/csf/es/koes-g.html

Bond, L. (1993). Comments on the O'Neill & McPeek paper. In P. W. Holland & H. Wainer (Eds.), *Differential item functioning* (pp. 277–280). Hillsdale, NJ: Lawrence Erlbaum Associates.

Borsboom, D., Mellenbergh, G. J., & van Heerden, J. (2004). The concept of validity. *Psychological Review, 111*(4), 1061–1071.

Bouton, L. (1988). A cross-cultural study of ability to interpret implicatures in English. *World Englishes, 17*, 183–196.

Bouton, L. (1994). Conversational implicature in the second language: Learned slowly when not deliberately taught. *Journal of Pragmatics, 22*, 157–167.

Bouton, L. (1999, March). *The amenability of implicature to focused classroom instruction.* Paper presented at TESOL 1999, New York.

Boyd, K., & Davies, A. (2002). Doctors' orders for language testers: The origin and purpose of ethical codes. *Language Testing, 19*(3), 296–322.

Breen, M. P., Barratt-Pugh, C., Derewianka, B., House, H., Hudson, C., Lumley, T., et al. (1997). *Profiling ESL children: How teachers interpret and use national and state assessment frameworks: Key issues and findings* (Vol. 1). Canberra: DEETYA.

Brennan, R. L. (2001). *Generalizability theory.* New York: Springer.

Breslow, N. (1981). Odds ratio estimates when the data are sparse. *Psychometrika, 46*, 443–460.

Brindley, G. (1998). Outcomes-based assessment and reporting in language learning programs: A review of the issues. *Language Testing, 15*, 45–85.

Brindley, G. (2000). Task difficulty and task generalisability in competency-based writing assessment. In G. Brindley (Ed.), *Issues in immigrant English language assessment* (Vol. 1, pp. 45–80). Sydney: National Centre for English Language Teaching and Research, Macquarie University.

Brindley, G. (2001). Outcomes-based assessment in practice: Some examples and emerging insights. *Language Testing, 18*(4), 393–407.

Brindley, G., & Wigglesworth, G. (Eds.). (1997). *access: Issues in English language test design and delivery*. Sydney: National Centre for English Language Teaching and Research, Macquarie University.

British Council, IDP: IELTS Australia, & University of Cambridge ESOL Examinations. (2005). *International English Language Testing System (IELTS): Handbook*. Cambridge: Cambridge ESOL.

Brown, A. (2003). Interviewer variation and the co-construction of speaking proficiency. *Language Testing, 20*(1), 1–25.

Brown, A. (2005). *Interviewer variability in language proficiency interviews*. Frankfurt: Peter Lang.

Brown, A., & McNamara, T. (2004). "The devil is in the detail": Researching gender issues in language assessment. *TESOL Quarterly, 38*(3), 524–538.

Brown, J. D. (1999). The relative importance of persons, items, subtests and languages to TOEFL test variance. *Language Testing, 16*(2), 217–238.

Brown, J. D. (2001). Six types of pragmatics tests in two different contexts. In K. Rose & G. Kasper (Eds.), *Pragmatics in language teaching* (pp. 301–325). Cambridge: Cambridge University Press.

Brown, J. D., & Hudson, T. (2004). *Criterion referenced language testing*. Cambridge: Cambridge University Press.

Buck, G. (2001). *Assessing listening*. Cambridge: Cambridge University Press.

Butler, F. A., & Stevens, R. (2001). Standardized assessment of the content knowledge of English language learners K–12: Current trends and old dilemmas. *Language Testing, 18*(4), 409–427.

Butler, J. (1990). *Gender trouble: Feminism and the subversion of identity*. New York: Routledge.

Cahill, D., Bouma, G., Dellal, H., & Leahy, M. (2004). *Religion, cultural diversity and safeguarding Australia*. Canberra: Department of Immigration and Multicultural and Indigenous Affairs and Australian Multicultural Foundation.

Calvet, L.-J. (1998). *Language wars and linguistic politics* (M. Petheram, Trans.). Oxford: Oxford University Press. (Original work published 1987).

Cameron, D. (1999). Communication skills as a gendered discourse. In S. Wertheim, A. Bailey, & M. Corston-Oliver (Eds.), *Engendering communication*. Berkeley, CA: Berkeley Women and Language Group.

Cameron, D. (2001). *Working with spoken discourse*. London: Sage.

Camilli, G., & Shepard, L. A. (1994). *Methods for identifying biased test items*. Thousand Oaks, CA: Sage.

Canagarajah, S. (2005, August). *Changing communicative needs, revised assessment objectives*. Paper presented at the AILA Congress, Madison, WI.

Canale, M. (1983). From communicative competence to communicative language pedagogy. In J. C. Richards & R. W. Schmidt (Eds.), *Language and communication* (pp. 2–27). London: Longman.

Canale, M., & Swain, M. (1980). Theoretical bases of communicative approaches to second language teaching and testing. *Applied Linguistics*, *1*(1), 1–47.

Chalhoub-Deville, M. (2003). Second language interaction: Current perspectives and future trends. *Language Testing*, *20*(4), 369–383.

Chalhoub-Deville, M., & Deville, C. (2004). A look back at and forward to what language testers measure. In E. Hinkel (Ed.), *Handbook of research in second language teaching and learning* (pp. 815–831). Mahwah, NJ: Lawrence Erlbaum Associates.

Chapelle, C. A. (1994). Are C-tests valid measures for L2 vocabulary research? *Second Language Research*, *10*(2), 157–187.

Chapelle, C. A. (1998). Construct definition and validity inquiry in SLA and research. In L. F. Bachman & A. D. Cohen (Eds.), *Interfaces between second language acquisition and language testing research* (pp. 32–70). Cambridge: Cambridge University Press.

Chapelle, C. A., Enright, M. K., & Jamieson, J. (2004, March). *Issues in developing a TOEFL validity argument*. Paper presented at the Language Testing Research Colloquium, Temecula, CA.

Chen, Z., & Henning, G. (1985). Linguistic and cultural bias in language proficiency tests. *Language Testing*, *2*(2), 155–163.

Cheng, L. (1997). How does washback influence teaching? Implications for Hong Kong. *Language and Education*, *11*, 38–54.

Cheng, L., Watanabe, Y., & Curtis, A. (2004). *Washback in language testing: Research contexts and methods*. Mahwah, NJ: Lawrence Erlbaum Associates.

Christie, F. (1998). Learning the literacies of primary and secondary schooling. In F. Christie & R. Misson (Eds.), *Literacy and schooling*. London: Routledge.

Clapham, C. (1996). *The development of IELTS. Studies in Language Testing, 4.* Cambridge: UCLES/Cambridge University Press.

Clapham, C. M., & Corson, D. (Eds.). (1997). *Language testing and assessment: Encyclopaedia of language and education* (Vol. 7). Dordrecht: Kluwer Academic.

Cleveland, J. (1658). *The rustick rampant, or, rurall anarchy affronting monarchy in the insurrection of Wat Tiler.* London: Printed for F. C. and are to be sold at Westminster-Hall and the Royall Exchange.

Cohen, J. (1988). *Statistical power analysis for the behavioral sciences.* Hillsdale, NJ: Lawrence Erlbaum Associates.

Colby, C. (2001). *An investigation of two types of question prompts in a language proficiency interview test and their effects on elicited discourse.* Unpublished master's thesis, McGill University, Montréal.

Commonwealth of Australia. (1994). *ESL development: Language and literacy in schools project* (2nd ed.). Canberra: National Languages and Literacy Institute of Australia/Department of Employment, Education and Training.

Contenté, J. (1978). *L'aigle des Caraïbes.* Paris: Robert Laffont.

Cook, H. M. (2001). Why can't learners of JFL distinguish polite from impolite speech styles? In K. Rose & G. Kasper (Eds.), *Pragmatics in language teaching* (pp. 80–102). Cambridge: Cambridge University Press.

Cooper, R. L. (1968). An elaborated language testing model. *Language Learning* (Special issue No. 7), 57–72.

Corcoran, C. (2003, August). *The role of linguistic expertise in asylum applications: A case study of a Sierra Leonean asylum seeker in the Netherlands.* Paper presented at the Conference of the Society for Pidgin and Creole Linguistics, Hawai'i.

Coulmas, F. (Ed.). (1981). *A Festschrift for native speaker.* The Hague: Mouton.

Council of Europe. (2001). *Common European framework of reference for languages: Learning, teaching and assessment.* Cambridge: Cambridge University Press.

Crawford, F. M. (1900). *The rulers of the south: Sicily, Calabria, Malta.* London: Macmillan.

Cronbach, L. J. (1971). Validity. In R. L. Thorndike (Ed.). *Educational measurement* (2nd ed., pp. 443–597). Washington, DC: American Council on Education.

Cronbach, L. J. (1988). Five perspectives on the validity argument. In H. Wainer & H. I. Braun (Eds.), *Test validity* (pp. 3–18). Hillsdale, NJ: Lawrence Erlbaum Associates.

Cronbach, L. J. (1989). Construct validity after thirty years. In R. L. Linn (Ed.), *Intelligence: Measurement, theory, and public policy* (pp. 147–171). Urbana: University of Illinois Press.

Cronbach, L. J. (1990). *Essentials of psychological testing.* New York: Harper Collins.

Cronbach, L. J., Ambron, S. R., Dornbusch, S. M., Hess, R. D., Hornik, R. C., Philips, D. C., et al. (1980). *Toward reform of program evaluation.* San Francisco: Jossey-Bass.

Cronbach, L. J., & Meehl, P. E. (1955). Construct validity in psychological tests. *Psychological Bulletin, 52*, 281–302.

Curriculum Corporation. (1994). *ESL Scales.* Carlton, Victoria, Australia: Curriculum Corporation.

Curriculum Corporation. (2000). *Literacy benchmarks years 3, 5 & 7.* Retrieved March 15, 2006, from http://online.curriculum.edu.au/litbench/default.asp

Davies, A. (1977). The construction of language tests. In J. P. B. Allen & A. Davies (Eds.), *Testing and experimental methods. The Edinburgh Course in Applied Linguistics* (Vol. 4, pp. 38–104). Oxford: Oxford University Press.

Davies, A. (1991). *The native speaker in applied linguistics.* Edinburgh: Edinburgh University Press.

Davies, A. (1995). Testing communicative language or testing language communicatively: What? How? *Melbourne Papers in Language Testing, 4*, 1–20.

Davies, A. (1997a) (Guest Ed.). Ethics in language testing. [Special issue] *Language Testing, 14*, 3.

Davies, A. (1997b). Australian immigrant gatekeeping through English language tests: How important is proficiency? In A. Huhta, V. Kohonen, L. Kurki-Suonio, & S. Luoma (Eds.), *Current developments and alternatives in language assessment* (pp. 71–84). Jyväskylä, Finland: University of Jyväskylä and University of Tampere.

Davies, A. (1997c). Demands of being professional in language testing. *Language Testing, 14*(3), 328–339.

Davies, A. (2004) (Guest Ed.). The ethics of language assessment [Special issues]. *Language Assessment Quarterly, 1*(2/3).

Davies, A., Hamp-Lyons, L., & Kemp, C. (2003). Whose norms? International proficiency tests in English. *World Englishes, 22*(4), 571–584.

de Lemos, M. (2002). *Closing the gap between research and practice: Foundations for the acquisition of literacy.* Camberwell: Australian Council for Educational Research. Retrieved March 15, 2006, from http://www.acer.edu.au/research/reports/documents/deLemos_ClosingTheGap.pdf

DfEE/QCA (Department for Education and Employment–Qualifications and Curriculum Authority). (2000). *The national curriculum for England, key stages 1–4*. London: The Stationery Office.

Department of Immigration and Multicultural Affairs. (1999). *Review of the independent and skilled-Australian linked categories*. Canberra: Author.

Deville, C., & Chalhoub-Deville, M. (2006). Test score variability: Implications for reliability and validity. In M. Chalhoub-Deville, C. Chapelle, & P. Duff (Eds.), *Inference and generalizability in applied linguistics: Multiple research perspectives* (pp. 9–25). Amsterdam: John Benjamins.

Dilena, M., & van Kraayenoord, C. E. (1995). Whole school approaches to literacy assessment and reporting. *Australian Journal of Language and Literacy, 2*, 136–143.

Dilena, M., & van Kraayenoord, C. E. (Eds.). (1996). *Whole school approaches to assessing and reporting literacy: Report of Children's Literacy Project No. 1 (1993–1994)* (Vols. 1–3). Canberra: Department of Education, Training and Youth Affairs.

Dorans, N. J. (1989). Two new approaches to assessing differential item functioning: Standardization and the Mantel-Haenszel method. *Applied Measurement in Education, 2*, 217–233.

Dorans, N. J., & Holland, P. W. (1993). DIF detection and description: Mantel-Haenszel and standardization. In P. W. Holland & H. Wainer (Eds.), *Differential item functioning* (pp. 35–66). Hillsdale, NJ: Lawrence Erlbaum Associates.

Douglas, D. (2000). *Assessing language for specific purposes*. Cambridge: Cambridge University Press.

Drasgow, F., & Probst, T. M. (2005). The psychometrics of adaptation: Evaluating measurement equivalence across languages and cultures. In R. K. Hambleton, P. F. Merenda, & C. D. Spielberger (Eds.), *Adapting educational and psychological tests for cross-cultural assessment* (pp. 265–296). Mahwah, NJ: Lawrence Erlbaum Associates.

Ducasse, A. M. (2006). *Assessing interaction in paired oral proficiency assessments in Spanish*. Unpublished doctoral dissertation, The University of Melbourne, Australia. Manuscript in preparation.

Dutton, D. (1998). *Strangers and citizens: The boundaries of Australian citizenship 1901–1973*. Unpublished doctoral dissertation, The University of Melbourne, Australia.

Eades, D., Fraser, H., Siegel, J., McNamara, T., & Baker, B. (2003). Linguistic identification in the determination of nationality: A preliminary report. *Language Policy, 2*(2), 179–199.

Earley, P. C., & Ang, S. (2003). *Cultural intelligence*. Stanford, CA: Stanford University Press.

Edgeworth, F. Y. (1888). The statistics of examinations. *Journal of the Royal Statistical Society, 51*, 599–635.

Edgeworth, F. Y. (1890). The element of chance in competitive examinations. *Journal of the Royal Statistical Society, 53*, 644–663.

Educational Testing Service. (2003). *Fairness review guidelines.* Princeton, NJ: Author. Available from http://www.ets.org/Media/About_ETS/pdf/overview.pdf

Educational Testing Service. (2004). *ETS international principles for fairness review of assessments.* Princeton, NJ: Author. Available from http://www.ets.org/Media/About_ETS/pdf/frintl.pdf

Educational Testing Service. (2005). *TOEFL iBT.* Princeton, NJ: Author.

Edwards, G. (1977). *L2 retention in the Public Service of Canada.* Ottawa: Public Service Commission of Canada.

Eells, K., Davis, A., Havighurst, R. J., Herrick, V. E., & Tyler, R. W. (1951). *Intelligence and cultural differences.* Chicago: University of Chicago Press.

Ehlich, K. (Ed.). (2005). *Anforderungen an Verfahren der regelmäßigen Sprachstandsfeststellung als Grundlage für die frühe und individuelle Sprachförderung von Kindern mit und ohne Migrationshintergrund.* [Requirements that procedures of continuous evaluation of the status of language development have to fulfill to serve as a basis for early and individual linguistic fostering of children without and with immigration background.] *Bildungsreform Band 11.* Berlin: Bundesministerium für Bildung und Forschung (BMBF) [German Federal Ministry of Education and Research, series on Education Reform].

Elder, C. (1996). The effect of language background on "foreign" language test performance: The case of Chinese, Italian, and Modern Greek. *Language Learning, 46*(2), 233–282.

Elder, C. (1997a). *The background speaker as learner of Italian, Modern Greek and Chinese: Implications for foreign language assessment.* Unpublished doctoral dissertation, The University of Melbourne, Australia.

Elder, C. (1997b). What does test bias have to do with fairness? *Language Testing, 14*(3), 261–277.

Elder, C., & Davies, A. (2006). Assessing English as a lingua franca. *Annual Review of Applied Linguistics, 26*, 232–301.

Elder, C., McNamara, T. F., & Congdon, P. (2003). Understanding Rasch measurement: Rasch techniques for detecting bias in performance assessments: An example comparing the performance of native and non-native speakers on a test of academic English. *Journal of Applied Measurement, 4*, 181–197.

Evans, B., & Hornberger, N. H. (2005). No Child Left Behind: Repealing and unpeeling federal language education policy in the United States. *Language Policy, 4,* 87–106.

Evans, N. (2002). Country and the word: Linguistic evidence in the Croker Island sea claim. In J. Henderson & D. Nash (Eds.), *Language in native title* (pp. 53–99). Canberra: Aboriginal Studies Press.

Extra, G. & van Avermaet, P. (2007). *Testing régimes: Cross-national perspectives on language, migration and citizenship.* Manuscript in preparation.

Faggen, J. (1987). Golden rule revisited: Introduction. *Educational Measurement: Issues and Practice, 6,* 5–8.

Feuerstein, R. (1979) *The dynamic assessment of retarded performers: The learning potential assessment device, theory, instruments, and techniques.* Baltimore: University Park Press.

Fogtmann, C. (2006). *The co-establishment of understanding in Danish naturalization interviews.* Unpublished manuscript, University of Southern Denmark, Odense.

Foucault, M. (1972). *The archaeology of knowledge* (A. M. S. Smith, Trans.) (pp. 50–55). London: Routledge. (Original work published 1969).

Foucault, M. (1977). *Discipline and punish: The birth of the prison* (A. Sheridan, Trans.). London: Allen Lane (Original work published 1975).

Freebody, P., & Gilbert, P. (1999). Research into language and literacy. In J. Keeves & K. Marjoribanks (Eds.), *Australian education: Review of research 1965–1998.* Camberwell, Victoria, Australia: ACER Press.

Freeman, D., & Riley, K. (2005). When the law goes local: One state's view on NCLB in practice. *The Modern Language Journal, 89,* 264–268.

Fulcher, G. (2004). Deluded by artifices? The Common European Framework and harmonization. *Language Assessment Quarterly, 1*(4), 253–266.

Gardner, S., & Rea-Dickins, P. (1999). Literacy and oracy assessment in an early years intervention project: The roles of English language stages. *British Studies in Applied Linguistics, 14,* 14–25.

Gee, J. (2003). Literacy and social minds. In G. Bull & M. Anstey (Eds.), *The literacy lexicon* (2nd ed.). French's Forest, NSW: Pearson Education Australia.

Gendaishi no kai. (1996). *Dokyumento Kanto Dishinsai.* Tokyo: Souhukan.

Giles, H., Coupland, J., & Coupland, N. (1991). *Contexts of accommodation.* Cambridge: Cambridge University Press.

Goffman, E. (1959). *The presentation of self in everyday life.* New York: Doubleday.

Goffman, E. (1964). The neglected situation. *American Anthropologist, 66,* 133–136.

Goffman, E. (1983). The interaction order. *American Sociological Review, 48,* 1–17.

Golato, A. (2003). Studying compliment responses: A comparison of DCTs and naturally occurring talk. *Applied Linguistics, 24*, 90–121.

Grice, H. P. (1975). Logic and conversation. In P. Cole & J. Morgan (Eds.), *Syntax and semantics* (Vol. 3, pp. 41–58). New York: Academic Press.

Gumperz, J. (1982a). *Discourse strategies.* Cambridge: Cambridge University Press.

Gumperz, J. (1982b). *Language and social identity.* Cambridge: Cambridge University Press.

Hagan, P., Hood, S., Jackson, E., Jones, M., Joyce, H., & Manidis, M. (1993). *Certificate in spoken and written English.* Sydney: NSW Adult Migrant English Service and the National Centre for English Language Teaching and Research, Macquarie University.

Halliday, M. A. K. (1978). *Language as social semiotic: The social interpretation of language and meaning.* London: Edward Arnold.

Halliday, M. A. K., & Martin, J. R. (1993). *Writing science: Literacy and discursive power.* London: Falmer Press.

Hambleton, R. K., Swaminathan, H., & Rogers, H. J. (1991). *Fundamentals of item response theory.* Newbury Park, CA: Sage.

Hammond, J., & Macken-Horarik, M. (1999). Critical literacy: Challenges and questions for ESL classrooms. *TESOL Quarterly, 33*(3), 528–543.

Hamp-Lyons, L. (1997). Ethics in language testing. In C. M. Clapham & D. Corson (Eds.), *Language testing and assessment: Encyclopaedia of language and education* (Vol. 7, pp. 323–333). Dordrecht: Kluwer Academic.

Hartog, P., & Rhodes, E. C. (1936). *The marks of examiners, being a comparison of marks allotted to examination scripts by independent examiners and boards of examiners, together with a section on viva voce examinations.* London: Macmillan.

Hawthorne, L. (2005a). "Picking winners": The recent transformation of Australia's skilled migration policy. *International Migration Review, 39*(3), 663–696.

Hawthorne, L. (2005b, November). *Evaluation of general skilled migration.* Presentation at DIMIA General Skilled Migration Symposium, Parliament House, Canberra.

Heath, J. (1663). *Flagellum, or, the life and death, birth and burial of Oliver Cromwel: Faithfully described in an exact account of his policies and successes, not heretofore published or discovered by S. T.* London: Printed for L. R.

Heath, S. B. (1982). What no bedtime story means: Narrative skills at home and school. *Language in Society, 11*(2), 49–76.

Heath, S. B. (1983). *Ways with words: Language, life and work in communities and classrooms.* London: Cambridge University Press.

Heubert, J., & Hauser, R. (Eds.). (1999). *High stakes: Testing for tracking, promotion, and graduation.* Washington, DC: National Academies Press.

Hill, K., Iwashita, N., McNamara, T., Scarino, A., & Scrimgeour, A. (2003). *A report on assessing and reporting student outcomes in Asian languages (Japanese and Indonesian).* Adelaide: Research Centre for Languages and Cultures Education, University of South Australia.

Hill, K., & McNamara, T. (2003). Supporting curriculum initiatives in second languages. In J. P. Keeves & R. Watanabe (Eds.), *International handbook of educational research in the Asia-Pacific region* (pp. 629–640). Dordrecht: Kluwer Academic.

Holland, P. W., & Thayer, D. T. (1988). Differential item performance and the Mantel-Haenszel procedure. In H. Wainer & H. Braun (Eds.), *Test validity* (pp. 129–145). Hillsdale, NJ: Lawrence Erlbaum Associates.

Hood, C. P. (2001). *Japanese educational reform.* London: Routledge.

Horio, T. (1988). *Educational thought and ideology in modern Japan* (S. Platzer, Ed./Trans.). Tokyo: University of Tokyo Press.

Horowitz, D. L. (2001). *The deadly ethnic riot.* Berkeley: University of California Press.

House, J. (1996). Developing pragmatic fluency in English as a foreign language: Routines and metapragmatic awareness. *Studies in Second Language Acquisition, 18,* 225–252.

Hudson, T. (2001). Indicators for cross-cultural pragmatic instruction: Some quantitative tools. In K. Rose & G. Kasper (Eds.), *Pragmatics in language teaching* (pp. 283–300). Cambridge: Cambridge University Press.

Hudson, T., Detmer, E., & Brown, J. D. (1995). *Developing prototypic measures of cross-cultural pragmatics* (Tech. Rep. No. 7). Honolulu: University of Hawai'i, Second Language Teaching and Curriculum Center.

Hymes, D. H. (1967). Models of the interection of language and social setting. *Journal of Social Issues, 23*(2), 8–38.

Hymes, D. H. (1972). On communicative competence. In J. B. Pride & J. Holmes (Eds.), *Sociolinguistics* (pp. 269–293). Harmondsworth, UK: Penguin.

Ingram, D. E., & Wylie, E. (1979). Australian Second Language Proficiency Ratings (ASLPR). In *Adult Migrant Education Program Teachers Manual.* Canberra: Department of Immigration and Ethnic Affairs.

International Language Testing Association. (2000, March). *Code of ethics for ILTA.* Retrieved February 22, 2006, from http://www.iltaonline.com/code.pdf

International Language Testing Association. (2005, July). *ILTA: Draft code of practice: Version 3.* Retrieved February 22, 2006, from http://www.iltaonline.com/CoP_3.1.htm

Jacoby, S. (1998). *Science as performance: Socializing scientific discourse through conference talk rehearsals.* Unpublished doctoral dissertation, University of California, Los Angeles.

Jacoby, S., & McNamara, T. F. (1999). Locating competence. *English for Specific Purposes, 18*(3), 213–241.

Jacoby, S., & Ochs, E. (1995). Co-construction: An introduction. *Research on Language and Social Interaction, 28*(3), 171–183.

Jaeger, R. (1987). NCME opposition to proposed Golden Rule legislation. *Educational Measurement: Issues and Practice, 6*(2), 21–22.

Jasinskaja-Lahti, I., & Liebkind, K. (1998). Content and predictors of the ethnic identity of Russian-speaking immigrant adolescents in Finland. *Scandinavian Journal of Psychology, 39*(4), 209–219.

Jenkins, J. (2000). *The phonology of English as an international language.* Oxford: Oxford University Press.

Latham, H. (1877). *On the action of examinations considered as a means of selection.* Cambridge: Dieghton, Bell and Company.

Johnson, M. (2001). *The art of non-conversation: A re-examination of the validity of the oral proficiency interview.* New Haven, CT: Yale University Press.

Johnston, B., Kasper, G., & Ross, S. (1998). Effect of rejoinders in production questionnaires. *Applied Linguistics, 19*(2), 157–182.

Joint Committee on Fair Testing Practices. (2004). *Code of fair testing practices in education.* Retrieved February 22, 2006, from http://www. apa.org/science/fairtestcode.html

Jones, C. F. (2002). The Arabic language: Its place in the Middle East's culture and politics. *American Diplomacy, 7*(3). Retrieved June 9, 2006, from http://www.unc.edu/depts/diplomat/archives_roll/2002_07-09/ jones_arabic/jones_arabic.html

Jones, P. A. (1998). *Alien acts: The White Australia Policy, 1901 to 1939.* Unpublished doctoral dissertation, The University of Melbourne, Australia.

Jenkins, J. (2006). The spreading of EIL: A testing time for testers. *ELT Journal, 60*(1), 42–50.

Kane, M. (1992). An argument-based approach to validity. *Psychological Bulletin, 112*(3), 527–535.

Kane, M. (2001). Current concerns in validity theory. *Journal of Educational Measurement, 38*(4), 319–342.

Kane, M. (2002). Validating high-stakes testing programs. *Educational Measurement: Issues and Practice, 21*(1), 31–41.

Kane, M., Crooks, T., & Cohen, A. (1999). Validating measures of performance. *Educational Measurement: Issues and Practice, 18*(2), 5–17.

Kasper, G., & Roever, C. (2005). Pragmatics in second language learning. In E. Hinkel (Ed.), *Handbook of research in second language learning and teaching* (pp. 317–334). Mahwah, NJ: Lawrence Erlbaum Associates.

Kay, H. C. (1892). *Yaman: Its early mediaeval history*. London: Arnold.

Kelley, C., & Meyers, J. (1993). *Cross-cultural adaptibility inventory manual*. Minneapolis, MN: National Computer Systems.

Kim, M. (2001). Detecting DIF across the different language groups in a speaking test. *Language Testing, 18*(1), 89–114.

Kim, S.-H., Cohen, A. S., & Park, T.-H. (1995). Detection of differential item functioning in multiple groups. *Journal of Educational Measurement, 32*, 261–276.

Kinsman, G. (2004). The Canadian Cold War on queers: Sexual regulation and resistance. In R. Cavell (Ed.) *Love, hate and fear in Canada's Cold War* (pp. 108–132). Toronto: University of Toronto Press.

Kirsch, I. S., & Mosenthal, P. B. (1990). Exploring document literacy: Variables underlying the performance of young adults. *Reading Research Quarterly, 25*, 5–30.

Koike, I. (2000). Sogosenyaku toshiteno gengokyouikuseisaku [The need to implement comprehensive language policy in Japan]. *ELEC Bulletin, 107*, 24–27.

Kolga, M., Tõnurist, I., Vaba, L., & Viikberg, J. (2002). *The red book of the people of the Russian Empire*. Tallinn: NGO Red Book. Retrieved January 31, 2005, from http://www.eki.ee/books/redbook/ingrians.shtml

König, K., & Perchinig, B. (2005). Austria. In J. Niessen, Y. Schibel, & C. Thompson (Eds.), *Current immigration debates in Europe: A publication of the European Migration Dialogue*. Brussels: Migration Policy Group.

Kunnan, A. J. (1990). DIF in native language and gender groups in an ESL placement test. *TESOL Quarterly, 24*, 741–746.

Kunnan, A. J. (2000). Fairness and justice for all. In A. J. Kunnan (Ed.), *Fairness and validation in language assessment* (pp. 1–14). Cambridge: Cambridge University Press.

Kunnan, A. J. (2003). Test fairness. In M. Milanovic & C. Weir (Eds.), *Select papers from the European Year of Languages Conference, Barcelona* (pp. 27–48). Cambridge: Cambridge University Press.

Kunnan, A. J. (2005). Language assessment from a wider context. In E. Hinkel (Ed.), *Handbook of research in second language learning* (pp. 779–794). Mahwah, NJ: Lawrence Erlbaum Associates.

Lado, R. (1949). *Measurement in English as a foreign language*. Unpublished doctoral dissertation, University of Michigan, Ann Arbor.

Lado, R. (1961). *Language testing: The construction and use of foreign language tests*. London: Longmans Green & Co.

Lane-Poole, S. (1901). *A history of Egypt in the Middle Ages*. London: Methuen.

Language and National Origin Group. (2004). Guidelines for the use of language analysis in relation to questions of national origin in refugee cases. *The International Journal of Speech, Language and the Law, 11*(2), 261–266.

Lantolf, J. P., & Poehner, M. (2004). Dynamic assessment of L2 development: Bringing the past into the future. *Journal of Applied Linguistics, 1*(1), 49–72.

Lantolf, J. P., & Thorne, S. L. (2006). *Sociocultural theory and the genesis of second language development*. New York: Oxford University Press.

Jones, R. L., & Spolsky, B. (1975). *Testing language proficiency*. Arlington, VA: Center for Applied Linguistics.

Law, G. (1995). Ideologies of English language education in Japan. *JALT Journal, 17*(2), 213–224.

Lee, Y. W., Breland, H., & Muraki, E. (2004). *Comparability of TOEFL CBT writing prompts for different native language groups* (TOEFL Research Report No. RR-77). Princeton, NJ: Educational Testing Service. Retrieved February 22, 2006, from http://www.ets.org/Media/Research/pdf/RR-04-24.pdf

Leech, G. (1983). *Principles of pragmatics*. London: Longman.

Leibowitz, A. H. (1969). English literacy: Legal sanction for discrimination. *Notre Dame Lawyer, 45*(1), 7–66.

Leung, C. (1999). Teachers' response to linguistic diversity. In A. Tosi & C. Leung (Eds.), *Rethinking language education: From a monolingual to a multilingual perspective* (pp. 225–240). London: Centre for Information on Language Teaching and Research.

Leung, C. (2005). Classroom teacher assessment of second language development: Construct as practice. In E. Hinkel (Ed.), *Handbook of research in second language teaching and learning* (pp. 869–888). Mahwah, NJ: Lawrence Erlbaum Associates.

Leung, C., & Teasdale, T. (1997). What do teachers mean by speaking and listening: A contextualised study of assessment in the English National Curriculum. In A. Huhta, V. Kohonen, L. Kurki-Suonio, & S. Louma (Eds.), *New contexts, goals and alternatives in language assessment* (pp. 291–324). Jyväskylä, Finland: University of Jyväskylä.

Levinson, S. (1983). *Pragmatics*. Cambridge: Cambridge University Press.

Linacre, J. M., & Wright, B. D. (1993). *A user's guide to FACETS: Rasch measurement computer program (Version 3.2.)*. Chicago: MESA Press.

Linn, R. L. (1997). Evaluating the validity of assessments: The consequences of use. *Educational Measurement: Issues and Practice, 16*(2), 14–16.

Linn, R., Baker, E., & Betebenner, D. (2002). Accountability systems: Implications of requirements of the No Child Left Behind Act of 2001. *Educational Researcher*, *31*, 3–16.

Linn, R. L., & Drasgow, F. (1987). Implications of the Golden Rule settlement for test construction. *Educational Measurement: Issues and Practice*, *6*, 13–17.

Liu, J. (2006). *Measuring interlanguage pragmatic knowledge of EFL learners*. Frankfurt: Peter Lang.

Losen, D. J. (2005). *Racial inequity in graduation rates*. Research presented during Connect for Kids and National Education Association conference call on the Dropout Crisis.

Luke, A. (1993). The social construction of literacy in the primary school. In L. Unsworth (Ed.), *Literacy learning and teaching: Language as social practice in the primary school*. Sydney: University of Sydney.

Luke, A. (1996). Genres of power? Literacy education and the production of capital. In R. Hasan & G. Williams (Eds.), *Literacy in society* (pp. 308–338). New York: Longman.

Luke, A., Comber, B., & Grant, H. (2003). Critical literacies and cultural studies. In G. Bull & M. Anstey (Eds.), *The literacy lexicon* (2nd ed). French's Forest, NSW: Pearson Education Australia.

Lumley, T., Mincham, L., & Raso, E. (1994). Exemplar assessment tasks and observation guides. In Commonwealth of Australia (1996), *ESL development: Language and literacy in schools project*, 2nd edition, Vol. 1: Teacher's Manual. Canberra: National Languages and Literacy Institute of Australia/Department of Employment, Education and Training.

Luoma, S. (2003). *Assessing speaking*. Cambridge: Cambridge University Press.

Lynch, B. K. (1997). In search of the ethical language test. *Language Testing*, *14*, 315–327.

Lynch, B. K. (2001). Rethinking assessment from a critical perspective. *Language Testing*, *18*, 351–372.

Lynch, B. K., & McNamara, T. F. (1998). Using G-theory and Many-Facet Rasch measurement in the development of performance assessments of the ESL speaking skills of immigrants. *Language Testing*, *15*(2), 158–180.

Madaus, G. F., & Kellaghan, T. (1992). Curriculum evaluation and assessment. In P. W. Jackson (Ed.), *Handbook on research on curriculum* (pp. 119–154). New York: Macmillan.

Manley, R. (1691). *The history of the rebellions: In England, Scotland and Ireland: wherein, the most material passages, sieges, battles, policies and stratagems of war, are impartially related on both sides; from the year 1640 to the beheading of the Duke of Monmouth in 1685. In three parts.*

London: printed for L. Meredith at the Angel in Amen-Corner and for T. Newborough at the Golden Ball in St. Paul's-Church-Yard.

Marinelli, V. (2005). The Netherlands. In J. Niessen, Y. Schibel, & C. Thompson (Eds.), *Current immigration debates in Europe: A publication of the European Migration Dialogue*. Brussels: Migration Policy Group.

Martel, A. (1999). La politique linguistique canadienne et québécoise: Entre stratégie de pouvoir et identitiés. *Globe, 2*(2), 37–64.

Martin, J. R. (1989). *Factual writing: Exploring and challenging social reality*. Oxford: Oxford University Press.

Martin, J. R. (2000). Design and practice: Enacting functional literacies. *Annual Review of Applied Linguistics, 20*, 116–126.

Maryns, K., & Blommaert, J. (2001). Stylistic and thematic shifting as a narrative resource: Assessing asylum seekers' repertoires. *Multilingua, 20*, 61–84.

Masters, G., & Foster, M. (1997). *Mapping literacy achievement: Results of the 1996 National School English Literacy Survey*. Canberra: Department of Education, Training and Youth Affairs.

Matthiessen, C. M. I. M., Slade, D., & Macken, M. (1992). Language in context: A new model for evaluating student writing. *Linguistics in Education, 4*(2), 173–195.

McKay, P. (2000). On ESL standards for school-age learners. *Language Testing, 17*(2), 185–214.

McNamara, T. F. (1996). *Measuring second language performance*. London: Addison Wesley Longman.

McNamara, T. F. (1997). "Interaction" in second language performance assessment: Whose performance? *Applied Linguistics, 18*, 446–466.

McNamara, T. F. (1998). Policy and social considerations in language assessment. *Annual Review of Applied Linguistics, 18*, 304–319.

McNamara, T. F. (2000). *Evaluation of the OECD/PISA reading framework. Final report submitted to the OECD*. Paris: Organisation for Economic Co-operation and Development.

McNamara, T. F. (2001). Language assessment as social practice: Challenges for research. *Language Testing, 18*(4), 333–349.

McNamara, T. F. (2003). Knowing your limits: Conceptual and policy constraints on evidence centred test design in language testing research. *Measurement: Interdisciplinary Research and Perspectives, 1*(1), 85–87.

McNamara, T. F. (2005). 21st century shibboleth: Language tests, identity and intergroup conflict. *Language Policy, 4*(4), 1–20.

McNamara, T. F. (2006). Validity in language testing: The challenge of Sam Messick's legacy. *Language Assessment Quarterly, 3*(1), 31–51.

McNamara, T. F., & Eades, D. (2004, May). *Linguistic identification of asylum seekers: A flawed test?* Presentation in the invited symposium on "Enforcing citizenship policy through language tests" at the annual meeting of the American Association for Applied Linguistics, Portland, OR.

McNamara, T. F., Hill, K., & May, L. (2002). Discourse and assessment. *Annual Review of Applied Linguistics, 22,* 221–242.

McNamara, T. F., & Shohamy, E. (Guest Eds.). (2008, in preparation). Language testing for citizenship and immigration [Special Issue]. *Language Assessment Quarterly,* 5.

McQueen, J., & Mendelovits, J. (2003). PISA reading: Cultural equivalence in a cross-cultural study. *Language Testing, 20*(2), 208–224.

McVeigh, B. J. (2002). *Japanese higher education as myth.* Armonk, NY: M. E. Sharpe.

Mehrens, W. A. (1997). The consequences of consequential validity. *Educational Measurement: Issues and Practice, 16*(2), 16–18.

Messick, S. (1980). Test validation and the ethics of assessment. *American Psychologist, 35,* 1012–1027.

Messick, S. (1989). Validity. In R. L. Linn (Ed.), *Educational measurement* (3rd ed.) (pp. 13–103). New York: American Council on Education & Macmillan.

Messick, S. (1996). Validity and washback in language testing. *Language Testing, 13*(3), 241–256.

Mey, J. L. (2001). *Pragmatics.* Oxford: Blackwell.

Mincham, L. (1995). ESL student needs procedures: An approach to language assessment in primary and secondary school contexts. In G. Brindley (Ed.), *Language assessment in action* (pp. 65–91). Sydney: National Centre for English Language Teaching and Research, Macquarie University.

Ministry of Education, Culture, Sports, Science and Technology. (1998). *Chugakuko Gakushu Shidoyoryo.* [The course of study for junior high schools]. Tokyo: Kairyudo.

Ministry of Education, Culture, Sports, Science and Technology. (1999). *Kotogako Gakushu Shidoyouyou-Kaisetu* [The course of study for senior high schools]. Tokyo: Kairyudo.

Ministry of Education, Culture, Sports, Science and Technology. (2003). *Regarding the establishment of an action plan to cultivate "Japanese with English abilities."* Retrieved March 15, 2006, from http://www.mext.go.jp/english/topics/03072801.htm

Mislevy, R. J. (1996). Test theory reconceived. *Journal of Educational Measurement, 33*(4), 379–416.

Mislevy, R. J., Steinberg, L. S., & Almond, R. G. (2002). Design and analysis in task-based language assessment. *Language Testing, 19*(4), 477–496.

Mislevy, R. J., Steinberg, L. S., & Almond, R. G. (2003). On the structure of assessment arguments. *Measurement: Interdisciplinary Research and Perspectives, 1*(1), 3–62.

Mitchell, J. R. (2005). *Toward a new vision for language training in the Public Service: A discussion paper prepared for the ADM Working Group.* Ottawa: Public Service Human Resources Management Agency of Canada. Retrieved November 30, 2005, from http://www.hrma-agrh.gc.ca/ollo/or-ar/vision/vision01-PR_e.asp?printable=True

Moore, H. M. (2005a). *Identifying "the target population": A genealogy of policy-making for English as a second language (ESL) in Australian schools (1947–1997).* Unpublished doctoral dissertation, University of Toronto, Toronto, Canada.

Moore, H. M. (2005b, September). *What can equality mean? Conflicting interpretations of provision for ESL students in Australian schools.* Plenary address, Queensland Association of Teachers of English to Speakers of other Languages Conference, Brisbane, Australia.

Moss, P., Pullin, D., Gee, J., & Haertel, E. (2005). The idea of testing: Psychometric and sociocultural perspectives. *Measurement: Interdisciplinary Research and Perspectives, 3*(2), 63–83.

Moss, P. A. (1998). The role of consequences in validity theory. *Educational Measurement: Issues and Practice, 17*(2), 6–12.

Muniz, J., Hambleton, R. K., & Xing, D. (2001). Small sample studies to detect flaws in item translations. *International Journal of Testing, 1*(2), 115–135.

National Reading Panel. (2000). *Teaching children to read: An evidence-based assessment of the scientific research literature on reading and its implications for reading instruction.* Retrieved March 15, 2006, from http://www.nichd.nih.gov/publications/nrp/report.pdf

North, B. (2000). *The development of a common reference scale of language proficiency.* New York: Peter Lang.

North, B. (in press). *Scales for rating language performance: Descriptive models, formulation styles, and presentation formats.* Princeton, NJ: Educational Testing Service.

North, B., & Schneider, G. (1998). Scaling descriptors for language proficiency scales. *Language Testing, 15*(2), 217–263.

Northern Association of Support Services for Equality and Achievement. (2001). *EAL assessment: Guidance on the NASSEA EAL assessment system.* Milton Keynes, UK: Milton Keynes Council.

Office for Standards in Education. (2003a). *Good assessment in secondary school* (Document reference no. HMI 462). Retrieved March 15, 2006, from http://www.ofsted.gov.uk/publications/docs/3205.pdf

Office for Standards in Education. (2003b). *Good assessment practice in English* (Document reference no. HMI 1473). Retrieved March 15, 2006, from http://www.ofsted.gov.uk/publications/index.cfm?fuseaction=pubs. summary&id=3209

Olson, D. (1994). *The world on paper: The conceptual and cognitive implications of writing and reading.* Cambridge: Cambridge University Press.

O'Neill, K. A., & McPeek, W. M. (1993). Item and test characteristics that are associated with differential item functioning. In P. W. Holland & H. Wainer (Eds.), *Differential item functioning* (pp. 255–276). Hillsdale, NJ: Lawrence Erlbaum Associates.

Organisation for Economic Co-operation and Development. (1999). *Measuring student knowledge and skills: A new framework for assessment.* Paris: Author.

Organisation for Economic Co-operation and Development. (2000). *Measuring student knowledge and skills: The PISA 2000 assessment of reading, mathematical and scientific literacy.* Paris: Author.

Organisation for Economic Co-operation and Development. (2002). *PISA 2000 technical report.* Paris: Author.

Organisation for Economic Co-operation and Development. (2005). *The OECD.* Paris: Author.

Painter, C. (1996). The development of language as a resource for thinking: A linguistic view of learning. In R. Hasan & G. Williams (Eds.), *Literacy in society.* Harlow, Essex: Longman.

Palmer, L., & Spolsky, B. (Eds.). (1975). *Papers in language testing 1967–74.* Washington, DC: TESOL.

Penfield, R. D. (2001). Assessing differential item functioning among multiple groups: A comparison of three Mantel-Haenszel procedures. *Applied Measurement in Education, 14*(3), 235–259.

Pennycook, A. (1994). Incommensurable discourses? *Applied Linguistics, 15*(2), 115–138.

Piller, I. (2001). Naturalisation language testing and its basis in ideologies of national identity and citizenship. *International Journal of Bilingualism, 5*(3), 259–278.

Popham, W. J. (1997). Consequential validity: Right concern—wrong concept. *Educational Measurement: Issues and Practice, 16*(2), 9–13.

Popham, W. J. (2001). *The truth about testing.* Alexandria, VA: Association for Supervision and Curriculum Development.

Popper, K. R. (1962). *Conjectures and refutations: The growth of scientific knowledge.* New York: Harper & Row.

Purpura, J. (2004). *Assessing grammar.* Cambridge: Cambridge University Press.

Qualifications and Curriculum Authority. (2000). *A language in common: Assessing English as an additional language.* Sudbury, UK: QCA Publications.

Ramsey, P. A. (1993). Sensitivity review: The ETS experience as a case study. In P. W. Holland & H. Wainer (Eds.), *Differential item functioning* (pp. 367–389). Hillsdale, NJ: Lawrence Earlbaum Associates.

Ravitch, D. (2003). *The language police.* New York: Alfred Knopf.

Read, J. (2000). *Assessing vocabulary.* Cambridge: Cambridge University Press.

Rea-Dickins, P. (2001). Mirror, mirror on the wall: Identifying processes of classroom assessment. *Language Testing, 18*(4), 429–462.

Rea-Dickins, P. (2004). Understanding teachers as agents of assessment. *Language Testing, 21*(3), 249–258.

Rea-Dickins, P., Gardner, S., & Clayton, E. (1998). *Investigating EAL language assessment in an early years bilingual intervention project.* Unpublished manuscript, University of Warwick, Warwick, UK.

Reath, A. (2004). Language analysis in the context of the asylum process: Procedures, validity, and consequences. *Language Assessment Quarterly, 1*(4), 209–233.

Richardson, S., Robertson, F., & Ilsley, D. (2001). *The Labour Force experience of new migrants.* Canberra: Department of Immigration and Multicultural Affairs.

Robinson, P. (2002a). Effects of individual differences in intelligence, aptitude and working memory on adult incidental SLA: A replication and extension of Reber, Walkenfield and Hernstadt (1991). In P. Robinson (Ed.), *Individual differences and instructed second language learning* (pp. 211–266). Amsterdam: John Benjamins.

Robinson, P. (2002b). Learning conditions, aptitude complexes, and SLA: A framework for research and pedagogy. In P. Robinson (Ed.), *Individual differences and instructed language learning* (pp. 113–133). Amsterdam: John Benjamins.

Robinson, P. (2005). Aptitude and second language acquisition. *Annual Review of Applied Linguistics, 25*, 46–73.

Roever, C. (1996). Linguistische Routinen: Systematische, psycholinguistische und fremdsprachendidaktische Überlegungen. *Fremdsprachen und Hochschule, 46*, 43–60.

Roever, C. (2004, May). *Adaptation of a test of ESL pragmatics from American English to Australian English.* Paper presented at the American Association for Applied Linguistics Conference, Portland, OR.

Roever, C. (2005). *Testing ESL pragmatics.* Frankfurt: Peter Lang.

Roever, C. (2006a, June). *Differential item functioning in an ESL pragmatics test*. Paper presented at Language Testing Research Colloquium, Melbourne, Australia.

Roever, C. (2006b). Validation of a web-based test of ESL pragmalinguistics. *Language Testing, 23*(2), 229–256.

Rooney, J. P. (1987). A response from Golden Rule to "ETS on 'Golden Rule.'" *Educational Measurement: Issues and Practice, 6*, 5–8.

Rose, K. (1994). On the validity of discourse completion tests in non-Western contexts. *Applied Linguistics, 15*, 1–14.

Rose, K., & Ono, R. (1995). Eliciting speech act data in Japanese: The effect of questionnaire type. *Language Learning, 45*, 191–223.

Rosenbusch, M. H. (2005). The No Child Left Behind Act and teaching and learning languages in U.S. schools. *The Modern Language Journal, 89*(2), 250–261.

Rubeling, H. (2002, May). *Test Deutsch alfa: A German as a foreign language test for people who cannot read and write*. Paper presented at the Language Assessment Ethics Conference, Pasadena, CA. Retrieved June 4, 2006, from http://www.studentgroups.ucla.edu/scalar/Scalar5/LAEC_program.html

Runciman, S.. (1958) *The Sicilian Vespers: A history of the Mediterranean world in the later thirteenth century*. Cambridge: Cambridge University Press.

Ryan, K., & Bachman, L. F. (1992). Differential item functioning on two tests of EFL proficiency. *Language Testing, 9*(1), 12–29.

Samejima, F. (1969). *Estimation of latent ability using a response pattern of graded scores. Psychometric Monograph 17*. Richmond, VA: William Byrd Press.

Samejima, F. (1996). Graded response model. In W. van der Linden & R. K. Hambleton (Eds.), *Handbook of modern item response theory* (pp. 85–100). New York: Springer.

Sasaki, M. (1991). A comparison of two methods for detecting differential item functioning in an ESL placement test. *Language Testing, 8*(2), 95–111.

Saville, N. (2003). The process of test development and revision within UCLES EFL. In C. Weir & M. Milanovic (Eds.), *Continuity and innovation: Revising the Cambridge Proficiency in English examination 1913–2002* (pp. 57–120). Cambridge: Cambridge University Press.

Saville, N. (2005). Setting and monitoring professional standards: A QMS approach. *Cambridge ESOL Research Notes, 22*, 2–5.

Schegloff, E. A. (1982). Discourse as an interactional achievement: Some uses of "uh huh" and other things that come between sentences. In D. Tannen

(Ed.), *Georgetown University Roundtable on Languages and Linguistics* (pp. 71–93). Washington, DC: Georgetown University Press.

Schegloff, E. A. (1988). Discourse as an interactional achievement II: An exercise in conversation analysis. In D. Tannen (Ed.), *Linguistics in context: Connecting observation and understanding* (pp. 135–158). Norwood NJ: Ablex.

Schegloff, E. A. (1995). Discourse as an interactional achievement III: The omnirelevance of action. *Research on Language and Social Interaction*, *28*(3), 185–211.

Schegloff, E. A. (1997). Whose text? Whose context? *Discourse and Society*, *8*, 165–187.

Schegloff, E. A. (1998). Reply to Wetherell. *Discourse and Society*, *9*(3), 413–416.

Schegloff, E. A. (1999). "Schegloff's texts" as "Billig's data": A critical reply. *Discourse and Society*, *10*(4), 558–572.

Scheuneman, J. D. (1979). A method of assessing bias in test items. *Journal of Educational Measurement*, *16*, 143–152.

Schmidt, R. (1983). Interaction, acculturation and the acquisition of communicative competence: A case study of an adult. In N. Wolfson & E. Judd (Eds.), *Sociolinguistics and language acquisition* (pp. 137–174). Rowley, MA: Newbury House.

Schmitt, A. P. (1988). Language and cultural characteristics that explain differential item functioning for Hispanic examinees on the Scholastic Aptitude Test. *Journal of Educational Measurement*, *25*, 1–13.

Seidlhofer, B. (2001). Closing a conceptual gap: The case for a description of English as a lingua franca. *International Journal of Applied Linguistics*, *11*(2), 133–158.

Seidlhofer, B. (2004). Research perspectives on teaching English as a lingua franca. *Annual Review of Applied Linguistics*, *24*, 209–239.

Shavelson, R. A., & Webb, N. M. (1991). *Generalizability theory: A primer*. Newbury Park, CA: Sage.

Shell, M. (2001). Language wars. *CR: The New Centennial Review*, *1*(2), 1–17.

Shepard, L. A. (1997). The centrality of test use and consequences for test validity. *Educational Measurement: Issues and Practice*, *16*(2), 5–13.

Shepard, L. A., Camilli, G., & Averill, M. (1981). Comparison of procedures for detecting test-item bias with both internal and external ability criteria. *Journal of Educational Statistics*, *6*, 317–375.

Shohamy, E. (1998). Critical language testing and beyond. *Studies in Educational Evaluation*, *24*, 331–345.

Shohamy, E. (2000). Fairness in language testing. In A. J. Kunnan (Ed.), *Fairness and validation in language assessment* (pp. 15–19). Cambridge: Cambridge University Press.

Shohamy, E. (2001). *The power of tests: A critical perspective on the uses of language tests*. London: Pearson.

Siegal, M. (1994). The role of learner subjectivity in second language sociolinguistic competency: Western women learning Japanese. *Applied Linguistics, 17*, 356–382.

Singler, J. V. (2003, August). *The "linguistic" asylum interview: The role of the interviewer and the role of the analyst*. Paper presented at the Conference of the Society for Pidgin and Creole Linguistics, Hawai'i.

Sireci, S. G., Patsula, L., & Hambleton, R. K. (2005). Statistical methods for identifying flaws in the test adaptation process. In R. K. Hambleton, P. F. Merenda, & C. D. Spielberger (Eds.), *Adapting educational and psychological tests for cross-cultural assessment* (pp. 93–116). Mahwah, NJ: Lawrence Erlbaum Associates.

Skehan, P. (2002). Theorising and updating aptitude. In P. Robinson (Ed.), *Individual differences and instructed language learning* (pp. 69–93). Amsterdam: John Benjamins.

Smith, G. T. (2005). On construct validity: Issues of method and measurement. *Psychological Assessment, 17*(4), 396–408.

South Australia. (2002). *South Australian curriculum, standards and accountability framework: English as a second language scope and scales*. Adelaide: Department of Education, Training and Employment.

Spolsky, B. (1967). Do they know enough English? In D. Wigglesworth (Ed.), *ATESL Selected Conference Papers*. Washington, DC: NAFSA Studies and Papers, English Language Series.

Spolsky, B. (1981). Some ethical questions about language testing. In C. Klein-Braley & D. K. Stevenson (Eds.), *Practice and problems in language testing* (pp. 5–21). Frankfurt: Peter Lang.

Spolsky, B. (1995). *Measured words*. Oxford: Oxford University Press.

Spreitzer, M. G., McCall, M. W., & Mahoney, J. D. (1997). Early identification of international executive potential. *Journal of Applied Psychology, 82*(1), 6–29.

Stern, W. (1914). *The psychological methods of testing intelligence*. Baltimore: Warwick & York.

Sternberg, R. J., & Grigorenko, E. L. (2002). *Dynamic testing*. New York: Cambridge University Press.

Stevenson, D. K. (1985). Authenticity, validity and a tea-party. *Language Testing, 2*(1), 41–47.

Street, B. (1995) *Social literacies: Critical approaches to literacy in development, ethnography and education*. London: Longman.

Sugimoto, Y. (1997). *An introduction to Japanese society: Contemporary Japanese society*. Cambridge: Cambridge University Press.

Suleiman, Y. (2004). *A war of words: Language and conflict in the Middle East*. New York: Cambridge University Press.

Sunderman, G. L., Kim, J. S., & Orfield, G. (2005). *NCLB meets school realities: Lessons from the field*. Thousand Oaks, CA: Corwin Press.

Sutherland, G. (1973). *Elementary education in the nineteenth century*. London: London Historical Association.

Takala, S., & Kaftandjieva, F. (2000). Test fairness: A DIF analysis of an L2 vocabulary test. *Language Testing, 17*(3), 323–340.

Tanabe, Y. (1997). Nyushi to eigokyouiku-Gakko Eigo no Shitennkara [Entrance examinations and the teaching of English]. *ELEC Bulletin, 104*, 15–18.

Teachers of English to Speakers of Other Languages (TESOL). (1998). *The ESL standards for pre-K–12 students*. Alexandria, VA: Author.

Teasdale, A., & Leung, C. (2000). Teacher assessment and psychometric theory: A case of paradigm crossing? *Language Testing, 17*(2), 163–184.

Thissen, D., Steinberg, L., & Wainer, H. (1993). Detection of differential item functioning using the parameters of item response models. In P. W. Holland & H. Wainer (Eds.), *Differential item functioning* (pp. 67–113). Hillsdale, NJ: Lawrence Erlbaum Associates.

Toronto Board of Education. (1988). *Benchmarks: Standards of student achievement*. Toronto, Ontario: Toronto Board of Education.

Trim, J. L. M. (1997). The proposed Common European Framework for the description of language learning, teaching and assessment. In A. Huhta, V. Kohonen, L. Kurki-Suonio, & S. Luoma (Eds.), *Current developments and alternatives in language assessment* (pp. 415–421). Jyväskylä, Finland: University of Jyväskylä and University of Tampere.

Tucker, M. F. (1999). Self-awareness and development using the overseas assignment inventory. In S. M. Fowler & M. G. Mumford (Eds.), *Intercultural sourcebook: Cross-cultural training methods 2* (pp. 45–52). Yarmouth, ME: Intercultural Press.

Van Avermaet, P., Kujper, H., & Saville, N. (2004). A code of practice and quality management system for international language examinations. *Language Assessment Quarterly, 1*(2/3), 137–150.

Van Ek, J., & Trim, J. L. M. (1996). *Vantage level*. Strasbourg: Council of Europe.

Van Ek, J., & Trim, J. L. M. (1998). *Waystage 1990*. Cambridge: Cambridge University Press.

Van Ek, J. A. (1975). *The threshold level in a European unit / credit system for modern language learning by adults.* Strasbourg: Council of Europe.

van Kraayenoord, C. E. (2003). Literacy assessment. In G. Bull & M. Anstey (Eds.), *The literacy lexicon* (2nd ed.) (pp. 273–287). French's Forest, NSW: Pearson Education Australia.

van Kraayenoord, C. E., Luke, A., Elkins, J., & Land, R. (1999). The Queensland year 2 diagnostic net: A critical commentary. *Journal of Research in Reading, 22,* 95–105.

Van Lier, L. (1989). Reeling, writhing, drawling, stretching, and fainting in coils: Oral proficiency interviews as conversation. *TESOL Quarterly, 23,* 489–508.

Victorian Curriculum and Assessment Authority. (2005). *Victorian essential learning standards.* Melbourne: Author. Retrieved March 15, 2006, from http://vels.vcaa.vic.edu.au/

Wall, D. (1997). Impact and washback in language testing. In C. M. Clapham & D. Corson (Eds.), *Language testing and assessment*: Encyclopaedia of *language and education* (Vol. 7, pp. 291–302). Dordrecht: Kluwer.

Watanabe, Y. (1996). Does grammar translation come from the entrance examination? Preliminary findings from classroom-based research. *Language Testing, 13*(3), 318–333.

Weigle, S. C. (2002). *Assessing writing.* Cambridge: Cambridge University Press.

Weinberg, M. (1995). *A chance to learn: A history of race and education in the United States* (2nd ed.). Long Beach: California State University Press.

Weintrob, J., & Weintrob, R. (1912). The influence of environment on mental ability as shown by Binet-Simon tests. *Journal of Educational Psychology, 3,* 577–583.

Weir, C. J. (1983). The Associated Examining Board's Test in English for Academic Purposes: An exercise in content validation. In A. Hughes & D. Porter (Eds.), *Current developments in language testing* (pp. 147–153). London: Academic Press.

Wetherell, M. (1998). Positioning and interpretative repertoires: Conversation analysis and poststructuralism in dialogue. *Discourse and Society, 9*(3), 387–412.

White, E. E. (1888). Examinations and promotions. *Education, 8,* 519–522.

Wiley, T. G. (2005). *Literacy and language diversity in the United States* (2nd ed.). Washington, DC: Center for Applied Linguistics.

Wilkins, D. 1973. *Notional syllabuses.* Oxford: Oxford University Press.

Winn, M. (2005). Collecting target discourse: The case of the US naturalization interview. In M. Long (Ed.), *Second language needs analysis* (pp. 265–304). Cambridge: Cambridge University Press.

Wright, B. D., & Stone, M. H. (1979). *Best test design*. Chicago: MESA Press.

Wucker, M. (1999). *Why the cocks fight: Dominicans, Haitians and the struggle for Hispaniola*. New York: Hill and Wang.

Yamagishi, S. (2002). *Kanto Daishinsai to Chosenjin Gyakusatsu: 80 Nengo no Tettei Keinshou*. Tokyo: Waseda shuppan.

Yamashita, S. O. (1996). *Six measures of JSL pragmatics* (Tech. Rep. No. 14). Honolulu: University of Hawai'i, Second Language Teaching and Curriculum Center.

Yell, M. L., & Drasgow, E. (2005). *No Child Left Behind: A guide for professionals*. Upper Saddle River, NJ: Prentice Hall.

Yoneyama, S. (1999). *The Japanese high school: Silence and resistance*. New York: Routledge.

Yoshitake, S. S. (1997). *Measuring interlanguage pragmatic competence of Japanese students of English as a foreign language: A multi-test framework evaluation*. Unpublished doctoral dissertation, Columbia Pacific University, Novata, CA.

Young, J., & Fletcher, M. (2000). A Queensland perspective on assessment in the early years: Teacher perceptions and the use of the Reading Development Continuum. *The Australian Journal of Language and Literacy, 23*, 212–229.

Young, L. (1994). *Crosstalk and culture in Sino-American communication*. Cambridge: Cambridge University Press.

Young, R., & He, A. W. (1998). *Talking and testing: Discourse approaches to the assessment of oral proficiency*. Amsterdam: John Benjamins.

Zieky, M. (1993). Practical questions in the use of DIF statistics in test development. In P. W. Holland & H. Wainer (Eds.), *Differential item functioning* (pp. 337–348). Hillsdale, NJ: Lawrence Erlbaum Associates.

Zumbo, B. D. (1999). *A handbook on the theory and methods of differential item functioning (DIF): Logistic regression modeling as a unitary framework for binary and Likert-type (ordinal) item scores*. Ottawa, Ontario: Directorate of Human Resources Research and Evaluation, Department of National Defense. Retrieved February 22, 2006, from http://www.educ.ubc.ca/faculty/zumbo/DIF/index.html

Index

Language Testing: The social dimension, by Tim McNamara and Carsten Roever. (Blackwell, 2006)

[Page numbers in italics indicate figures]

292